GAVIN NEWSHAM

TWO TRIBES

The Rebirth of the Ryder Cup

Atlantic Books

LONDON

First published in hardback in Great Britain in 2010 by Atlantic Books,
an imprint of Atlantic Books Ltd.

Copyright © Gavin Newsham 2010

1 2 3 4 5 6 7 8 9 10

A CIP catalogue record for this book is available from the British Library.

ISBN: 978 184887 700 9

Designed and typeset by Richard Marston
Printed in Great Britain by the MPG Books Group Ltd

Atlantic Books
An Imprint of Grove Atlantic Ltd
Ormond House
26–27 Boswell Street
London
WC1N 3JZ

www.atlantic-books.co.uk

TWO TRIBES

To the Lovely Ann – because she's worth it

Contents

List of Illustrations

Introduction

THEY called them the 'Twenty Million Dollar Team'. Twelve men, 36 major championship titles, and more awards, accolades, gongs and honours than the House of Lords. It was a US side unlike any other sent across the Atlantic to contest the Ryder Cup: Nicklaus, Watson, Floyd, Trevino, Irwin, Miller, Nelson – it wasn't so much a golf team as a living, breathing Hall of Fame, a crack unit of golf assassins dispatched to the UK, armed with every shot in the coaching manual and an in-built predisposition to flatten anyone and anything in their path. Against them was the new European Ryder Cup team. Twelve men and, with Tony Jacklin and the Spaniard Severiano Ballesteros both left out of the line-up, precisely no major championship titles between them. The 1981 Ryder Cup wasn't going to be pretty.

That the Ryder Cup was losing its lustre was clear. That it had a future, less so. Every two years, the USA and Great Britain and Ireland (and then Europe) would go head to head over three days of competition and every two years, it seemed the Americans just brushed them aside as though they were pestering kids, wrapping up victory with indecent haste and embarrassing ease.

British golf was at a crossroads. With little finance to promote the game, precious few corporate sponsors and little or no television coverage of the professional game, it had found itself caught in a void, without the wherewithal to challenge the hegemony of the American game. Yes, there were a few talented players coming through the ranks, both in Britain and Europe, but the gulf between the American game and the European version had never seemed so wide, never seemed so wholly gloomy. Only Tony Jacklin had carried the mantle for this side of the Atlantic, winning the Open Championship at Royal Lytham and St Anne's in 1969 and then becoming the first Briton in forty-three years to win the US Open, waltzing to a seven-stroke victory at Minnesota's Hazeltine National Country Club.

Jacklin's remarkable victory across the pond, however, was a rare success for British and European golf. In the States, the golfers were household names and millionaires to boot. They walked the walk and talked the talk and never was the contrast more marked than when they teed it up in the Ryder Cup. Sure, they could have gone easy on Britain (and Europe) but they never did. Instead, they just kept their foot on the opposition's throat until such time as they decided to bring an end to proceedings. It was ugly, one-sided and, for the most part, humiliating.

Yet change was afoot. In 1977, the game's administrators in the UK, the Professional Golfers Association (PGA), had left their suitably modest offices at The Oval cricket ground in Vauxhall, London, and headed north to the West Midlands and to a development called The Belfry, where they had signed a new ninety-nine-year lease. There would be two new golf courses, a modern hotel and sports complex and the access was terrific, with the M1, M5 and M6 all passing nearby.

If it seemed too good to be true, it was. Though it would host the 1978 Hennessy Cup and the 1979 English Open, the new and immature Brabazon course had come in for some harsh criticism during both events and, come the 1981 Ryder Cup, it was hardly suitable for a rugby match, yet alone an international golf competition. It was, its critics maintained, what you got for building a golf course on a potato patch, although Brian Barnes, the forthright Sussex professional, said it best when he likened it to a 'ploughed field'.

There was little option but to move the 1981 Ryder Cup and with Walton Heath, the celebrated old heathland course secreted away in deepest Surrey, drafted in as the replacement venue, work continued on The Belfry. Fairways were relaid, new drainage installed and the layout strengthened; they even planted another 100 trees to improve the aesthetics.

For The Belfry, now six years and several million pounds into its redevelopment, though, the loss of the Ryder Cup was a blessing in disguise. 'I look back and think how lucky The Belfry was,' suggests the PGA's then Secretary Colin Snape. 'If that match had been at The Belfry there's every chance you would never have heard of the Ryder Cup again.'

But if The Belfry was in no fit state to host the Ryder Cup, so Walton Heath would find itself rendered virtually unplayable, only this time it would be Mother Nature stepping in to have her say. 'It was just like the Somme,' adds Snape. 'It was so muddy. You would never have played a normal tournament on that course but we plodded on because we had to. We were in a situation where we had just a week's slot to fit in with everyone's schedules so everybody gritted their teeth and got on with it.'

If the European team thought that the sodden conditions might have levelled the playing field, they were wrong. Though they edged the first day 4½–3½, the visitors stepped up their game on a soaking Saturday, and with the likes of Ray Floyd playing with his trousers tucked into his socks, took seven out of the eight points on offer and all but quashed any fanciful thought that Europe could somehow overcome the strongest US Ryder Cup team ever assembled.

Typically, the US team tore into the home side in the Sunday singles too. With the previous day's rain making the greens extremely receptive, it was US captain Dave Marr's team that hammered home their advantage. While there were some notable scalps for the European side – Howard Clark's 4&3 win over the reigning Masters champion Tom Watson perhaps the most impressive ('He beat me up pretty heavily that day,' laughs Watson) – the Americans were simply irresistible.

A case in point was Tom Kite's victory over Sandy Lyle in the second game out. Though Lyle was in commanding form, he was simply steamrollered by his Texan opponent. After ten holes, the young Scot was 6 under par for his round but still found himself all-square. When the game finished at the 16th hole, Lyle was 8-under, while Kite was 10-under. Between them, the pair had plundered seventeen birdies and three eagles in their 16 holes and, later, Lyle admitted he was powerless to do anything about the outcome, concluding that he had 'never played better in being roundly cuffed'.

The final scoreline, meanwhile – a record 18½–9½ win for the US team – suggested that Europe, even with an entire continent to pick from, were as far away from competing with the Americans as they ever were. Certainly, the Americans still assumed an inherent supe-riority in the event. 'We went into the Ryder Cup with the idea that it was a foregone conclusion – that we were going to win,' explains Tom Watson. 'That's not to be bigheaded about it. It was just a matter of fact. It was a one-sided competition for the most part.'

For all their efforts and determination to play their part in the biennial event, Great Britain and Ireland had turned into little more than a perennial punchbag, a mere training tool for the chiselled-jawed celebrities of the US professional circuit. It wasn't that the game wasn't being taken seriously, more that it was no longer the competi-tion it once was. Inevitably, people drifted away or became distracted. Sometimes the Ryder Cup just seemed to be a means to an altogether different end. At times, for instance, the PGA's Colin Snape would use his position to help facilitate his lifelong passion for Bury Football Club. At Laurel Valley in 1975, they changed the scoreboard during the Saturday foursomes to 'Fulham 1 Bury 1' to keep him up to speed with the football back home and then, on the way home, he had the plane stop off in Manchester so he could get back in time for Bury's next match. 'It was a big game,' he reflects. 'Mansfield at home.'

Today, schedules are rearranged, guts busted and hearts broken as players strive to claim a place on their teams but by 1977 and the game at Royal Lytham and St Anne's, it had become clear, painfully so, that for many of the American players at least, there was little to be gained from playing in the event. The 1973 Open champion Tom Weiskopf, for instance, opted out of the trip to the Lancashire coast in favour of an expedition hunting bears in Alaska, citing a lack of competition – and fading interest – in the contest. 'It's the lions against the Christians,' he explained. 'Lop-sided. I've done it before. Let someone else have a chance to play.'

Though he was criticized for his decision, Weiskopf had been blunt but essentially accurate. In the twenty-two contests since the first Ryder Cup in 1923, the US had won all but three. If the Americans were finding excuses not to play, morale in the British camp was lower than a plugged Titleist in a trap. After the latest British evisceration in 1977, the *Observer*'s Peter Dobereiner concluded that 'In America the Ryder Cup now rates somewhere between Tennessee Frog Jumping and the Alabama Melon-Pip Spitting Championship.'

Enthusiasm was waning and the crowds dwindling. In the United States, meanwhile, it seemed the contest was all but dead and buried. It wasn't even the fact that the players appeared without payment that was putting players off. It just seemed like there was often something better to do.

While the matches at Lytham went ahead as planned, ending in another comprehensive defeat for Great Britain and Ireland, moves were already afoot to try and salvage the Ryder Cup. During the week, meetings had taken place between the British PGA President Lord Derby and his American counterpart Henry Poe, prompted by a suggestion from Jack Nicklaus that the Great Britain and Ireland team be expanded into a team featuring players from the forerunner to the European Tour, the European Tournament Players' Division. That meant promising new players like Spain's Severiano Ballesteros, who had bulldozed his way into the professional game at the Open at Royal Birkdale in 1976, would now be eligible for the Ryder Cup team and maybe, just maybe, the Americans would have a game on their hands. 'The Americans,' said Nicklaus, 'are quite happy to treat this match as a goodwill gesture, a get together, a bit of fun. But here in

Britain it's treated differently. The people here seem to want a serious, knock-em-down match. If that's what's wanted, there has to be stronger opposition. Something has to be done to make it more of a match for the Americans.'

With the proposal ratified, the all-new European team headed to the United States in mid-September 1979 and to The Greenbrier in White Sulphur Springs, West Virginia. With Ballesteros, the new Open champion, in their ranks, John Jacobs's side took to the tee with a new-found confidence. Three days and twenty-eight hard-fought games later, Europe returned home – on the wrong end of a 17–11 drubbing. Great Britain, Great Britain and Ireland, and now Europe – the more things changed the more they stayed the same.

Here was a competition, or, more precisely, a lack of a competition, that seemed to be heading only one way. At Walton Heath, for example, just 16,000 people came through the gates during the week. Contrast that with the last Ryder Cup at Valhalla in Louisville, Kentucky, when over 200,000 swarmed on to the golf course. Yes, it's a different era, but it's also an entirely different competition.

Of course, it wasn't meant to be this way. Fifty years earlier, the inaugural Ryder Cup had taken place at the Worcester Country Club in Boston, Massachusetts, and, after a week of hard-fought but good-natured competition, it had seemed as though a glorious new chapter in international golf had begun. Certainly, the man behind the event, British entrepreneur Samuel Ryder, seemed justifiably pleased with how it had gone, even if the Brits had come out on the wrong end of a 9½–2½ mauling.

The son of a Manchester corn merchant, Sam Ryder came to golf relatively late in his life. Having moved south to St Albans in 1895, Ryder's new penny packet seed business, the Heath and Heather Company Ltd, had flourished but the demands of his company, not to mention his role as Mayor of St Albans and his commitment to his local church, found Ryder stretched and, increasingly, unwell. On the advice of his family, Ryder had visited his doctor who prescribed fresh air and exercise, and when it was suggested to him that golf might be the ideal way to combine both, Ryder was reluctant, not least because cricket remained his first love.

But when he grudgingly agreed to give the game a go, Ryder soon found himself hooked. Six days a week he would practise, stopping only to observe the Sabbath. At the golf club, on the carpet in his house, or flopping chips over the hedges in the garden at his home, Marlborough House, Ryder threw himself into it with the same gusto he had for his business. Within a year, he boasted a handicap of just six and had also been appointed as the new captain of Verulam Golf Club.

Though he had come to golf in middle age, Ryder had found not just a new hobby but something that would, in time, come to define his life. By the early 1920s, he had even taken to promoting professional tournaments, stumping up a £50 first prize and a guaranteed £5 appearance fee for each player who teed it up in the competition at Verulam. Soon, all the biggest names in golf would come to play in Sam's shows: Harry Vardon, James Braid, J. H. Taylor, Ted Ray, not to mention the Kent professional whose services as a coach he had retained at £1000 a year, Abe Mitchell.

A club professional at North Foreland Golf Club in Kent, Mitchell had twice won the British Matchplay Championship and while he had never won the Open Championship he had come extremely close, landing three top five finishes by the time Sam Ryder enlisted his help in 1925. Together, Ryder and Mitchell's passion for the game would prove to be the catalyst for a new international professional tournament – the Ryder Cup.

While international matches had been tried before, most notably in the informal trans-Atlantic game on the King's Course at Gleneagles, Scotland in 1921, Ryder was intent on establishing a new, permanent date in the professional golfing calendar, not least because amateurs from the US and Great Britain already had the new Walker Cup to contest. With Ryder's backing, Abe Mitchell would begin to moot the idea of the event on the professional circuit, finding the best possible ally in the world's most famous golfer, America's Walter Hagen. The Open champion in 1922 and then 1924, Hagen was at the very peak of his powers, a confident, cocksure champion with the gift of the gab but, crucially, the game to back it up. Hagen was taken with Ryder's proposition in that there was no money at stake, nor would there be any appearance fee paid to players. Yes, there would be some chicken sandwiches and a couple of ales at the end of the day but this was something more, this was about playing for your country. It was about honour. 'Match play, team play, individual play, the Ryder Cup is a pure form of competition – the original form of competition,' adds Tom Watson today. 'Head to head, playing for your country, that's it.'

With the idea of an international match agreed in principle, Sam Ryder set about creating a trophy for the event, commissioning a new £250 trophy from the royal jewellers, Mappin and Webb, bearing his name and Abe Mitchell's likeness on the top of the lid. The only obstacle now seemed to be finding a suitable date in the calendar, but when a new qualifying event was launched to cope with the oversubscribed 1926 Open Championship, Ryder finally had a window.

With many Americans making the long journey over the Atlantic to take part in qualifying, there was now a break between the qualifying and the Open itself and, with time on their hands, Walter Hagen assembled a team to play in an unofficial game at Wentworth, Surrey – against a British team led by Ted Ray and featuring Sam Ryder's friend, tutor and co-conspirator Abe Mitchell.

While the home side eased to a comprehensive victory, 13½–1½, it would be another year before the first official Ryder Cup began in earnest. Great Britain, captained by the redoubtable Ted Ray, headed over to the United States on the RMS *Aquitania*, with Sam Ryder in tow, for the matches at Worcester Country Club, Massachusetts, to be greeted by the kind of fanfare that welcomed troops coming home from the front line, not professional golfers arriving for a competition nobody had heard of.

This time, the result would go the way of the hosts as Walter Hagen's men exacted revenge for Wentworth with a thumping, emphatic 9½–2½ win. But it mattered little to Ryder. For him, the very fact that the trophy that bore his name was now in play and up for grabs was enough, for the meantime at least.

By 1939, the scoreline in the Ryder Cup matches read Great Britain 2–USA 3, and everything that Sam Ryder had envisioned for the competition – his competition – appeared to be coming to fruition. The outbreak of the Second World War, however, would very nearly signal the end of the Ryder Cup, not just for the duration of the conflict, but forever. With the event suspended, challenge competitions were played instead as part of the war effort, featuring some of the star players who would, ordinarily, have taken part and normal service wouldn't be resumed until the matches in Portland, Oregon, in 1947.

But in the aftermath of the war, golf, quite rightly, seemed to be the last thing on anyone's mind. As Britain struggled to recover from the massive social and economic devastation, the idea that they would or could send a team to the United States to play in the 1947 event seemed unimaginable, even perverse, not least because there were so many better things that needed attention and investment.

Enter the American millionaire Robert Hudson. A successful, self-made man, Hudson, like Sam Ryder, was a golf fanatic who had also taken to sponsoring professional events around his hometown of Portland, Oregon, including the Portland Open in 1944 and 1945. It was during the 1946 PGA Championship – another event that he had sponsored and the scene of Ben Hogan's maiden major win – that Hudson had first learned of the financial difficulties threatening the future of the event. Rather than let the competition wither on the vine, he decided to step in and bankroll the 1947 Ryder Cup.

'British golf had a terrible time of it for fifteen or twenty years after the war. We were always the poor relations, always needing a hand-out,' explains the golf commentator Bruce Critchley. 'There just wasn't any money for golf courses. Golf was still a rich man's pastime and golf equipment was expensive. But it was different in America where golf and the country club was part of the culture and where golfers tended to be well off.'

The Ryder Cup captain and player Tony Jacklin agrees. 'After the war it was quite a struggle,' he says. 'It was much more difficult for the British to show up and give them a game. There were food stamps and coupons and the like, none of which was very conducive to giving you confidence. It's hardly surprising America recovered after the war a lot quicker than we did.'

Robert Hudson would pick up the tab for everything and the British team wanted for nothing. First-class travel on the *Queen Mary*, parties at New York's Waldorf Astoria, luxury train travel over to Oregon; everything was done in style, everything was laid on for Henry Cotton's team. Perhaps, though, they were just too comfortable. On a track drenched by the worst deluge in Portland in sixty-five years, it was as one-sided a contest as had been seen in the Ryder Cup. Outplayed, out-thought and out-fought, the British team very nearly suffered the first and only whitewash in the history of the Ryder Cup. It was only thanks to Sam King, the Kent professional fresh from a spell in the Home Guard, that Britain's blushes were spared. King won the very last game against Herman Keiser 4&3, registering the visitors' only point in an 11–1 annihilation.

While Robert Hudson's generosity had reignited the Ryder Cup, the scale of the defeat had laid bare the gulf in talent between the two nations. Many of the Americans, now armed with the latest designs in clubs and balls, had been able to play competitive golf throughout much of the war, while across the Atlantic, golfers had downed clubs to join the war effort instead.

While the matches were closer in 1949 – there really was no way they couldn't be – the US team, with Snead, Mangrum and Demaret, and skippered once more by Ben Hogan (who was still recovering from a near-fatal car crash and unable to play) overcame a spirited effort by Charles Whitcombe's British side, winning the final four singles matches to chalk up yet another victory, albeit a narrow one.

Yet if it seemed as though Britain could mount something resembling a fight on home turf, the matches in the States were invariably one-sided, and often embarrassingly so. In 1951, the US, marshalled by 'Slammin' Sam Snead, cruised to a 9½–2½ triumph at Pinehurst Country Club, while in 1955, they notched another straightforward 8–4 win and this despite a new selection process for the British team based on a points list drawn up on the players' performances over a set list of tournaments, the idea being that the best team would emerge from the new system. While that may have been the case, with players like Ireland's Christy O'Connor and the future Ryder Cup captain John Jacobs benefiting from the changes, it was never enough to compete with the Americans who, despite having five debutants in their eight-man side, still ambled to victory.

Britain's continued inability to win was beginning to become something more than merely a matter of misfortune. If anything, those years of turning up and being beaten like a drum were now playing havoc with the mindset of the players, to the point where it felt like they were already 1-down when they stepped on to the first tee. Even when Britain got close to winning, such as in 1953 at Wentworth, they always seemed to be lacking that key ingredient, that killer instinct, needed to carry them over the winning line. The experience of the twenty-two-year-old Peter Alliss in that game seemed to typify the British malaise. With the score level at five points apiece, Alliss went down the last 1-down, but with his opponent Jim Turnesa making a hash of the final hole appeared set to snatch a half point.

But if Turnesa seemed intent on handing Alliss a lifeline, Alliss seemed equally set on passing up the offer, duffing his third shot just a few inches, before finding the green with his fourth and leaving himself with a short putt for his par. That putt, however, would drift by the hole, and by halving the hole with a miserable six, Alliss had given his opponent the point. Moments later, Alliss's fellow debutant Bernard Hunt, who seemed to be afflicted by the same nerves, needed just a half at his final hole to secure a win, which would have given

Britain a draw. But Hunt three-putted from the back of the green, giving Douglas a half and the USA a one point win, 6½–5½.

Two years later, Alliss and Hunter would be overlooked for selection for the game at Palm Springs' Thunderbird Golf and Country Club, sacrificed in an ultimately futile bid to wrestle the trophy back from Chick Harbert's team. The passing of time, it seemed, did little to improve the chances of the British team. Every time a Snead or a Hogan finally moved aside, there was always a Palmer or a Nicklaus waiting in the wings. It was a never-ending conveyor belt of golfing greats. A ceaseless line of legends.

All of which made a rare British victory in 1957 all the more remarkable. Held at the short course at Lindrick, fifteen miles or so east of Sheffield; captained by the Welshman Dai Rees, perhaps the greatest British golfer never to win the Open Championship, it was a match where another defeat seemed inevitable. Three points to one down after the first day of foursomes and with just the singles to play, it was, given America's peerless record in the final day head-to-heads, another victory just waiting to be sealed. Remarkably, though, Rees and his team rallied on the last day, winning six of the eight games and turning a two point deficit into a conclusive 7½–4½ victory. They were not narrow victories either. Rees himself thumped Ed Furgol 7&6, Christy O'Connor eased past Don Finsterwald by the same margin and Bernard Hunt, one of the villains of the piece four years earlier, coasted to a 6&5 win over Doug Ford. For the first time since 1933, Britain had, quite unexpectedly, won the Ryder Cup.

A sure sign that Great Britain had, for once, got the measure of the Americans came during the game where Scotland's Eric Brown beat the tempestuous talent of Tommy 'Thunder' Bolt by 4&3. The American, a player known for his penchant for hurling clubs whenever a shot failed to go the way he had planned, found himself on the receiving end of some good-natured ribbing from the Lindrick galleries. After shaking hands on the 15th green, Bolt had turned to Brown and said: 'I guess you won but I didn't enjoy it one bit.' Brown, though, was quick off the mark. 'And nor would I after the licking I have just given you,' he replied. Apoplectic, Bolt stormed off the course, snapping another of his long-suffering clubs.

Indeed, whenever Britain came close to winning, such as in 1969, the more the Americans seemed to take it personally. That year at Royal Birkdale, the youngest British player to play in the Ryder Cup, twenty-year-old Bernard Gallacher, defeated Lee Trevino 4&3 in his singles match, but only, as Trevino suggested, because the American had an injured foot. 'I don't know if there was anything wrong with his foot,' retorted the cocksure young Scot, 'but there was certainly something wrong with his swing!'

Yet for every bitter exchange, for every withering wisecrack, there was still the kind of sportsmanship and camaraderie that had first persuaded Sam Ryder that the event had a real future, and in 1969 one moment that, for all the years of batterings handed out by the Americans, suggested that, when it really mattered, the game itself was more important.

In a tense finish at Royal Birkdale, the new Open champion, Tony Jacklin, and the seven-time major winner, Jack Nicklaus, went down the last with the match all-square. When Nicklaus missed his short putt to win the match, Jacklin found himself staring at a 2ft putt that would either guarantee a tie or lose the Ryder Cup once more. As Jacklin sized up his putt, though, Nicklaus simply stepped forward, picked up his opponent's marker and offered his hand, saying: 'I don't think you would have missed that putt Tony, but in the circumstances I would never give you the opportunity.'

While it was a genuine act of sportsmanship, typical of a man of Nicklaus's stature, it meant little to the outcome of the match. Yes, the result was officially a tie – the best result Europe had managed in twelve years – but under the rules a tie meant that the holders retained the trophy and when Sam Snead took his troops back across the pond, he did so with the Ryder Cup once more in his keep.

While Lindrick and, to a lesser extent, Royal Birkdale, had been just blips in the Ryder Cup scheme of things, they had come at an important time not merely for Britain, but for the competition itself. Yes, it was piecemeal success, but it was enough to sustain it for a little while longer, even if the 1970s saw the results revert to type as a fresh wave of merciless US talent, like Watson, Weiskopf and Wadkins, continued where generation after generation of American golfers before them had left off, winning each and every contest in the decade that fashion forgot.

But it was delaying the inevitable and the quagmire of Walton Heath had seemed to be the final nail in a coffin being lowered slowly under the sod, with precious few mourners in attendance. Over the decades, this unique competition had been tweaked, toyed and tinkered with. The format had changed and then changed again and the selection criteria had been modified. They had added countries and then an entire continent. But still the result was the same. Still, the Americans, with their smart shoes and Hollywood haircuts, always seemed to walk away with Sam Ryder's trophy...

The Awakening

PGA NATIONAL, PALM BEACH, FLORIDA

14–16 October 1983

TONY Jacklin had had a gutful of the Ryder Cup. Played seven, lost six, tied one, won none. But for *that* tie in 1969 when Jack Nicklaus's concession had given Great Britain and Ireland a share of the spoils at Royal Birkdale, the greatest British golfer of his generation had given his all to the event and for what? Fourteen years on from his debut, the brutal truth now was that Tony Jacklin didn't want to be the whipping boy any more. He didn't want to be the good sport or the plucky underdog. It was, as he explains, 'not much fun getting beaten like a drum every time'.

When he was thirteen years old, the young Tony Jacklin and his father, Arthur, had travelled the sixty miles or so from the family home in Scunthorpe to Lindrick Golf Club in Worksop to watch Dai Rees's Great Britain and Ireland team take on a US side, led by the 1956 Masters and PGA champion, Jack Burke, in the 1957 Ryder Cup. That day, those feted names he only ever saw on the back pages of his dad's newspaper – Alliss and Faulkner, Brown and O'Connor, Furgol and Bolt – became living, breathing reality, right there in front of his eyes. The day over, and with Great Britain claiming a rare and special victory, an inspired Jacklin returned home, squeezing in nine holes before bedtime and shooting the lowest score of his young life.

A quarter of a century later and everything had changed. While Jacklin's childhood dream of becoming a professional golfer had been fulfilled, way beyond the dreams he enjoyed as a kid, the competition that had inspired him as a boy had lost its lustre. The 1981 debacle at Walton Heath had been the final straw. Left out of the team for the first time since 1967, Jacklin assumed that it was the end of the road for him and the Ryder Cup. With only the top ten players in the qualification table guaranteed a place in the team, it had been left to captain John Jacobs to pick his final two team members. The experienced Peter Oosterhuis had been an obvious choice, not least as he was now playing virtually full time in America. However, Jacobs's decision to pick Mark James, one of the villains of the piece at The Greenbrier in 1979, as his second wild card, rankled with Jacklin, so much so that the two-time major winner, left out for the first time since 1967, had all but called time on his Ryder Cup career. Jacklin's only consolation, not that he took any pleasure in it, was that he wasn't a member of a team that would suffer a record defeat at the hands of the USA.

Two events after Great Britain and Ireland had become a European team, nothing much had changed. If anything, things had got worse. A 17–11 drubbing at The Greenbrier followed by the record 18–11 defeat at Walton Heath suggested that the Ryder Cup, while notionally still alive, had become an anachronistic knockabout at best, a practice session for the Americans at worst. It had long since ceased to be a contest. It was now a cull.

With the team failing, spectacularly so, and the event itself fast losing its appeal among fans, players and sponsors alike, the job of European skipper had become not so much a poisoned chalice, as the cup of no hope. When the PGA asked Jacklin to be captain for the 1983 matches at the PGA National Course, Palm Beach, Florida, he was taken aback. Jackin had been hitting some balls on the range prior to the Car Care Plan Tournament at Moortown Golf Club in May 1983 when Ken Schofield, the European Tour's Executive Director, and his counterpart at the PGA, Colin Snape, ambled over to him and asked him to lead the

European team. 'I was quite shocked when they asked me to be the captain,' he recalls. 'It was all a bit last minute so I didn't give them an answer immediately but thought about it overnight.'

Though time was of the essence – there were now just six months to go before the match – Jacklin knew he was in a strong position, not least because, as he admits, he 'didn't really give a damn whether I did it or not'. That night, though, Jacklin pondered the offer, concluding that even though he still harboured the residual grudges from two years previously, here was an opportunity to make a real difference to the European team and, crucially, the way they approached the competition. It was also, as he explains, a chance to 'make some demands'.

Throughout his sixteen years' experience of playing in the competition, Jacklin had looked on as the American opposition repeatedly outclassed them on the golf course, and, equally importantly, off it too. At each event, the USA team, with its multiple major winners and millionaires, would turn up with their catalogue haircuts, sharp suits and ice-white teeth and wipe the floor with the GB and Ireland team. They looked and felt the part and played like it too. The GB and Ireland team, meanwhile, were a rag-tag bunch in comparison, an assembly of seemingly disparate individuals thrown together, united by polyester blazers, and expected to compete against the very best players in the world. 'Through the years I did it, the PGA officialdom organized it, in their wisdom, and they never had to play. So everything was done in an amateurish way. We wore what they thought was right, which was more or less anything that they could get that was free, and a lot of it was quite obviously rubbish,' says Jacklin, a player whose Stylo plastic shoes bade farewell to their soles during his singles match with Ray Floyd in 1975 at Laurel Valley. 'There was no self-esteem. And then these Americans would turn up in cashmere sweaters with leather golf bags. They did everything first class. And we were 2-down before we had hit a shot, just on the basis of how we felt or how we were made to feel.'

For a player like Jacklin, who until Graeme MacDowell won in 2010, was the only British winner of the US Open since 1924 and only the third Englishman since the war to win the Open Championship, the way the Ryder Cup was being approached was little more than an embarrassment. The following day, Jacklin notified Ken Schofield and his counterpart at the PGA, Colin Snape, of his decision. 'I knew if I was to accept the job I wanted to do it on my own terms,' he explains. 'And when I went back to them I prefaced my answer on that basis. I said, if I do it, it has got to be the way the Americans do it.'

There would be conditions and caveats, directives and demands. From better clothes and equipment to hotel inspections and return travel on Concorde for the players, their wives and their caddies, Jacklin was seeking a raft of assurances, including a designated team room at the competition itself. Previously, team meetings had always been huddles in the corner of the locker room or stolen summits by the side of the practice green. Not now, though. As far as Jacklin was concerned, it was first class or forget it.

While the desire to replicate the super-slick operation favoured by the Americans was admirable, there was the small matter of just who was going to foot the bill for it all – not that that was Tony Jacklin's problem. Money, or the lack of it, had long been a problem in the Ryder Cup. In 1951, for example, Arthur Lacey's Great Britain and Ireland team had sailed to the United States on the *Queen Mary*, staying in cabin class, rather than first, achieving a saving of some £1250 on the trip. Soon after, they were on their way home, only this time with a thumping 9–2 defeat to contemplate on the long, uncomfortable journey back.

But golf in 1983, and, more particularly, the Ryder Cup, was yet to be wholly consumed by corporate sponsorship. It was hardly surprising. With defeat after predictable defeat, and humiliation piled on embarrassment, it was hardly an attractive proposition for any potential commercial partners. Indeed, after the crushing defeat in 1981 at Walton Heath, the PGA's main sponsor, Sun Alliance, had even called time on their agreement, deciding that the effort and the expense simply weren't warranted any more.

Television companies had all but lost interest too. In the States the 1983 match would be shown on local channels only, while in the UK a short highlights programme was the most anyone could hope for. Assuming there were any highlights, of course.

Today, it's taken for granted that countless companies queue up to pay handsomely for the privilege of association with the Ryder Cup. From official clothing suppliers to camera equipment, travel agents to Ryder Cup wine, there's no shortage of offers on the table of the organizing bodies; in 2010, there was even an official helicopter supplier to the event. Back in the dark days of the 1970s and early 1980s, though, when it was not so much a cash cow as a dead duck, the PGA had to find the funds to pay for everything. That job went to the PGA's Secretary and wheeler-dealer-in-chief, Colin Snape. 'You look back on it with affection but the clothing really was crap,' he says. 'I really was going round almost with a barrow persuading people; "Can I have free suitcases?" and "How many cashmere sweaters?" and so on but that is the way it was. It was fun really but it was seat of the pants stuff.'

It had been a testing time for Snape and the PGA. Having lost their main sponsor in the wake of the 1981 debacle, it had fallen upon the Lancastrian to seek new backing for the Ryder Cup and he would spend much of 1982 on the road, hawking the event around largely uninterested parties. After six months' selling, all Snape had to show was a useless offer of £80,000 in cigarette coupons.

With less than a year until the 1983 Ryder Cup was due to take place, the PGA still didn't have a sponsor on board. At the 1982 PGA Championship at Southern Hills, Tulsa, Oklahoma, Colin Snape and his counterparts at the PGA of America would meet for an update on what was becoming an increasingly gloomy situation, concluding that if a sponsor could not be found – and quick – the very future of the Ryder Cup could be in doubt. But as the players made contingency plans – a worried Bernard Gallacher even offered to pay his own way to Florida – Snape received a tip-off from his fellow Ryder Cup committee member Bill Watson that Raymond Miquel, the head of Bell's Scotch

Whisky and an avid golf fan to boot, might be worth pursuing in his search for a new sponsor. 'Bernard was always DOOM,' laughs Snape. 'There was always a DOOM scenario on everything.'

With the groundwork done, Snape boarded a train in February 1982 and made the 500-mile journey from London to Perth, Scotland, to meet with Miquel. Hard of nose and light on sentiment, Miquel had been responsible for increasing Bell's sales sevenfold and making it the best-selling whisky in the UK. They called him 'Ruthless Raymond' – and that was just his friends.

While Snape was open to offers, as long as it wasn't just free whisky to go with his cigarette coupons, it seemed that Miquel was taken with the idea of selling Bell's across the pond. A deal, and an improbably good one at that, was struck. For making Bell's the official sponsor of the Ryder Cup, the PGA would receive £300,000, spread over the 1983 contest and the following event at The Belfry in 1985. 'I had to persuade the PGA (of America) to allow Bell's name to be identified with the Ryder Cup in America which was complete anathema,' adds Snape. 'The sponsoring of the Ryder Cup by a drinks company had never happened before but they were very helpful because they realized that if I didn't get that sponsorship the matches were literally finished.'

With the Ryder Cup's immediate future assured, it was clear that a few other little local difficulties needed reconciling, not least the matter of Seve Ballesteros's place on the team. After the savaging at Walton Heath, a game from which the Spaniard had been dropped, it was painfully clear that the European team needed Seve Ballesteros much more than he needed it. This, after all, was the greatest player of his generation. A brooding, swashbuckling, mono-browed magician, armed with every shot in the coaching manual and many more besides. 'He could get it up and down from a ball-washer,' said the 1973 Open champion Tom Weiskopf, 'and walk away without a drop of water on his hands.'

Moreover, Ballesteros had that kind of natural, intrinsic belief in his own ability allied to a matchplay strategy ideally suited to the frenzy of a Ryder Cup contest. 'I go to the 1st tee, I clap my opponent on the back, I wish him a good game,' he once said, adding, '[Then] I look into his eyes and I think, "I will bury you".'

On the recommendation of Lord Derby, the President of the PGA and Chairman of the Ryder Cup committee, Jacklin set about trying to sweet-talk the Spaniard back into the Ryder Cup fold. During that summer's Open Championship at Royal Birkdale, Southport, the European captain convened a meeting with Ballesteros over breakfast at the Prince of Wales Hotel. 'He [Ballesteros] was pretty peed off and quite rightly so,' recalls Jacklin. 'He vented for about an hour, on this, that and the other, and I said, "I understand all that but it is going to be different now because I have got the reins and I think with your talents and abilities and with me on the inside organizing we can make a difference".'

Since quitting the European Tour, Ballesteros's image had taken a battering in Europe. He had been cast in the role of the turncoat, apparently more interested in making money than playing for his country and continent. Jacklin now told Ballesteros that here was the perfect opportunity for him not merely to address his personal PR problem but in doing so, to lead Europe into a glorious new age of Ryder Cup golf. 'I said, "Look, if we can turn this around you will get treated like a real hero, as you should be",' says Jacklin.

Eventually, Jacklin's impassioned sales pitch began to work. Ballesteros mulled the idea over and a fortnight later, he informed Jacklin that if the offer remained open, he would be honoured to play for the European Ryder Cup team once more. The return of Seve Ballesteros to the fold gave the European Ryder Cup campaign a much-needed fillip. One by one, the pieces of Jacklin's masterplan were falling into place. That summer, Jacklin would visit West Palm Beach to check the team's hotel to ensure that the rooms were up to the standard he required. Colin Snape even sourced some decent clothes from Austin Reed, but not before Tony Jacklin and his fashion-conscious wife Vivien had given them the once-over. 'As far as I was concerned

I needed to check the clothing and that everything was right, in terms of quality and colour,' says Jacklin. 'I chose the colours for television [because] I wanted them to look the part on TV. We went to a lot of trouble.'

Not surprisingly, Jacklin also got his way with the travel arrangements so when he and his team finally left for Florida they did so in supersonic style – on Concorde. On board with him were twelve not so angry men, and a team more focused than it had been in decades. With a new qualification process, eliminating the two wild-card picks, Jacklin had no option but to take the twelve men who had finished at the top of the final qualification table (the points system used by the Tour to determine the team).

There were five survivors from the team that had been so roundly thrashed at Walton Heath – Faldo, Langer, Lyle, Gallacher and Cañizares, but they were different players from the ones who had capitulated in 1981. Nick Faldo was winning and winning regularly, as was Sandy Lyle, while Bernhard Langer was beginning to realize some of his undoubted potential, taking three Tour titles in the summer of 1983.

Elsewhere, Sam Torrance, sixth on the European Tour money list in 1983, was selected for his second appearance, while another of his colleagues from The Greenbrier, Ken Brown, would also be back for another shot at Ryder Cup redemption.

And, of course, there was the return of Severiano Ballesteros. 'In 1983 I think we all felt America had quite a strong team at West Palm Beach,' says Bernard Gallacher, who would be making his eighth and final appearance as a player. 'In the past I always felt the Americans had the best players in the world and certainly *the* best player in the world by a long way in Jack Nicklaus. But now in our locker room we had the best player in the world and it made all the difference.'

There would also be four rookies in Jacklin's team in the shape of England's Gordon J. Brand, Wales's Ian Woosnam, forty-three-year-old Brian Waites, who had propelled himself into the reckoning by winning the 1982 Car Care Plan International at Moor Allerton, and a young man who two years earlier had begged, stolen and borrowed his tickets to go and watch the Ryder Cup at Walton Heath – Paul Way.

Hailing from Tonbridge, Kent, Way was young, blond and good to go. Aged 20, he had turned pro after playing in the Walker Cup and winning the English Amateur strokeplay championship. In his first season on the Tour, he had hit the ground running, winning the KLM Dutch Open and comfortably securing his berth in Tony Jacklin's first Ryder Cup team. 'I wasn't really intimidated,' he says. 'I was only twenty or so, so I was full of confidence. I guess I hadn't really experienced anything like it before so I knew no better.'

For players like Gordon J. Brand, though, the 25th Ryder Cup would offer little more than a cameo role. Captain Tony Jacklin had long been concerned that the qualification process for the European team appeared to reward consistency, rather than proven winners, and for players like Brand, who had snuck into the team in twelfth place in the qualification standings, it meant little or no action. Even before they landed in Florida, Jacklin had informed Brand that, barring injuries or exceptional circumstances, the twenty-eight-year-old would not feature in the games until the singles on Sunday. 'I had no problem making those decisions on choosing players,' says Jacklin. 'It wasn't about being Mr Nice Guy.'

When the team touched down at JFK airport, they bade farewell to Concorde to take an Eastern Airlines flight down to Florida. Blessed with half a dozen courses, sumptuous hotels and year-round sunshine, the PGA of America's home at Palm Beach Gardens was everything The Belfry aspired to be. It was somehow fitting that Jacklin's bow as European team captain would pit him against the man who had famously and magnanimously conceded his putt to him at Royal Birkdale in 1969 – Jack Nicklaus.

The sage-like Tom Weiskopf once said that going head to head with Jack Nicklaus 'was like trying to drain the Pacific Ocean with a teacup'. He had a point. If there was one thing Nicklaus couldn't abide it was losing. Alongside an unassailable record of seventeen major titles – he would go on to add an eighteenth at the Masters in 1986 – the Golden Bear had also chalked up nineteen runners-up finishes in the big four events, the latest of which had come at the PGA Championship at Riviera Country Club, Los Angeles just a month or so earlier, when Hal Sutton had pipped him by a single stroke. Nicklaus's Ryder Cup record, too, was up there with the best, with seventeen wins from twenty-eight games played over six Ryder Cups between 1969 and 1981. Crucially, it had been Nicklaus – reluctant to see the competition die – who had proposed the expansion of the Great Britain and Ireland team into a European one. Without his input, without his vision, Tony Jacklin and his team might never have made it to Florida.

It would be a busy week for the Europeans, and this was before they got down to the serious business of playing some golf. Even for young bucks like Paul Way, the demands on the players' time proved exhausting. 'It's a long, long week and there's a hell of a lot of pressure,' he explains. 'You're up at 6 o'clock and then there's dinners in the evening and all sorts of other functions to attend. Then, if you're playing 36 holes a day as well, as I did, it can be really tiring. I was knackered and I was a young twenty-year-old.'

The European team certainly looked better than they had in some time. Tony Jacklin had finally got his cashmere sweaters, which, had the game been played at Wentworth in October, would have been ideal. But this was Florida, the so-called Sunshine State, where it was always humid, where the average daily temperature was still in the 70s and where slipping on a cashmere sweater felt like wearing a sleeping bag.

It wouldn't be the only faux pas in the tailoring department. Though better quality clothing (although no less unfashionable) had been procured, there still wasn't enough of it to go round. Each of the European players would have just one shirt to play in each day, which was fine for those players who were called into action just once (or, in the case of Gordon Brand not at all) but for 36-holes-a-day players, it presented a real problem. 'It was so humid there that after the morning round that shirt was bloody wringing wet so we had to nip into the pro shop and buy some new ones,' explains Paul Way. 'It was still all about money and there wasn't very much of it knocking around.'

When play got underway in the first morning's foursomes, it was as though nothing much had changed at all. Despite the best-laid plans, the endless negotiations and the lovely, soft cashmere sweaters, Bernard Gallacher and Sandy Lyle went out in the first game and promptly got battered 5&4 by the formidable partnership of Tom Watson and Ben Crenshaw. This, however, was a team blessed not just with a crop of the best young players in Europe but, thanks to Tony Jacklin, a new purpose and a new belief.

The session would end level, with each side recording two wins. Having sat out the morning foursomes, an anxious Ian Woosnam, meanwhile, found himself paired with Sam Torrance for the afternoon fourballs game against Ben Crenshaw and Calvin Peete. It was a smart move by Tony Jacklin. Sensing Woosnam's nerves – the Welshman said later that he had almost vomited on the first tee – he had teamed him with a player who knew the Ryder Cup ropes and who could hold Woosnam's hand as he made his bow in the event. For his part, Torrance too was keen to ease the pressure on his playing partner, insisting that he take the lead on the 1st tee and show Woosnam how it was done.

At least that was the theory. With his tee shot, Torrance succeeded only in pushing his drive straight right and out of bounds. With a shrug of his shoulders, Torrance moved aside and watched as Woosnam stung a 1-iron right down the middle before hitting his approach to three feet and holing his putt for a birdie. His nerves gone, Woosnam was up and running in what would be a long and illustrious career in the Ryder Cup.

The afternoon would belong to Europe. Wins for Brian Waites and Ken Brown over Gil Morgan and Fuzzy Zoeller, and Seve Ballesteros and Paul Way over Ray Floyd and Curtis Strange, and a half point for Torrance and Woosnam, had given the visitors a 4–3 advantage.

By the interval on Saturday, and with 1½ points from their three games, Ballesteros and Way had proved to be a not entirely unsuccessful, if unlikely, pairing. Not everybody was happy, though. That lunchtime, a friend of Ballesteros and fellow Spanish professional, Angel Gallardo, approached Tony Jacklin with a troubled look on his face. 'I think you need to talk to Seve,' he said.

Perplexed, Jacklin found his leading man, and took him to one side in the locker room. 'Have you got a problem?' asked the captain.

Ballesteros looked flustered, agitated. 'This boy,' he said referring to his new partner Paul Way. 'I am holding his hand all the time, I feel like his father.'

'In here,' replied Jacklin, tapping Ballesteros's head, 'you are.'

The penny had dropped. 'Look what's happening. You are winning points,' added Jacklin. 'You are his father, that's why you are playing with him. Is it a problem?'

With a Latin shrug, Ballesteros turned on his heels and set about preparing for the afternoon foursomes. 'For me,' he said, 'it is not a problem.'

That afternoon, Ballesteros and Way, father and son, went out again to play the reigning Open champion Tom Watson and Bob Gilder, a player who won four times on the PGA Tour in a little over a year. 'After three games I thought I'd probably get the chance to sit out the afternoon on Saturday and take a breather,' recalls Paul Way, 'but Jacklin said, "No, you're out with Seve again and you're playing Tom Watson and Bob Gilder". Watson was my hero but we went 5-up after six holes and won quite comfortably.'

The trouble with Seve Ballesteros was that he was, perhaps, just too good. For lesser players – and in Seve's heyday that meant pretty much everybody else on the planet – the sheer quality of his play, allied to the power of his personality, could be more than a little daunting. 'Seve wasn't easy to partner, as great a player as he was. Even his own teammates were intimidated by him because of his persona. He had a lot of charisma, he was a strong character,' adds Jacklin. 'But the

[Ballesteros and Way] partnership was very strong and the main reason was that Paul Way was not intimidated by Seve. He was twenty or so and I suppose in his heart of hearts he thought he might be better than Seve.'

Paul Way agrees. 'I wasn't really intimidated. I was young so I was full of confidence and I hadn't really experienced anything like it before so I knew no better,' he says. Unquestionably, it had been an astonishing start to his Ryder Cup career. More than a quarter of a century later, he's still grateful for the opportunity that Tony Jacklin gave him. 'Getting paired with Seve was incredible,' he says. 'He was the reigning Masters champion at the time and the best player in the world. It was like playing with Tiger Woods today.'

If Tony Jacklin felt as though his masterplan was coming together and heading towards a glorious conclusion come Sunday evening, his opposite number Jack Nicklaus was feeling the Florida heat. Before he sent his team out for the singles on Sunday, he gathered them together and, in no uncertain terms, told them all exactly what he expected of them. 'I will not be the first captain to blow this thing,' he insisted. 'Now you guys show me some brass.'

Though the scores were tied at eight points each, Nicklaus had genuine cause for concern. With the exception of Tom Watson, most of his box-office names seemed to be ill, injured or off form; Fuzzy Zoeller's back was playing up, Tom Kite had been felled by flu and Ray Floyd was suffering from a rare loss of touch.

Certainly, the singles order given by each captain betrayed the way they were thinking. Jacklin went out with all of his big guns blazing, loading the top half with big names like Ballesteros, Faldo and Langer in a bid to win some early points and wrestle the momentum away from the US team. Nicklaus, meanwhile, anticipating a tight finish, listed his more reliable, big match performers like Lanny Wadkins and Tom Watson at the bottom of the order, in the hope that they would pull the US through the tape and over the finishing line.

It was a given that Ballesteros would head off first for Europe. Why, figured Jacklin, leave your best player to play late in the day when the matter might already have been settled by then? Up against Ballesteros would be Fuzzy Zoeller, the man he had succeeded as Masters champion in 1980. 'When Jack [Nicklaus] told me I had to play Seve, I took so many pills I'm glad they don't have drug tests for golfers,' he said later.

Zoeller had just cause for concern. Initially, Ballesteros would be in imperious form and looked as though he would make short work of his opponent. With seven holes to play, the European No. 1 was three holes to the good and closing in on the perfect start for his team. Suddenly, though, errors began to creep into his game. One hole went Zoeller's way, followed by another and then another. By the time they reached the final hole, the pair, improbably, were all-square.

At the final hole, it had seemed as though Ballesteros's collapse was complete. A hefty, hooked drive into the punishing rough saw the Spaniard hack out, only to find a fairway bunker, the green still some 240 yards distant. His ball was going nowhere. Sat under the lip, with an eight-foot rise ahead of him, the wind against and water guarding the putting surface, right and back, the percentage shot, maybe the only shot, was to take a short iron out and start digging.

Ballesteros was now on the verge of an embarrassing reverse. Desperate times required desperate measures. Or perhaps divine intervention. To audible gasps from the galleries, Ballesteros pulled his wooden-faced Tony Penna No. 3 out of the bag and settled his stance in the trap. Lashing at his ball, he swept it out of the sand, staring it down as it arced through the air, over the water, before landing pin high on the edge of the green, just 20 feet from the hole. A delicate chip and a solid putt later and the Spaniard had his par and snatched an unlikely half point from the jaws of both defeat and victory. Jack Nicklaus would later call Ballesteros's 3-wood the greatest shot he had ever seen – and he'd seen a few.

Miraculous though it was, however, it was, in reality, a half point lost, not won, and a half point that would prove crucial come the end of the day. Ballesteros had been in such a dominant position that given his stature and his ability he should never have allowed Zoeller back into the game.

Initially, though, Ballesteros's failure to complete a victory seemed to have done little to dent European hopes, as Nick Faldo soon wrapped up a 2&1 win over Jay Haas. But as had happened all week, as soon as one side gained an advantage the other would invariably respond and tie the scores once more. Faldo's point, for example, would soon be matched by Ben Crenshaw's 3&1 win over Sandy Lyle. Then, as Bernhard Langer restored the European lead, Gordon Brand, getting his clubs out for the first time in the week, lost out to Bob Gilder 2&1, in a game that would mark the beginning and the end of the shortest Ryder Cup career possible.

It was too tight to call. Now, for the first time in a generation, the American team found themselves in a real game, a genuine contest. When Ian Woosnam was outgunned 3&2 by the man they called 'The Walrus', the 1982 Masters champion Craig Stadler, it left two games out on the course with the scores tied at 13 apiece. In the final game, Tom Watson was stuttering to a victory over Bernard Gallacher, leaving the match ahead of them between José María Cañizares and Lanny Wadkins as the pivotal game. With seven to play, Cañizares had been 3-up which, against any other opponent, may have been sufficient to see him home. But this was Lanny Wadkins.

Born Jerry Lanston Wadkins, the Wake Forest University graduate had long held a reputation as one of the grittiest, gutsiest players in the modern game. Brought up in Richmond, Virginia, he had learned to play as a kid, 'beating the crap out of' his younger brother Bobby, who would also become a professional. In 1974, three years after he had turned pro, Wadkins had spent a fortnight in hospital as doctors removed his appendix and gall bladder, leaving his fledgling career in the balance. An inevitable slump followed, but without a coach and trusting his own instincts, he clawed his way back into contention, culminating in his maiden major win in 1977, where he overturned a six-shot deficit in the PGA Championship at Pebble Beach to defeat Gene Littler in a play-off.

When he was inducted onto the World Golf Hall of Fame in 2009, Wadkins put his success down to the twin attributes of 'perseverance and meanness'. Others were more forthright. Lee Trevino said Wadkins was 'the gutsiest sonofabitch I've ever met', while his future Ryder Cup skipper, Dave Stockton, said that playing him was 'like having a bulldog tied to your ankle'.

Certainly, José María Cañizares knew he would have to work for his win but as the afternoon turned into evening, it had seemed as though the man from Malaga was enjoying one of those days where everything seemed to be going in his favour, as Lanny Wadkins explains:

'It was one of those matches where I felt like I should have been winning the whole day but Cañizares was pulling his magic and holing shots from everywhere. The two holes that come to mind were the 1st hole [where] he drove it into the woods, chipped out and hit it on the green to fifty feet and holed it for par, while I drove it down the middle, hit it to six feet and missed a birdie putt and we tied the hole. Then I was 1-down going to the 16th and hit a 2-iron about twelve feet past the hole and he puts it to the edge of the lake and splashes it out thirty feet from the hole on the green and I miss a twelve-footer. He holes his and we tie again. It seemed like there was a bunch of holes like that during the day.'

One down at the 17th, Wadkins would hole a nervy six-footer to keep the game alive and the pair would head to the 18th, their captains and assembled teammates in tow. 'We all knew what the situation was,' says Wadkins. 'The only other match on the course was Tom Watson playing Bernard Gallacher and at that point Tom was 2-up with two to play and if Watson was 2-up he didn't lose matches. We weren't concerned about Tom – the one that made the difference was mine.'

The 18th at the PGA National was a par-5, into the wind; a dogleg-left monster and a hideous hole to end with. Wadkins needed to win the hole, tie his game and claim the half point they needed to effectively win the Ryder Cup. Cañizares, meanwhile, needed to match Wadkins's score to win 1-up and give the European team a draw.

Wadkins would be longer off the final tee. Cañizares, meanwhile, found himself unable to reach the green in two, opting instead to lay up. Wadkins too would take the safer option, resisting his natural attacking instincts, and hitting a 3-wood into the narrow part of the fairway, short of the green. For his third shot, Cañizares could only find the front right edge of the putting surface. It was advantage Wadkins.

With 72 yards to the pin, Wadkins pulled his sand wedge out of his bag and with his teammates, their wives, and most of the caddies willing him on, clipped a startling, skipping shot over the greenside bunker and up to the pin, stopping it dead just a foot from the hole. Cañizares was powerless to do anything about it. Wadkins had his birdie, his tie and claimed his and the USA's all-important half point. 'The whole team were standing right there and pretty anxious as you can imagine,' he recalls. '[And] it was a tough shot because the pin was on a back ledge and it was too close to carry up there and spin with a 56-degree wedge. A shot that everybody hit at that time was a driving sand wedge where you skipped it back there and I played it perfectly.'

As the ball stopped dead, the US team engulfed Lanny Wadkins. Even team captain Jack Nicklaus, a man not prone to over-excitement, fell to his knees and kissed the divot Wadkins had just made. 'They were pretty excited,' laughs Wadkins.

The mood was jubilant, the relief palpable. Jack Nicklaus had narrowly avoided going down in history as the first US captain to lose the Ryder Cup on home soil – at least for now – and for that he had Jerry Lanston Wadkins to thank. 'That little son of a gun,' smiled Nicklaus, before adding, 'he needs a wheelbarrow to carry his brass around.'

Demoralizing though the result was for the Europeans, there was now a tangible sense, not simply that the apparently invincible Americans finally had a match on their hands, but that the Ryder Cup had come out of its coma. 'That year, that was the awakening for the European team,' says Tom Watson, undefeated in four Ryder Cup appearances for the US. 'They certainly had the ability that week to beat us, it was a very close match and it could have gone one way or the other on that last day, no question.'

While Tony Jacklin's Ryder Cup revolution had fallen tantalizingly short of ending the period of dominance of the United States, it had, undeniably, still been a performance to be proud of. Buoyed by the brilliance of Ballesteros, Europe had finally turned a corner, not because the result had changed – they had still lost after all – but because, for once, the Ryder Cup had been a proper match, only settled at the death by Wadkins and his wedge. 'We were a morbid bunch at the closing ceremony because we had gone so close. You can imagine what it felt like,' says Jacklin. 'We were gutted, all of us, but the fact of the matter was it was a hell of a result.'

Seve Ballesteros, moreover, had found his rightful place. Though still only twenty-six, he had assumed the mantle of Jacklin's General on the European team, partnering rookies like Paul Way and instilling in them the belief that they were every bit as good as the household names from across the pond. Even after the defeat, the Spaniard took it upon himself to address the long faces in the team room. '[He said] "This is not a loss – it is a victory. For the first time we have actually come close to beating the Americans",' recalls Jacklin.

'It was strange,' adds Paul Way. 'We were all pretty down but Seve just came into the team room and told everyone what a great result it had been. He just took all the positives out of the week and made everyone feel much, much better.'

Truth was, the European team had every reason to be proud of what they had just achieved in Florida. After three days and twenty-eight games, one point was all that had separated the two teams, one point between them and a little piece of history. Now, though, it was time to get back on Concorde, cashmere sweaters and all...

Sam's Town

LEE Trevino was at his effervescent and incorrigible best. He had just laid eyes on the new Brabazon course at The Belfry, venue for the 1985 Ryder Cup matches, and decided that it was a track that could have been built with his star-studded US team in mind. 'My guys love this course!' he beamed. 'It's so Americanized. It's what they're used to – with water hazards to fire over, rather than the bump-and-run golf we get at your Open.'

It had been a long time coming but, finally, The Belfry was ready for the Ryder Cup. Well, almost. After the embarrassment of missing out for the 1981 event when the course still looked like the aftermath of a music festival, some £8 million had been ploughed – quite literally – into making the PGA's home course a picture-perfect setting for an event that was, after the close call of West Palm Beach two years earlier, finally capturing the public's attention. 'There had never been a Ryder Cup match in the Midlands,' explains Colin Snape. 'The main reason why we took it to The Belfry was because of its location. It was slap bang in the middle of the country, the motorways had been finally connected up and the airport expanded and so on, so it became a natural venue for all the matches that followed.'

Now, the Americans too had taken on board the idea of travelling to the Ryder Cup in the best possible way, chartering Concorde for the first time and providing the recently expanded Birmingham International Airport with its first ever visit from the supersonic jet. Trevino's team, like so many before, featured a trio of men who had become part of the US Ryder Cup furniture as, once again, Lanny Wadkins, Ray Floyd and Tom Kite reported for duty, ably assisted by the likes of major winners such as Fuzzy Zoeller, Craig Stadler and that year's PGA champion, Hubert Green, not to mention US Open champion Andy North. 'We went out with a pretty good team in '85,' recalls Lanny Wadkins. 'I wouldn't say it was as good as some of the other ones we had but it was a good team [with] a lot of youngsters.'

And so what if there was no Tom Watson or Jack Nicklaus, both left out as they struggled for form; it was a solid, strong line-up, and one that in any other year could have also featured Trevino himself. Though he was 45 years old and with one eye already on the Seniors Tour, the man they called 'Super Mex' could still turn in some scintillating golf. At the 1984 PGA Championship at Shoal Creek in Birmingham, Alabama, he had eased to a four-stroke victory, collecting the last of his six majors when nearly everyone had pretty much written off his chances of even competing in a major again.

The countdown to The Belfry's first Ryder Cup would be interrupted, however, by something Colin Snape simply couldn't have foreseen. With less than a fortnight to go until the start of competition, Snape turned on the television to watch the news only to find that rioting had broken out in the Birmingham suburb of Handsworth, just ten miles or so from The Belfry.

Over several days in mid-September, hundreds of people, angered by heavy-handed policing of the local African-Caribbean population in their area, took to the streets, smashing windows, looting shops and setting fire to cars. Two people died, thirty-five were injured and over 1500 police were called in to help quell the disturbances. While the situation was defused within a few days, the riot sparked similar outbreaks of violence in other parts of Birmingham as well as in nearby

Coventry and Wolverhampton, and across the country, with clashes in London's Brixton and Peckham as well as Toxteth in Liverpool and in Bristol.

Even as the US team arrived at Birmingham International Airport on the Monday evening, 'half of Birmingham was still on fire', recalls Colin Snape. Faced with the task of trying to convince Lee Trevino and his players that they hadn't just flown into a war zone, Snape implemented an impromptu smoke and mirrors plan around The Belfry's hotel. 'I said, "Turn those televisions off for God's sake!" So they [the American team] were shepherded in that night, but I couldn't help wondering what the morning was going to bring.'

The following morning, Tuesday, matters got worse. As the first real test of The Belfry's much-vaunted transport infrastructure was about to take place, Snape and his right-hand man, the Ryder Cup director George O'Grady, were confident the venue could handle the anticipated crowds. They were wrong. 'The traffic plan completely broke down, the whole of the West Midlands was gridlocked with people trying to get into the site,' recalls Snape. 'George is looking at me and I said, "Come on George, what the fucking hell do you expect me to do about it?" The tension, as you can imagine, became quite tangible.' At the 1981 contest at Walton Heath, just 16,000 fans had watched the action. Now, four years on, in excess of 90,000 were expected to pour through The Belfry's gates.

At the Gala Dinner, US captain Lee Trevino, an incurable wise-cracker, made a typically gag-filled speech, as though he had found himself transplanted to the stand-up stage of a local working men's club. After the jokes, though, came the introductions the next day, at the Opening Ceremony. Trevino got up and introduced his players as 'the best twelve players in the world'. '[Tony] Jacklin decided to go totally the opposite way,' recalls Howard Clark. 'He invited his team to stand up and be applauded and just introduced us by name, nothing about our past or anything like that.'

When all but one of his players had taken a bow, Jacklin played his trump card, introducing his last player, Seve Ballesteros, as, quite simply, 'the best player in the world'.

Certainly, the anticipation and expectation of a European victory wasn't misplaced. Since the close call of West Palm Beach two years earlier, European golf had grown significantly stronger. Back-to-back European wins in the Open Championship, courtesy of Seve Ballesteros at St Andrews in 1984 and the Scot Sandy Lyle at Sandwich in 1985, and a debut major win for Germany's Bernhard Langer at the Masters in 1985 had seen all three players stroll into the Ryder Cup team, after a year which had seen the trio occupy the top three places in the European Tour Order of Merit.

Below them in the money list were the players who would become the backbone of the European Ryder Cup team: Ian Woosnam, Howard Clark and Sam Torrance. 'Sam was inspirational that week,' says Clark. 'He did so much to really rouse the players, I suppose, into a battle mode.'

Even the youngest player on Jacklin's side, Paul Way, had already experienced the terror of the 1st tee in a Ryder Cup and had acquitted himself admirably. The experience he had gained on his debut at Palm Beach in 1983, however, served to increase rather than diminish his pre-match anxiety at The Belfry. 'I was a lot more nervous in 1985 because I knew what to expect,' he reflects. 'I was suffering from ton-sillitis and the pressure was getting to me, I think. I'd won the PGA at Wentworth that year and I was pretty much the first person to qualify for the team and all these thoughts start getting into your head.'

Wisely, Way decided to put off an operation on his throat until after the Ryder Cup, later declaring it to be 'the best thing I ever did'. But if Way had been preoccupied by matters medical, his teammate Nick Faldo had more fundamental issues to fret about. Despite being heralded as the Next Big Thing in golf after he won his first profes-sional tournament at the Skol Lager Individual in August 1977, Faldo had failed to make the impact he and most commentators imagined he would. Yes, he had a successful career with some eleven Tour wins to his credit and his first in the US at the 1984 Sea Pines Heritage Classic, but in the big events, when the rewards – and the pressure – were at their greatest, he had developed a tendency to fall away in the final reckoning, most notably at the 1983 Open Championship at Royal Birkdale and in the following year's Masters, where he failed to convert genuine opportunities to win his first major title. The tabloids were even calling him 'Nick Foldo'.

Superficially, all seemed well with Faldo's game – he was still winning tournaments, after all – but having topped the Order of Merit in 1983 and registered three top ten finishes in the Open from 1982 onwards, he had dropped to twelfth in 1984 before falling further to 42nd in 1985. While the decline in his ranking was a cause for concern, the mere fact that he had to rely on a captain's pick to make the 1985 Ryder Cup team suggested that all was not well with Faldo's form.

In the winter of 1984/85, Faldo has decided that if he was going to fulfil his potential, he needed to take some drastic action. With his new coach in tow, the English swing guru David Leadbetter, Faldo spirited himself away to Grenelefe, south of Orlando, and set about deconstructing a swing he viewed as unreliable. It would be a long, arduous process, one that would take the best part of two years to reap any rewards.

Still, at least Tony Jacklin had Seve Ballesteros to fall back on. With four major titles now on his resumé, Ballesteros was, unquestionably, the biggest star in the golf firmament. A brilliant, idiosyncratic individual on the one hand, yet an irrepressible, irreplaceable team player on the other, the Spaniard had become the lynchpin of the European Ryder Cup team, the kind of player whose mere presence in the team room set the rest of the team at ease.

While Ballesteros gave the team belief, the light relief in the locker room would be provided by Sam Torrance. They made the perfect combination: Ballesteros, the man who had been there and done it and had the medals to prove it, and, alongside him, Torrance, the sardonic Scot with a penchant for a good laugh and a good drink. 'There was a great atmosphere in the team room that week and Sam Torrance was instrumental [in that],' says Howard Clark.

The match got underway at 8.15 a.m. sharp with Seve Ballesteros – who else? – and his partner Manuel Piñero cruising effortlessly into a 4-up lead after just six holes against the debutant Mark O'Meara and Curtis Strange. Gradually, though, the Americans came back. By the time they reached the 10th hole, they were just 2-down and the focus turned to one of the most bewitching par-4s in golf.

In 1978, the Brabazon course had taken its international bow when it hosted the Hennessy Cup, an event that pitted a GB and Ireland team against the rest of Europe. When the game between Seve Ballesteros and Nick Faldo had reached the 10th hole, Faldo played safe, leaving himself a wedge in from the heart of the fairway. Ballesteros did not. He pulled his driver from his bag and drove the full 310 yards to the green, his ball stopping just eight feet from the hole.

Today, there is a plaque at The Belfry commemorating this breathtaking bit of magic from Ballesteros, and at the Ryder Cup seven years later, there was an assumption that even in a team game, Ballesteros would do the same again, even though he had struggled with his driving going into the tournament.

He didn't disappoint. With the hole shortened to just 275 yards in a bid to tempt more players to go for the green, the US captain, Lee Trevino, never the longest hitter himself, regarded it as a risk not worth taking and advised his team to take the fairway route to the hole. Tony Jacklin, meanwhile, left it up to each player and pairing to decide what to do – not that you could have really told Ballesteros to lay up anyway.

The sensible shot was to hit a comfortable 6- or 7-iron down the left on to the fairway, chip on with a wedge and hope to make birdie. But as with his bunker shot two years earlier against Fuzzy Zoeller, there was no hesitation, no wavering with Ballesteros. He took out a wood and nearly cracked the casing off his ball. Out it flew, high over the water guarding the putting surface, before rolling to the back of the green.

Two putts later, Ballesteros and Piñero had their birdie and went on to win the match 2&1.

Ballesteros and Piñero's victory would, surprisingly, be the only point Europe would take on the opening morning. Moreover, there would be another more concerning issue for Tony Jacklin to address. Paired with Bernhard Langer, Faldo had played poorly in a 3&2 loss to Calvin Peete and Tom Kite in the second game out. While the defeat was unexpected – Langer and Faldo were one of Tony Jacklin's strongest pairings – Faldo regarded his performance as so unacceptable that he sought out his captain straight after the game and insisted he be left out until the singles on Sunday.

With three sessions of pairs games yet to play, Tony Jacklin's team was, effectively, down to eleven men, and one of his strongest pairings, on paper at least, was over and done with, after just 16 holes together. What grated most was that it was a captain's pick wasted for Jacklin. Having demanded an extra wild card, he had chosen Faldo (along with Ken Brown and José Rivero), not least because he had played in the previous four contests.

Now, though, Jacklin would have to shuffle his pack. Since Faldo was back on the range, tinkering and tweaking, lost in introspection, the European captain decided to team Bernhard Langer with José María Cañizares, and also chose to bring in Paul Way and Ian Woosnam.

As Raymond Floyd took a well-earned break after his first-day success, Lanny Wadkins and his rookie partner Mark O'Meara made their way to the 1st tee for their fourball match against Seve Ballesteros and Manual Piñero. With two points on the first day, Wadkins was buzzing while the rookie O'Meara was still finding it hard to acclimatize. 'The whole grandstand just booed us,' recalls Wadkins. 'It was his [O'Meara's] first Ryder Cup and he was shocked.'

Wadkins, patently, was not. 'I was like, "Man, don't you love it? Let's go!" I love stuff like that.'

It wasn't just the home galleries that were intent on getting under the skins of the visiting team. Fifteen minutes later, the fourball reached the 1st green, and Wadkins found himself faced with an awkward 25-footer. In his way, however, was Ballesteros's marker and, as was his right, Wadkins asked his opponent to move it. The Spaniard duly obliged but when Wadkins hit his putt his ball flicked off the side of Ballesteros' marker and went right in the hole.

Ballesteros glared at Wadkins. 'He looked at me and said, "You did that on purpose. You had me move my coin so you could hit it and bounce in the hole".' 'Yes Seve,' countered Wadkins, with the devil in his eyes. 'I am that fucking good.'

With Wadkins clearly intent on giving as good as he got, he and O'Meara took the fight to Ballesteros and Piñero, eventually emerging with a comfortable 3&2 victory over the previously undefeated Spanish duo. 'Only a fool is going to aim at a coin when the hole is fifty times the size!' he says today. '[But] Seve was always going to dish it out – you just had to give it right back to him.'

Wadkins and O'Meara's victory had tied the scores once more at five half points each, with just one match, Bernhard Langer and Sandy Lyle versus Craig Stadler and Curtis Strange, left out on the course. It would prove to be a critical game. Up to this point, the American pair had remained comfortably ahead, successfully rebuffing any moves from their European opponents. Stadler especially looked assured and in command, holing putt after crucial putt.

With two holes to play, Stadler and Strange were 2-up and set fair for victory. A ridiculous, improbable Sandy Lyle eagle at the 17th, however, would reduce the Americans' advantage to just one, but still, they seemed odds-on to take the point. Off went the drives at the 18th, with Curtis Strange the only one to find trouble in a bunker on the right. Strange then laid up short of the water, while Stadler's approach found the green but was still some 60 feet shy of the flag. Langer and Lyle, meanwhile, would also find the bottom level of the green, closer than Stadler's but no less easy.

Strange was effectively out of the reckoning, but Stadler's first putt travelled up and over the final green, coming to rest a little more than a tap-in away. It was 18 inches, maybe a couple of feet. Straight too. It was a putt so short and so simple that, had it been on any other hole, it would have been conceded without a moment's thought from the opposition. But as the best they could do was a par-4, this was Langer and Lyle's last hope and the only thing they could cling to.

Barely pausing, Stadler stepped forward to tap in, but succeeded only in pulling the ball so wide that it didn't even touch the sides of the hole. As the ball dribbled past, Stadler simply turned his back and wrapped his left hand around the back of his neck, presumably measuring himself up for the noose that he might need.

It was a hideous miss. From being in control of the game, Stadler had gifted the Europeans a half point they should never have got. Suddenly, the mood around The Belfry changed. In the team room, the Europeans knew that the tide had turned. 'We took that and ran with it,' says Tony Jacklin. 'As a team we knew that was a sign, a chink in the armour, a weakness, and you have got to pounce on it.'

For a Ryder Cup veteran like Ray Floyd, who had watched the drama unfold at greenside, it was another of those crucial, seemingly pivotal moments when the momentum in a Ryder Cup suddenly, inexplicably, seems to change. 'There are little movements during the play that can change everything,' says Floyd. 'A half point loss or win, a stroke instead of getting a half, you win one and they get nothing, it's huge.'

That afternoon the European team, buoyed by this unexpected slice, or rather pull, of luck, stormed back in the foursomes, winning the session 3–1. Only Ian Woosnam and Paul Way failed to win their match, going down to Peter Jacobson and a clearly determined Curtis Strange. Now, having started the day a point in arrears, Europe had pulled clear with a two-point cushion.

This, though, was uncharted territory for Tony Jacklin and his European team. If the sense of expectation before the first tee shot had been struck on Friday had been huge, now it was off the scale. Come the clear skies and stiff breeze of Sunday, another 25,000 fans had squeezed into The Belfry. Around the 1st tee and all along the 1st fairway, the crowd was six deep, sometimes more. To those home fans who had squirmed through the last Ryder Cup held in Britain in 1981, it must have seemed as though they were watching an entirely different competition.

For the singles matches at PGA National two years earlier, Tony Jacklin had gambled on sending his strongest players out first in the hope that he could get quick points on the board and gather some momentum. This time, however, Jacklin would be more circumspect. Manuel Piñero, Ian Woosnam and Paul Way – reliable players who were all enjoying good form – were the first three out, followed by Ballesteros, Lyle and Langer. The hope was that Piñero, Woosnam and Way could steal a few points before the big guns' matches came into play.

Faced with having to claw back a deficit, Lee Trevino could not afford the luxury of holding back his bankers and, predictably, he sent out his heavyweights first, with Lanny Wadkins leading the way, followed by Craig Stadler, Ray Floyd and Tom Kite.

Emboldened by the exploits of his compatriot Seve Ballesteros, Piñero had been desperate to lead off, even if it meant coming up against one of the tougher American players. Tony Jacklin acceded to the Spaniard's request, and Piñero soon learned that he would be facing the toughest nut of them all, Lanny Wadkins.

True to his word, Piñero duly delivered, recording a 3&1 win over Wadkins while Paul Way continued his remarkable Ryder Cup career, conquering the conditions and his sore throat to defeat Ray Floyd, 2-up, and register another huge point for Europe. 'I took lots of major scalps in my Ryder Cup – Floyd, Watson, Zoeller – and they weren't too happy about it,' he says. 'But everybody struggled that day because the wind was up. I shot maybe a 73 or 74 but that was still good enough to beat Ray Floyd. Over eighteen holes, anyone can beat anyone. I was never as good a player as Ray Floyd or Curtis Strange [whom Way beat in 1983] but over 18 holes you've always got a chance.'

In his two appearances in the Ryder Cup Way had banked six and a half points out of a possible nine, which, he jokes, would have been more 'if my partners hadn't let me down'. His partners, lest it be forgotten, were Seve Ballesteros and Ian Woosnam.

The sole American player to win his game in the top half of the singles draw was Craig Stadler, who put Saturday's nightmare behind him to beat Ian Woosnam 2&1. The visitors' only other half point came from the dependable hands of Tom Kite, who slugged it out with Seve Ballesteros in one of the great Ryder Cup clashes.

Typically, Kite had begun as he had so many times before in the Ryder Cup, matching anything his opponent had to offer before easing imperiously into a 2-up lead by the turn. While he lacked the natural swagger of Lanny Wadkins, Kite was no less obdurate, a natural-born battler with a killer instinct and a healthy distrust of reputations, even if he was playing someone as gifted as Ballesteros.

With five to play, Kite, seemingly oblivious to the hoopla around him, looked certain to beat the man universally regarded as the best player in the world. Seve was on the verge of a crushing defeat, not just for him but for Europe as well. At the 14th, though, Ballesteros offered the first sign of a fightback as he drained a 35-foot putt to reduce the deficit to 2-down. At the next hole, the par-five 15th, the Spaniard birdied from 20 feet, then stormed off to the 16th tee only one hole behind and with an expression made of equal parts determination and madness. Following a half at the 16th, Ballesteros went through the back of the green at the par-5 17th in two, leaving himself in the long grass while Kite found the green in three. To the dismay of The Belfry crowds, Ballesteros fluffed his chip, succeeding only in nudging it up to the fringe of the green. Staring at his ball as though it had failed to act on orders, Ballesteros then stepped up and simply holed his putt from off the green, winning the hole with a birdie, leaving the galleries open-mouthed and awestruck.

All-square going down the last, Tom Kite could have been forgiven for crumbling but – champion that he was – he played the final hole superbly, a flushed tee shot leaving him a mere 9-iron into the green.

Both men found the putting surface, but neither could do better than a two-putt par, giving them a half point apiece. Some players would have been happy with a share of the spoils, but as Ballesteros left the green, he was still visibly angry with himself for not winning.

Watching from the greenside was Peter Jacobsen, who had already suffered a 3&2 reverse to Sandy Lyle. 'I admired Seve for his perform-ances,' he says. 'He was the most inspirational player that I have ever played with, watching him play, whether I was competing with him or against him or just in a tournament, a stroke-play tournament, whether it was the Open Championship, the US Open, the PGA Tour, I loved to watch this man play because of the way he directed his game.'

Kite's half point would have little effect on the way the match was clearly heading. With Lyle and Langer – respectively 3&2 and 5&4 winners over Jacobsen and Hal Sutton – already back in the clubhouse, Europe needed just one point from the remaining six matches to win the Ryder Cup, one point to finally make their own bit of history.

But where would it come from? At the 17th, Howard Clark had a 6-foot putt to register a 2&1 win over the debutant Mark O'Meara but his putt had caught the edge of the hole and stayed above the ground. Had that putt dropped, the Yorkshireman would have been the man who made history for Europe.

But it didn't. Instead, attention turned to the hole ahead, with the Scot Sam Torrance facing the towering 1985 US Open champion, Andy North. Both men had struggled in the breezy Belfry conditions, with their round scores nudging 80. The fact that they had both played poorly was irrelevant. One-down with two to play, Torrance had pulled level by bravely winning the 17th and had headed off to the 18th tee to be met by Tony Jacklin.

Jacklin smiled at Torrance, as if he knew that the moment – his moment – had finally arrived. Torrance pulled out his driver and handed it to his captain. 'You hit it!' he said.

'Don't be daft, laddie,' replied Jacklin, handing it back. Torrance's tee shot would be not just his best shot of the day, but 'the drive of my life'. When North followed, he could only ditch his drive into the water, which meant that the best he could do was a bogey 5. As Torrance reached his ball, sat safely in the heart of the fairway, he was joined briefly by his teammates Paul Way and Ian Woosnam, who updated him on the state of play and told him to go and win it. A sweet, swift 9-iron later and Torrance found himself with the luxury of two putts from 20 feet to take the trophy.

As he crossed the bridge to the green, Torrance felt emotion welling up inside him, as the wall of noise – and the enormity of what was about to happen – hit him like a tidal surge. His putt, meanwhile, was pure and perfect as it drifted towards the hole, curling deliciously before dropping, deadweight, into the cup. With tears streaming down his face, and catching in his moustache, Torrance held his arms aloft and as The Belfry erupted, Ian Woosnam ran on to the green, bear-hugging the Scotsman, as if to squeeze a few more tears of joy out of him.

While the champagne and the tears flowed at the 18th green, Howard Clark was a hole back, having sunk a putt that he believed had given Europe their long-awaited win. In short, it might actually have been Howard Clark who won the Ryder Cup in 1985, and not Sam Torrance, as Clark himself explains. 'Maybe I didn't get the recognition that I probably could have done,' says Clark, 'but I always thought, well, it was justified because Sam was on the 18th, he beat his player and I had halved the 17th which meant I was 1-up with one to play which meant I couldn't lose so I was guaranteed half a point. So they just took it upon themselves to award him the winning putt… maybe after all these years he could have said something about that but it's no big deal.'

But it was hard, if not impossible, to deny Torrance his moment in the rare West Midlands sunshine. For Tony Jacklin too, this was a vindication of everything he had strived for, a justification for Concorde and cashmere. Crucially, the experience gained two years earlier in Florida had strengthened his team, fostering belief and confidence and inspiring them to a fantastic victory. 'There had been anticipation that week in '85 but we weren't as much concerned with what other people were thinking. We were just all closer as a team, all in touch with each other. It was two years that had gone by so quickly. When we arrived at The Belfry it was like no time had passed. We just hit the ground running.'

Though the US rallied in the final games, Europe had coasted to a 16½–11½ win. For every member of the European team it was, as Paul Way described it, 'a historic, life-changing moment'. As the team clambered on to the roof of the clubhouse to celebrate, spraying champagne on the crowds below, Concorde, the big bird that had helped propel the team onwards and upwards, flew over The Belfry, dipping its wings in appreciation.

If Tony Jacklin was 'bawling like a baby', Lee Trevino was devastated. For all his many achievements in the game, he had become only the third man in history to captain a losing US Ryder Cup team. And how it hurt. The PGA's Executive Director Colin Snape recalls the celebrations of Europe's famous win. 'The victory dinner was really something special. The players got dressed up and all the sponsors and everybody that helped came,' he recalls. 'But Lee Trevino didn't acquit himself well. He couldn't take defeat. It was such a shock to him personally. He felt that he had let America down… defeat can show the character of a person.'

The victory dinner would only be the start of the celebrations. Long and hard they partied, deep into the night – and then into the swimming pool. Having played just two games and lost them both, Nick Faldo was less than keen to join in the revelry, preferring to sulk in the corner of the clubhouse and analyse just where his Ryder Cup had gone wrong. But when the players noticed his absence, a press gang was dispatched to find him. The next thing he knew, he had been slung in The Belfry's pool, fully clothed. 'We threw Faldo in the pool because he only played two games and lost both of them,' says Paul Way, matter-of-factly. 'He was going through his swing changes at the time and wasn't very confident, but we chucked him in the pool anyway.'

Next in line was the skipper, thrown in after Faldo, his pristine team suit ruined. 'It wasn't my idea of having a good time,' he reflects. Pulling himself out of the water, Jacklin shook himself down like a dog, before traipsing back to his hotel room, dripping as he went. After a quick shower, he slipped on his bathrobe, grabbed a tumbler and poured himself a very large whisky. 'It had,' he concludes, 'been emotional.'

Back to Jack

SIXTY long years had passed since Ted Ray and his team had stood on the deck of the *Aquitania*, posing for photographs as they set sail from Southampton docks to play in the first official Ryder Cup at Worcester Country Club, Massachusetts. After a rough and uncomfortable six-day voyage, during which most of the team were confined to their rooms with sea-sickness, the Great Britain team had arrived in the United States to a warm reception from the great and the good of American golf. But less than a week later they were on their way home again, with another six days at sea to ponder the devastating 9½–2½ rout that Walter Hagen's team had just handed them.

Twenty-six Ryder Cups and another World War later, Tony Jacklin's European team arrived in the United States in a shade over three hours having travelled in supersonic style on Concorde. But while the mode of transport had changed, the results, Stateside at least, had not. Following their momentous victory at The Belfry two years earlier Jacklin's team were now holders of the Ryder Cup, but no side, be it Great Britain, Great Britain and Ireland or Europe had ever ventured to the States and returned home with Sam Ryder's trophy in their possession. Winning at home was one thing, but winning in the United States was an entirely different proposition.

For the first time, though, the European Ryder Cup team had flown to the States with the Ryder Cup in their possession. With the monkey finally shaken off their back in 1985, the mood on Concorde was expectant, the atmosphere relaxed. During the flight, Sam Torrance even stood up and asked for quiet as he announced that he and his girlfriend, the actress Suzanne Danielle, had become engaged. The PGA was also celebrating. After the win in 1985, the Ryder Cup had grown exponentially. Concorde, for instance, was now paying for itself. Ingeniously, the PGA had enlisted the services of the ticketing agency Keith Prowse to sell tickets on the team flight to well-heeled fans at a cost of £5,000, the net result being that all of the PGA's Ryder Cup party now travelled for free. The clothing, too, was better and swisher than ever, Glenmuir having been retained as the official supplier of clothing to the European team. Tony Jacklin and his men stepped off Concorde wearing their new £600 cashmere jackets to be greeted at Columbus's Rickenbacker Airport by a clearly impressed Jack Nicklaus.

It had been a golden time for the Golden Bear. In April 1986 Nicklaus had won his eighteenth and final major championship – nearly a quarter of a century after his maiden win – when he took the 50th Masters at Augusta at the age of 46, shooting a miraculous 65 in the final round to win by one stroke. But Muirfield Village – looking lovely as ever in the September sunshine – presented Nicklaus with a special challenge. For he was here as US Ryder Cup captain for the second time, at the course he had designed and built himself – and in his home town as well. That was some test – even for a golfer as great as Nicklaus.

Of all the courses Nicklaus had designed, Muirfield Village was closest to his heart. A Colombus native, he had long nurtured the dream of building a course in his home town. Having acquired a 220-acre site in the suburb of Dublin, Ohio in 1966, that dream was finally realized in 1974 when the course was officially dedicated, an event he marked with an exhibition game between himself and the 1973 Open champion, Tom Weiskopf. For the record, Jack shot a course record 6-under round of 66 that day – a record that would stand until 1979.

Muirfield – it was named after the course in Scotland where he won his first Open Championship in 1966 – was a typically testing Nicklaus track. With its tight fairways, bold bunkering and greens so slick it was like putting on a table top, it had been nicknamed the 'Augusta of the North', which, in Nicklaus's mind, meant mission accomplished. 'I set out to build not only an outstanding golf course for every level of player, but a magnificent course for watching a tournament,' he said. 'I thought the Masters was a great thing for golf and that I'd like to do the same thing in Columbus.'

If the prospect of hosting the Ryder Cup on one's own course, and with the added pressure of being a team captain too, was the stuff of fraught days and sleepless nights, it didn't show with Nicklaus. Perhaps the fact that he had, since 1976, hosted his own annual tournament at Muirfield – the Memorial – which had become a well-attended stop on the PGA Tour, lessened his anxieties. But Nicklaus had things on his mind, nonetheless. Having seen his previous team come perilously close to losing in 1983, he harboured doubts not just about the strength of his team but about the way it was selected and even about the format of the Ryder Cup itself. The success of the European team, and the concomitant increase in the appeal of the competition, led Nicklaus to conclude that there was now a strong case for extending the Ryder Cup to four days by adding an extra day of singles. This made commercial sense, not least because of its appeal to the television network ABC – with whom the PGA had just struck a new deal to cover the Cup live – but it also played to the USA's natural strength in the singles games. That said, it was testament to the potency of Jacklin's team that Nicklaus and the USA were now seeking to change the format of the Cup in order to regain their old ascendancy.

Not surprisingly, the idea of extending the matches was given short shrift by Jacklin. While he could envisage some of his younger players enjoying one good round in the singles, the notion that they could do it twice was less likely. For Jacklin, the format was just fine and it would take a public threat from him to resign as European skipper for

Nicklaus and the PGA of America to scratch the idea. Nicklaus, though, was more successful with some of his other proposals, doubling the qualification period for the US team to two years and opening up a debate that would eventually see the right of the reigning US Open champion to qualify for the team removed.

Jack Nicklaus would be the perfect host. Nothing, it seemed, was too much trouble for him. He even invited several prospective members of the European team to play in his own Memorial tournament at Muirfield Village at the end of May, flying them from New York on a private jet and giving them the ultimate VIP tour of his home-town course. 'Jack made us very welcome as he and all the Americans always did,' explains Howard Clark. 'As a European player in those days we didn't get invites to play in tournaments unless we had won a major or we were top of the Order of Merit – it was highly unlikely that you were going to get invited to Muirfield Village let alone any other tournament for that matter.'

For some Americans, Nicklaus's welcome was too warm. The then PGA Commissioner, Deane Beman, felt that offering places to European players at the expense of home-grown talent wasn't appropriate. It was, as he pointed out, the PGA Tour and not the Jack Nicklaus Tour.

The members of the European Ryder Cup team were certainly made to feel like VIPs when they touched down in Ohio in September. At the airport, they were fast-tracked through immigration and led to a fleet of individual Cadillacs waiting to take them to Muirfield Village. When they arrived at their hotel, they were greeted by the Ohio State Marching Band, welcoming them to the strains of 'Three Cheers for the Red, White and Blue'. 'Everything was perfect,' says Tony Jacklin. 'The course was great. The accommodation was great. Our hosts, Barbara and Jack Nicklaus, were unfailingly gracious and generous while also being competitive in exactly the best way.'

If anything, Nicklaus shouldn't have made the visitors quite so welcome. After all, European golf had turned a corner and now it was their players making the headlines, not the Americans. With nine of the victors of 1985 in their 1987 team, Europe now possessed a spine that boasted some of the strongest players in the world. There was Ballesteros, still in his prime and still the same old Seve. There was Ian Woosnam, arguably the best ball striker in the world. There were Langer and Lyle and there was the new Open champion, Nick Faldo, whose time in the wilderness spent remodelling his swing had been rewarded with his first major at the Open Championship at the other, original, Muirfield. 'We had great confidence and natural partnerships,' explains Howard Clark, back for his fourth Ryder Cup appearance. 'Woosnam and Faldo, Lyle and Langer, were just fantastic players. There was a very strong top half of the team, with another team, if you like, that could back the top half up.'

There would also be debuts for the young Spaniard earmarked as golf's next big thing, José María Olazábal, and the dependable Scot who wasn't, Gordon Brand Jr. 'I think the Ryder Cup was always a draw for the Europeans because it was the Ryder Cup, it was as simple as that,' Brand explains. 'I don't think it was as big for the Americans but it was a concept we believed in... so it was a huge thing to be a member of the Ryder Cup.'

If the organization at Muirfield was faultless, the same couldn't be said of the European team. Despite the great strides (quite literally in the case of the team's trousers) made by Tony Jacklin and the PGA in the years since 1981, little things were still going wrong. When the team took delivery of their official golf bags, for instance, they found them to be the wrong size, prompting Tony Jacklin's assistant Bernard Gallacher to get on the phone to the manufacturer Titleist. He had two demands to make of them: first, that they deliver new bags of the desired size as soon as possible; secondly, that they made sure that the players' names on the bags were spelt correctly...

Of course, it didn't help that some of the European team were their own worst enemies. While some players, such as Bernhard Langer, were precise and organized, leaving nothing to chance, others, like Sam Torrance, were a little more laissez-faire in their approach. 'With

Langer, everything was perfect in that Germanic sort of way,' says Sandy Jones, the head of the PGA's Scottish operation, who was assisting Tony Jacklin for the week. 'At Muirfield, we got a message on one of the practice days that there was a threat of rain and I was sent back to all the players' rooms to get sweaters. Langer's room was laid out perfectly; here was Monday, here was Tuesday, here was Wednesday – it was perfection. I remember then going into Sam's room and there was stuff everywhere, I shouldn't pick on Sam, but you can imagine the situation, there was a shoe here, a shoe there...'

For the 1987 contest, the PGA of America had a new acting executive director in place. Jim Awtrey was a former professional who had played on the PGA Tour in 1970–71 and, latterly, coached the golf team at his alma mater, the University of Oklahoma. In 1986, he had been appointed as the PGA's manager of tournament operations and, within a year, had landed the position of acting executive director. As the new guy in the hot seat, taking over at a time when a resurgent Europe had made the event a real contest, there was now a new pressure that none of his predecessors had really experienced. 'The Ryder Cup in 1987 was my first as executive director,' he explains. 'It was a lot of responsibility... because it was taken for granted that it was always won by the Americans on home soil.'

Eight years after the Great Britain and Ireland team had become a European team, the team itself was becoming increasingly cosmopolitan in its make-up. Irrespective of nationality, the players were established, confident and comfortable, and partnerships emerged naturally. Well, almost. While the pairings of Faldo and Woosnam and Ballesteros and Olazábal appeared clear cut, the decision to partner Gordon Brand Jr with the Spaniard José Rivero was less obvious, not least to Gordon Brand. 'It was a complete mystery to me,' he shrugs, 'because you would have thought that in preparation – in practice rounds – that you would possibly be playing with someone you had been friends with or whose game you knew, or even, quite simply, someone who could speak your language. Sometimes captains just see your pairing and think they match. José and I weren't boom-boom hitters, we were very much steady Eddies, so he may well have actually looked at that. It would have been different if I had been playing with Sam Torrance or Howard Clark who were people I had gone out to dinner with or played World Cups with, so I would have had some knowledge of them, but even to this day I don't know why I played with Rivero.'

Truth was Brand and Rivero didn't need any luck. In their opening fourballs game on Friday afternoon they trumped Ben Crenshaw and Scott Simpson 3&2 and set up the perfect afternoon for the visitors as they whitewashed the USA to take a commanding 6–2 lead. 'We got a result,' adds Brand. 'I think at the time you are not really aware of what's happening. It sounds a bit blasé [but] I just looked at it as another game of golf. Maybe that naivety was a good thing.'

As Europe had roared into the lead on the first day, Jack Nicklaus had grown concerned, first, and understandably, by the scoreline, and secondly by the marked lack of support for his team around his course. Come the second day, Nicklaus had resolved to effect a change. On Saturday morning, he arranged for the galleries to be given Stars and Stripes flags to wave and, whether he ordered it or not, suddenly the players' wives and team officials, all in uniform, were noticeable by their presence rather than their absence.

That Nicklaus was finding new ways to inspire his team and his home crowd was a clear indication that even after just one day, the thought that he was in danger of becoming the first US captain to lose a Ryder Cup on American soil was clearly uppermost in his mind. Whatever he did, though, he knew that Tony Jacklin, especially with Ballesteros by his side, now possessed that invaluable commodity that counted for so much in Ryder Cup golf – confidence.

Jacklin's trust in Ballesteros was total. Under his captaincy, the Spaniard had played every session in 1983 and 1985, taking six and a half points from a possible ten and proving himself to be the keystone of the European team. While his partnerships, first with Paul Way and then with Manuel Piñero, had been undeniably successful, it would be his partnership with his compatriot, the twenty-one-year-old José María Olazábal, that would, arguably, come to define his Ryder Cup career.

Olazábal's rise through the professional ranks had been quicker than a six-foot downhiller at Augusta. Having joined the European Tour in 1986, he had won that year's European Masters and the Sanyo Open in close succession, propelling himself into the Ryder Cup reckoning, with a game based less on accurate driving and, like Ballesteros, more on laser-like iron play, imaginative recoveries and the most reliable of putting strokes.

The son of a farmer, Olazábal, it seemed, was always destined to play golf, born the day after a new golf course, Real Golf Club de San Sebastián, opened next to his house in Fuenterrabía in the Basque region of northern Spain. Most of Olazábal's family would pass through San Sebastián golf club. His grandfather would be the club's greens-keeper and when he passed away, Olazábal's father, Gaspar, took over the position. After school, 'Chemma', as his family called him, would take his cut-down clubs and, with his cross-handed grip, hit ball after ball or stroke putts on the practice green just 20 feet from his front door until the sun went down or his father called him in, whichever came first. By sixteen, he had decided to turn professional, much to his parents' amusement. 'You should have seen their faces,' he said.

Five years on, and Olazábal's parents were forced to concede that sometimes kids really do know best, and if Jacklin's hunches with Paul Way and José Rivero had paid off, the decision to pair Ballesteros and Olazábal was an almost preordained union. It was not so much father and son as inseparable siblings, with big brother Seve leading the way and little brother José María, keen to learn and ever eager to please. 'Seve was so dominant that the big problem was getting somebody to fit with him because Seve made his own team nervous,' explains Jacklin's assistant, Bernard Gallacher. 'It worked with Manuel Piñero, it worked with Paul Way, but the real combination was Seve and Olazábal,' You just can't put these superstars with just anybody because some of the lesser players get a bit jumpy and a bit nervous and don't play their own game playing with such a good player.'

It would be a partnership that reaped immediate dividends. The bond was instant, the trust implicit. After an opening foursomes victory over Larry Nelson and Payne Stewart the duo dispatched Curtis Strange and Tom Kite in the afternoon fourballs, with Ballesteros in imperious form. At the 1st he chipped in from 40 feet to take the hole, before notching up five more birdies, including a 45-foot putt to win the 10th and an outrageous 70-foot putt that took the 17th and finished the match 2&1. The first real test of their collaboration would come at the final hole of their Saturday foursomes match against Ben Crenshaw and Payne Stewart. With two putts for the match, Ballesteros stepped up and sent his 14-foot putt racing ten feet past the hole, leaving Olazábal with a beastly return putt to take the point. With a confidence that belied his age, the junior partner calmly knocked in the putt, sealing their third win in succession.

It was only on the Saturday afternoon, after two arduous days and four hard-fought rounds, that Ballesteros and Olazábal finally dropped a point, losing out 2&1 to Hal Sutton and Larry Mize, but with three wins from four, it was clear that here was a partnership for the future, a pairing that any European skipper in the years to come could bank on. 'The Ryder Cup involves a European team but you see some great national pairings, like Seve and Ollie,' says the commentator Bruce Critchley. 'So they represent Spain too. You have got to have a con-stituency, you have got to have something you represent to give you the impetus, something to be proud about.'

It was hard to believe that Ballesteros was still only thirty years old, such was his presence. Now playing his fourth Ryder Cup, the resurgence of the competition as a genuine contest hadn't just coincided with his participation but rather been largely driven by it. And in 1987, his influence in the European camp was inestimable. 'He was inspirational,' explains Sandy Jones. 'He was always the leader, he had that presence. I don't know how you explain it, it's instinctive, it is built into him. There is an aura about the guy. And not every-body has it.'

The seismic, talismanic impact of Seve Ballesteros had not merely translated into points on the scoreboard for Europe. Throughout the team, there was now a new-found self-assurance and a belief that so long as Seve was on board and making things happen, they were going to be just fine. 'The Europeans, especially Seve, made such a big difference,' says Howard Clark. 'They added such a lot because they brought a real confidence factor to the British players.'

Just as prolific as Ballasteros and Olazábal was the partnership of Germany's Bernhard Langer and Scotland's Sandy Lyle. Though they had been members of the three previous Ryder Cup teams, they had only played once together, sharing the points with Curtis Strange and Craig Stadler in Saturday fourballs at The Belfry in 1985. Yet Langer and Lyle were kindred spirits. Straight-talking, no-nonsense types, but both blessed with a dry sense of humour that could take the sting out of any situation, they had been thrown together after Ken Brown and Langer had stalled in their foursomes match against Hal Sutton and Dan Pohl. They now found themselves facing the toughest pairing that Jack Nicklaus could muster, Lanny Wadkins and Larry Nelson.

Wadkins and Nelson were the opponents if not from hell, then from somewhere in the nearby suburbs. In nine outings together stretching back to 1979, the US pair boasted a record of played nine, won nine. They were dogged and destructive, two golfing assassins likened by Lyle to the 'golfing twin brothers of Sylvester Stallone's Rocky Balboa'.

On the Saturday morning, the four of them went at it like tag-team wrestlers, the Europeans scraping through to a hard-fought 2&1 victory. When Langer and Lyle then found themselves drawn, inevita-bly, against Wadkins and Nelson in the afternoon fourballs, they picked up where they left off, winning a mesmerizing encounter 1-up. The game ebbed to and fro, but try as they might the Americans couldn't pull back the deficit. It wasn't for lack of trying. Wadkins would play the last five holes in 4 under par, but still couldn't make an impression on the Europeans' lead. At the 18th, Lyle seemed to have sealed the deal when, in the fading light, he stopped an 8-iron just six feet from the hole, leaving him with a slippery and very missable putt down the hill. But Wadkins wasn't done, responding with an approach that landed just a yard from the pin. As the home crowd sensed a snatched half point, screaming 'USA! USA! USA!', Bernhard Langer eyed up his own approach. 'Get inside that,' said Lyle, 'and I'll kiss you.'

The moment Langer's ball left the clubface it was all over the flag. When it hit the green, it rolled, stopping sweetly just inches from the cup. Langer looked across to his partner and smiled as he tossed his 8-iron back into the bag. Lyle, meanwhile, would backtrack on his promise, choosing to blow his partner a kiss instead.

Lyle and Langer's win meant that the afternoon's points were shared and that Europe would take a sizeable 10½–5½ lead into the final day. It was a heady moment for the Europeans. Winning at The Belfry in 1985 had propelled them into exciting new territory, but to be taking a five-point lead going into the Sunday of the Cup – and in the United States, to boot – well, that was almost like landing on Mars.

Typically, though, the Americans would come roaring and snarling back. Out first, Ian Woosnam's rotten record in the singles would continue as he lost to the man fully 12 inches taller than him, Andy Bean, while the US middle order then proceeded to rip Europe apart. Mark Calcavecchia snaffled the point from Nick Faldo, Payne Stewart held off José María Olazábal, José Rivero also lost out to Scott Simpson while the ever-dependable Tom Kite crushed Sandy Lyle 3&2, even though the Scot had been in sparkling form and was 6 under par for his round. Europe's huge lead had all but evaporated: there was now just a single point in it, with the scoreboard standing at 12–11 in Europe's favour. Only Howard Clark, with his win at the 18th against Dan Pohl, and Sam Torrance's half with Larry Mize, helped keep Europe's nose in front.

Gordon Brand Jr, meanwhile, was discovering how lonely the Sunday singles could be for the European players in America as he battled it out with Hal Sutton. At the 8th hole Brand had just dunked a 100-yard sand wedge straight into the hole to take a 4-up lead. 'As I walked off the green a typical fat American [was] sitting there in his chair with two burgers and four cokes and he said, "Hal, you've got him, you've got him, Hal". And I just looked at him and thought, "I'm 4-up mate, haven't you seen the scoreboard?" And then, of course, Hal Sutton goes eagle, birdie, par, eagle and we are just about all-square again... then you just go, "Oh, my God". I was in control of this game and then it was almost like somebody sucking the blood out of you. You just couldn't believe it.'

As attention turned to the eighth game, between Ireland's Eamonn Darcy and Ben Crenshaw, Tony Jacklin feared the worst. He had good reason, too. Darcy, after all, had never won a game in the Ryder Cup. In his three appearances in the competition, he had played nine games, had lost seven of them and taken a half point from the other two. Indeed, prior to Muirfield Village, his last game had been a singles game against Jack Nicklaus in the savaging at Walton Heath in 1981 where, with the victory already assured, Nicklaus twisted the knife still further, handing him a 5&3 drubbing.

As he walked on to the 1st tee with his opponent Ben Crenshaw, a voice rang out from the crowd surrounding the tee box. 'There was a big fat guy in the gallery,' remembered Darcy. 'He was frothing at the mouth and screaming, "Kill him, Ben, kill him. No prisoners today". I thought to myself, "Here we go" – it was going to be that kind of day.'

Darcy would survive but Ben Crenshaw's putter wasn't so fortunate. At the 6th hole, the man they called 'Gentle Ben' three-putted and as he left the green, incensed, he took his anger out on his Wilson 8802 putter, at which point the shaft snapped in two. 'I was absolutely stunned,' he commented later. 'Of course, the first thing you think is, "God, why now? Why, on the last day of the Ryder Cup, in a tight match?"'

On the following hole, Crenshaw was still seething when his captain, Jack Nicklaus, came by for a progress report. 'How're you doing,' asked the skipper.

Sheepishly, Crenshaw looked at the ground, muttering, 'Well, I broke my putter.'

'You did what?' asked the captain.

'I broke my putter on the 6th green.'

'Well,' shrugged Nicklaus, 'with the way things are going, I don't blame you.'

For the rest of the round, the Texan would have to putt using the leading edge of his sand wedge and, later, his 1-iron. It said much for his skill on the greens that he managed to take the game to the final hole where the two stood all-square. 'I wasn't aware that Ben had broken his putter,' said Darcy later. 'I thought he was putting with his 1-iron because the greens were so quick and he had missed a couple on the front nine.'

In a nervy final exchange, the best Crenshaw could manage would be a bogey five having tugged his drive into the creek running along the left side of the fairway. Darcy, meanwhile, was just as shaky, spearing his 3-wood approach into the greenside bunker, before splashing out to four feet. With a putt to win the hole and the match and with his hands visibly shaking, Darcy trickled his ball down the slope towards the hole. If it missed it would go 15 feet past, maybe more. When it finally dropped, Darcy had his first ever win in the Ryder Cup, some eleven games and twelve years after his very first shot in the event. 'In hindsight, the way it all happened was a fairytale. We all get a chance somewhere,' he explained. 'Even though we all claim the Ryder Cup is a team event... I was able to put my stamp on it.'

Eamonn Darcy's win took Europe to the brink of their first ever victory on American soil. Soon after, at 2.50 p.m., the Ryder Cup was Europe's once more. Seve Ballesteros – who else? – would be the player to close the deal, holing out on the 17th green against Curtis Strange to win 2&1 and take Tony Jacklin's team over the threshold. When Gordon Brand secured his half point with Hal Sutton in the final game, the European party could begin in earnest and as the team poured on to the green, Jacklin was picked up and plonked on the broad shoulders of one of the stars of the week (and the man with the lowest centre of gravity), Ian Woosnam.

After the tears of joy at The Belfry in 1985, the celebrations seemed somehow different; not muted, just different. There was an air of confidence, even superiority, and, for once, it wasn't misplaced. 'We were a well-armed force to have the first victory on American soil,' reflects Tony Jacklin. 'We were a formidable force. All of a sudden and we went and got it done.'

Howard Clark agrees. It was different in the respect that we weren't really expected to lose as we had for the previous twenty-eight years. The Americans put out a pretty strong team again with Nicklaus as captain on his own course [but] we had a fantastic nucleus with Seve and José, Langer and Lyle and Faldo and Woosnam – they were just immense characters. It was a special week.'

As Jacklin clambered down, his debutant José María Olazábal began dancing on the green. It was part flamenco, part drunken uncle at a wedding – and wholly embarrassing. Still, you could forgive him. It was a spontaneous outburst from a young player who had delivered in spectacular fashion and who was determined to enjoy this rare moment. Not everybody thought Olazábal's antics were funny, though, especially Paul Azinger who felt that the Spaniard should have reined in his celebrations. Message received and understood, Olazábal apologized for any offence caused, adding, for good measure, that the Americans should 'get a life and a sense of perspective'.

Besides, Jack Nicklaus had plans for the green. 'Jack came on to the green,' recalls Gordon Brand Jr, 'and said, "Don't worry lads, don't worry about the green. I'm going to dig it up on Monday".'

At the closing ceremony, Nicklaus was crestfallen. Four years earlier, his relief had been palpable as his team had escaped with the narrowest of wins at West Palm Beach. At Muirfield Village, however, he had been powerless to prevent a gifted European team from becoming the first in history to win the Ryder Cup on American soil. In his acceptance speech Lord Derby, the President of the PGA and the European

Tour, dwelt – rather undiplomatically, perhaps – on the difficulty of Nicklaus's position: not only had 'the Golden Bear' become the first American captain to lose the Ryder Cup at home, but had contrived to do so on his home course. 'The American players were just sitting there and you could see them sick in their chair,' recalls Jim Awtrey, who was sitting behind them. 'Now was Lord Derby trying to be mean-spirited? No, that was just his joy and it was kind of tongue in cheek… but you know, you look back over those things and you laugh [although] at the time you may have a different view.'

The carousing would continue apace in the public bar as the European team joined their jubilant fans. Bernhard Langer found a German flag, matched by Torrance's Scottish Lion Rampant, while Seve Ballesteros tried to teach Sandy Lyle the fundamentals of the flamenco. Even Nick Faldo started dancing – badly – on the tables. On the way back to the team room, a gang of European players reconvened in Muirfield Village's car park like naughty schoolboys, and, armed with penknives, began to unscrew the 'Ryder Cup '87' registration plates from the courtesy cars. Tony Jacklin, meanwhile, had slipped away once more, preferring a Glenmorangie with his wife Viv in his hotel room to a night on the tiles. Later, he would call the victory 'the greatest week of my life'.

The following morning, the team awoke, hungover but happy. They soon found, however, after a week of being treated like superstars, of wanting for nothing (apart from bigger golf bags) and having their every whim catered for, that there was something different, and less welcoming, about the atmosphere in the team house, as Gordon Brand Jr explains. 'Every morning that week someone would come in at five o'clock in the morning, put the kettle on and then all the papers were laid out and all the Danish pastries. So every morning you would wake up and you could at least start your day with a cup of coffee and read the papers. Of course, on the Monday after the tournament, there was no Danish, no coffee, no papers. It was like, yeah, right, go home… I wouldn't quite say it was go back home you bloody Europeans, but…'

The End of an Era

THE BELFRY, SUTTON COLDFIELD

22–24 September 1989

SAM Torrance had warned Gordon Brand Jr. After the win at Muirfield Village and the Beatles-like reception the team had received on their return home to Heathrow, Brand had thought that life as a professional golfer couldn't really get much better. Enter Torrance with his two-penn'orth. 'You just wait until we get to The Belfry,' Torrance told his compatriot. But just how different could it be? thought Brand. After all, he had just become one of only twelve men in history to have ever won a Ryder Cup on American soil. Compared with playing in the States, the West Midlands would surely be a doddle.

Back at The Belfry, the European team were steeling themselves for their defence of the Ryder Cup. Preparations had gone well, very well, in fact. Tony Jacklin had been coerced and cajoled into one last fling as European captain and his side appeared confident and relaxed, balanced and resolute. On the morning of Friday 22 September, a little after 6 a.m., Gordon Brand Jr awoke in his hotel room at The Belfry and wandered over to the window to see what the weather held in store for the first day's play of the Ryder Cup. 'I don't know whether you have ever seen the scene in *Monty Python's Life of Brian*, when he opens up the curtains,' he says. 'But it was like, "Oh my God, all those fucking people," and you go, "Oh dear" and you realize that you are in a really big tournament. It was just completely different and people had set their stall out for the day and they were banging their feet on the stands already… well, it was very exciting.'

Billed, hyperbolically, as 'The Match of the Century', the 1989 Ryder Cup would demonstrate just how much the event had grown in such a short time. Indeed, it was hard to believe that less than a decade earlier, the PGA's Colin Snape had been scouring the country desperately trying to drum up interest – and cash – from many, mostly indifferent, sources. By 1989, everything was changing. The Belfry's owners, De Vere, had sanctioned an £8 million redevelopment of the Brabazon course, with new mounds springing up around the course to improve the view for spectators and two new lakes created to help control the water flow and, well, look pretty.

But if proof were needed of how big the event had become in such a short space of time, one only needed to look at the scale of the tented village that had been erected at The Belfry for the match. Instead of just a few bars and food outlets, there were 226 tents, housing 300 hospitality suites and covering some 350,000 square feet, while the total number of staff on hand to help was nearing 5,000.

In the United States, too, the media had cottoned on to the fact that the event had become one of the must-see contests of the sporting calendar. On top of a new television deal, secured by Jim Awtrey, CEO of the PGA of America, with the cable TV channel USA Network, there was clear evidence of an increasing interest in the event on the part of the print media. Once the Ryder Cup would have been secreted away in the 'News in Brief' sections of the US newspapers, but now more than 50 American journalists would make the trip to the West Midlands for the 1989 competition.

After an eight-year absence, Mark James was returning to a team and to an event that had changed beyond all recognition. In his last appearance amid the misery and the mud of Walton Heath in 1981, James had been part of a team decimated by the strongest US side in history. Now, though, he found himself in a side that was, improbably, looking to win a third consecutive Ryder Cup. 'The difference was blatantly obvious at The Belfry in '89,' he reflects. 'The whole thing had just become an awful lot bigger. The players were feted a bit more, the press interest was enormous and the crowds were a lot bigger.'

While Europe's success had transformed the Ryder Cup, so too had the European Tour grown in size and stature. In 1983, when Tony Jacklin took Europe to within a whisker of victory, there were just twenty-seven events on the Tour, with the players playing for a total prize fund of £2,819,185. Seven years later, the Tour announced that their professionals would be playing in thirty-seven tournaments, with prize money pushing through the £16 million mark. It was a testament to the efforts of Ballesteros, Faldo, Langer and Lyle, that Europe's players were now considered the best in the world and their home Tour reflected that. A new winning mentality had washed over European golf, a fact recognized by Jack Nicklaus. 'Winning is winning,' he said. 'It doesn't matter if it's the Hong Kong fourballs. The Europeans are more used to it than we are.'

Not everybody agreed though. At Birmingham's Metropole Hotel, the teams gathered for the now traditional curtain-raiser, the Gala Dinner. Twenty-two years earlier, the US captain and nine-time major winner Ben Hogan had boasted that his team were the 'best players in the world' and, true to his word, they romped home, 23½–8½, against Dai Rees's GB and Ireland side. Now, Ray Floyd took Hogan's lead once more, introducing his players as 'the twelve greatest players in the world', which, as Jacklin later pointed out, presumably made 'Seve Ballesteros 13th on his list'.

Understandably, Jacklin was incredulous. Looking along his line-up, he could see four of the top ten ranked players in his team, seven major titles and, in Nick Faldo, the reigning Masters champion. Besides, was Dan Pohl *really* better than Bernhard Langer? As opening gambits go, it was quite a statement of intent, albeit one that served only to act as the perfect motivational tool for Tony Jacklin. Even some of Floyd's team members seemed a little uneasy with their captain's proclamation. 'We were as embarrassed as all of you,' said Curtis Strange.

But it wasn't in Floyd's nature to be deliberately inflammatory. Yes, he was as durable and intransigent an opponent as any out there, but he was also one of the Tour's nice guys, a man who knew and appreciated the traditions of the game and who loved the camaraderie off the course as much as the competition on it.

Raymond Floyd had seemed to be a US captain-in-waiting for decades. Now 45, he had already played in six Ryder Cups (and would go on to play two more after 1989) and was still in the kind of commanding form that could have made him a valuable playing asset to any US team. If anything, he was getting better as he headed ever closer to the Seniors Tour. In June 1986, for example, Floyd had taken the US Open title at Shinnecock Hills, New York, claiming his fourth major title, aged 43 years, 9 months and 11 days. But if it was Ryder Cup experience that was the key to a successful application, then Floyd was a shoo-in. 'I have been so fortunate to have played eight, captained one and [been] assistant in one,' he says. 'To think I have had ten experiences and I can take something from each and every one. Of course the captaincy was something I will never forget ever, it was an honour… I think that was obviously my most special.'

Floyd, like Lanny Wadkins, was one of those players who lived for the Ryder Cup. Since his debut in the event, in the black and white walkover days of the 1960s, he had gone out of his way to make himself available for the event when other senior players, like Tom Weiskopf, had preferred to be elsewhere. 'It is *the* golf event,' he says. 'I think it has been not only the most rewarding but the most exciting golf through the years and you are representing your country – I mean that is the utmost, especially as an American.'

With more than a little help from his wife, Maria, Floyd would adopt a new, inclusive approach to his Ryder Cup captaincy, ushering in a new spirit, a new bond. Team meetings were frequent and informal, preparations thorough yet relaxed, and where once only the US players would be allowed in the team room, now the wives and the caddies too would be welcomed.

'Maria said, "Look, we are a team. When guys are playing tournament golf, their wives are part of what is going on. You know, we ought to make things more comfortable for the players, make sure their wives are part of it". As a player you want to have your wife and your caddy, basically, and so '89 is when we embraced the caddies and brought them into the team room so they were as much a part of it as the wives and the players. That is something that I credit my wife with because up to then it was always a guys' thing: the guys in the meetings together, the guys in the team room. Not that that still doesn't happen, but you know you sit around now with the caddies in the room, or the wives in the room and you throw out things and everybody has an influence.'

With two wins and the narrowest of defeats, Tony Jacklin's record as the most successful British or European Ryder Cup captain was already assured and, superficially at least, there seemed little to be gained from taking charge of the side for one last hurrah. But faced with an overwhelming demand from players, administrators and supporters alike, the captain signed on once more. In his 2006 autobiography, Jacklin revealed the thinking behind his decision. 'I suppose my reasoning, even if it was only partly conscious at the time, was, "What's left to do? If we won, which I fully expected us to, it would be three in a row, and if we lost, then that was likely to be a signal some new blood was needed anyway. Probably with that partly in mind, I was determined we were going to make it one to remember.'

But there had also been tragedy in Jacklin's personal life that had put the Ryder Cup in stark perspective. At the end of April 1988, six months after the win at Muirfield Village, Jacklin's wife, Viv, had died suddenly after suffering a brain haemorrhage while driving in Spain. She was just forty-four. As the woman who had been by his side throughout all of his many great triumphs, Viv Jacklin had been the backbone of Jacklin's golf career and her passing had left him distraught and desolate. 'Every single thing I'd done and achieved in my life had been accomplished with and through her,' he wrote. 'And then one day... it was all gone.'

The Ryder Cup captaincy, then, would prove to be a valuable distraction for Jacklin and by the end of the year his thoughts had once more turned to the task of securing an unprecedented hat-trick of victories. While his team still had that stellar nucleus of Ballesteros and Olazábal, Faldo and Woosnam, it was now missing Sandy Lyle whose game, by his own admission, was in 'terrible decline'. The Scot remarked that the prospect of playing in the 1989 match was tying his 'stomach in knots'.

After a miraculous last-hole victory at the Masters in April 1988, Lyle had turned his attention to playing in the United States, thereby bypassing the opportunity to amass any qualification points in Europe. But it would be a move that did for his chances of playing at The Belfry and, indeed, for his game itself. After two runner-up finishes and one third place on the PGA Tour, Lyle fell into the kind of deep slump that lesser players never manage to climb out of, hitting a run of bad form that saw seven missed cuts and one disqualification in nine starts. When it was mooted that he might be in line for one of Jacklin's three picks, Lyle made it known that it was probably best if the captain looked elsewhere if he was keen to get some points on the board.

Jacklin's first pick, Bernhard Langer, was a given, while his second, the ever-reliable Howard Clark, considered himself 'fortunate' to get into the team. While he had been in the prime of his career for the last five years, his form going into 1989 was decidedly sub-prime. Clark had taken a leaf out of Nick Faldo's book and employed the services of the swing doctor David Leadbetter in a bid to get his game back on track. The move was not a success, however. 'It put me back,' says Clark. 'I'm not having a go at David – he tried his best with me – but it just didn't work for me.'

The man charged with taking Lyle's 'place', meanwhile, would be the most unlikely of wild cards. Forty-one year-old Christy O'Connor Jr was the nephew of the Christy O'Connor who had played in every Ryder Cup from 1955 to 1973. O'Connor Jr had come agonizingly close to making the side in 1985 and, while he was further down the qualification list in 1989, Tony Jacklin had followed one of his now legendary hunches and given the silver-haired Irishman his place in the team, some fourteen years after a dismal debut in the competition at Laurel Valley, Pennsylvania, where his record read played two, lost two.

Tony Jacklin too had reason to be cheerful. Joining him at The Belfry was his new wife, Astrid. The couple had met at a neighbour's house in August 1988 and married soon after. As his Ryder Cup career came to an end, a new chapter in Jacklin's life was beginning.

With the best twelve players in the world – supposedly – at his disposal, Ray Floyd's team began in confident fashion. By pairing the players he thought would best complement each other's games – and personalities – Floyd hit upon a formula that would see his team ease into a 2½–1½ lead after the alternate shot session. 'I think that pairing the guys that are compatible and get along easy and have a personality that works with each other, I think that's important,' he explains.

After a dispiriting start, Europe roared back in the afternoon fourballs. Spurred on by a lunchtime team talk from Tony Jacklin, the home side would win each and every match against arguably the strongest pairings that Ray Floyd could have sent out. Clark and James eased past Couples and Wadkins, Faldo and Woosnam beat Calcavecchia and McCumber 2-up and Ballesteros and Olazábal demolished Watson and O'Meara 6&5. There would also be a last-hole victory for Sam Torrance and Gordon Brand Jr over Paul Azinger and Curtis Strange in the first of the fourballs, but, as Brand recalls, the game and the event largely passed him by:

I have got this putt for a four and to win a very vital point. Eventually I look at it, left edge, and think whatever you do, make it firm and just hit the bloody thing. So I hit it straight in the middle of the hole and we win the match, but funnily enough I didn't remember anything about that putt going in until I saw the video about four months later. I couldn't remember anything. Seve ran over to me and he patted me on the back and said, 'Gordon, remember your player partners'. It was just a blank, from the moment that ball went in I couldn't remember a thing. I spoke to a friend of mine that had come to watch me at The Belfry a couple of weeks later and he said, 'How did you enjoy The Belfry?' And I said, 'Oh, it was fantastic. Did you go up?' And he said, 'What do you mean, did I go up?' I said, 'Well, I didn't see you,' and he said, 'Gordon, you must have brushed past me twice and you almost walked through me'. I said, 'Well, I didn't even see you'. You are so focused on what you are doing. When people say, do the crowds annoy you? I didn't even know one of my best friends was there. Were there 25,000 people there or was there nobody there? It probably wouldn't have made much difference actually, I didn't see them or hear them.

Foursomes is a difficult form of the game, as Howard Clark points out:

Though I didn't play badly I never really gelled in a foursomes partnership. It was one of the most difficult if not the most difficult form of golf to play. You can end up going four or five holes without having a putt, or go three or four holes without having a chip shot, things like that. So it's difficult to get into your stride. In Ryder Cup foursomes everybody would go back and discuss shots which became a bit tiresome and tedious. You know, we wanted to get on with it but the captains wanted us to be together to make decisions. But what decisions have you got to make? To take a driver out? But it's the next shot that is the decision and if you are waiting for the guy who has hit the drive 280 yards down the fairway to make a decision then you are out of your stride.

Saturday's spoils would be shared, with nothing to divide the two teams. In the morning fourballs, Ballesteros and Olazábal cruised into a 3-up lead against Kite and Strange, but managed – just – to hang on in the face of a spirited fightback from the Americans, winning at the last as Olazábal manufactured a magical bunker shot that gifted his partner a tap-in and their team an invaluable point.

The afternoon session, meanwhile, would hinge on a marathon fourball match between Howard Clark and Mark James and Payne Stewart and Curtis Strange. With four holes to play and with the match score at 8–7 in Europe's favour, the Americans were one hole to the good, but back-to-back birdies at the 16th and 17th allowed the Yorkshire duo to pull ahead as the game neared its conclusion. With the light fading and nerves shredded, Howard Clark launched his drive off the 18th tee, clearing the water by less than a club length, before James followed with a 3-iron that found the green and set up a match-winning par. It had been a vital point in Europe's defence of the Ryder Cup.

'Jessie James and myself beat Strange and Stewart on that Saturday evening but it took over six hours to play, and you know, it wiped me out for the next day,' says Howard Clark.

At 9–7 – the same lead they had held four years earlier – Tony Jacklin and Europe stood poised to write another memorable chapter in the history of the Ryder Cup. Jacklin's singles line-up would, on the face of it, seem like a case of spreading his bets. Up front went Ballesteros, a strangely subdued and still pointless Bernhard Langer and José María Olazábal. At the bottom, Torrance, Faldo and Woosnam, just in case things got sticky.

The first match out on Sunday would see the birth of one of the Ryder Cup's great rivalries. Although Tony Jacklin had earmarked Ian Woosnam to take the lead role in the singles, the Welshman had been reluctant and with few other takers coming forward, Seve Ballesteros stepped up and offered his services. Against him would be a man who didn't give a castanet who he went toe to toe with – Paul Azinger.

It wouldn't be long before the two started squabbling. At the 2nd hole, Ballesteros had thinned a shot with a sand wedge and the old square grooves on the club face had cut up his ball. As was his right, Ballesteros showed the ball to his opponent and asked if he could change it. Looking at the ball, Azinger disagreed and – with Ballesteros fuming – the referee was summoned. He agreed with the American. 'OK,' said Ballesteros. 'If that's the way you want it, it's all right with me.'

Azinger's behaviour irked Ballesteros, presumably because it was precisely the kind of thing that he could and would have done himself. Later, Ballesteros would accuse Azinger of taking a bad drop at the final hole after the American found the water from the tee. Azinger, though, would have the last laugh, snaffling a one-hole victory as the Spaniard found the water at the 18th. It would be the start of a rivalry that would entertain and enthral for years to come. 'I never set out to be controversial or anything like that,' Azinger reflected. 'I was just passionate, like everybody else. When I played Seve, somehow I was never nervous. I was always just hyped and motivated. You know, we're both very patriotic, and occasionally we had run-ins.'

The opening exchanges would be tight, with three of the first four games being settled at the 18th. The same, however, could not be said about Howard Clark's match with Tom Kite. Whether it was the adverse effects of that six-hour match against Stewart and Strange or merely Kite's steely matchplay pedigree, Clark found himself completely consumed by his opponent. And as Sandy Lyle had found two years earlier at Muirfield Village, Clark was powerless to do anything about a mauling unprecedented in Ryder Cup history.

With the support and security of his playing partner Mark James, Clark had won two points from his three games on Friday and Saturday, but now, with nobody to bounce off, his concerns over his form were cruelly exposed. 'I wasn't so bad when I was playing with somebody. There was a bit of confidence there, there was a bit of back-up,' he explains. 'But on my own I was very fragile.'

Kite would complete his victory with indecent haste, running out an 8&7 winner and recording the largest winning margin in modern Ryder Cup history. Twenty years later, at the 2009 Seniors Open Championship at Sunningdale, Clark and Kite bumped into each other during the practice rounds. The American reminded him of an incident in their game in 1989 which, Kite maintained, may have had some bearing on the final result, as Clark himself explains.

'We were on the 2nd green and I had putted up dead and he has got a putt for a win. [So] he picked up my ball and threw it across to me. I wasn't paying attention and as I glanced away the ball hit me straight in the middle of the head. He still thinks that that affected me. It was one of those things but he still feels a little bit guilty about that.'

In the seventh game, the veteran Christy O'Connor Jr was embroiled in a titanic tussle with Fred Couples. The American had managed to keep O'Connor at bay, leading all the way to the 16th whereupon a birdie from the Irishman had levelled matters. Having halved the 17th, the two went down the last all-square. O'Connor, with the honour, found the fairway but was sixty yards shorter than Couples off the tee, Forced to go for the green with a long-iron, O'Connor speared a 2-iron into the heart of the green and watched as the crowd screamed its approval as it stopped just four feet from the hole. Years later, they would install a plaque in the 18th fairway commemorating O'Connor's 2-iron. It was that good.

It was a crushing blow for Couples. He had bagged the advantage with the longest drive of the week at the final hole only to see O'Connor turn the tables with a career-defining shot. The American's second shot was a shaky effort, falling wide and to the right of the green. The chip that followed wasn't much better either and, with a five being the best Couples could manage, the American held out his hand to concede O'Connor's putt and the game.

O'Connor's conjuring trick had taken the score to 13–10 in Europe's favour and, once again, The Belfry waited expectantly. Soon after, when José María Cañizares snatched the full point from Ken Green on the 18th green, Europe knew Sam Ryder's trophy would be staying on this side of the Atlantic.

With four matches still out on the course, the scoreboard reading 14–10, and with the Ryder Cup retained (at the very least) for Europe, the BBC's Steve Rider approached the USA's Tom Kite near the 18th green and asked him how he felt about another European victory. 'Not yet,' replied Kite, quite correctly. 'Let's get this straight.'

He had a point. Though Europe stood on the verge of another victory, they still required a half point from somewhere to seal the outright win. It seemed inappropriate – and premature – for Tony Jacklin to be seen celebrating with the crowd. But with a party atmosphere enveloping the course, some of the players who were still involved in matches found themselves in an uncertain position. Should they shake hands on a half? Should they continue? 'No one seemed to know what to do when we'd retained it,' says Mark James. 'I will be careful not to slag anyone off here, but I think the players who were still out on the course were left wondering what on earth to do, whether to play or not to play, whereas someone should have gone out and said, come on, we haven't won it, get stuck in, think of your Ryder Cup record, we want to win this, not halve it.'

One by one, though, the remaining Americans rose to the challenge. In the ninth game out, Mark McCumber pipped Gordon Brand Jr by one hole, Tom Watson beat Sam Torrance 3&1 and Lanny Wadkins battled to a last-hole win over Nick Faldo after the Englishman, like Ballesteros, found the water at the 18th. By the time Ian Woosnam and Curtis Strange reached the 18th tee in the final game left out on the course, an hour had passed since José María Cañizares's victory over Ken Green had secured the point that had retained the Ryder Cup for Europe. It had been an hour during which, gradually, the party atmosphere had given way to concern and the anticipation of another European victory had ebbed away.

For Woosnam, without a singles win in his three previous Ryder Cup outings, it was a crucial game. With three to play, the Welshman was 1-up and set to help himself and Europe to at least the half point they needed to cross the finishing line. Enter Curtis Strange. At the 16th, the Virginian rattled in a 25-footer for birdie to level the match. Another birdie at the penultimate hole then gave Strange the lead, leaving Woosnam needing a win at the final hole to get the half point.

Both men would find the fairway, Woosnam comfortably outdriving his opponent and giving himself the best possible opportunity to win the hole. As Woosnam waited, Strange surveyed the scene, looking out over the lake guarding the final green as 20,000 pairs of eyes stared back at him. While history has remembered Christy O'Connor's 2-iron, Strange's 2-iron approach that followed, given the match situation, was every bit as impressive, perhaps more so, as it cleared the water and ran up to four feet from the flag. When he then stepped up and holed his putt for his third birdie in a row and a two-hole victory, it gave the USA a tie that had seemed little more than a distant dream an hour or so earlier. 'We had basically lucked into a tie,' says Tom Watson. 'It was one of those matches where it didn't look very good for the US team at all during those matches but we pulled it out in the end and got the tie.'

For the first time in Tony Jacklin's tenure, Europe had been caught out by complacency, guilty, perhaps of believing that fortune, fate and an adoring home crowd would be sufficient to carry them home. While the Ryder Cup was staying put at The Belfry, the sheen of what had promised to be another golden Sunday at The Belfry had been taken off and dumped in the lake by the 18th green. Sam Torrance felt that Europe had 'let the Americans off the hook' and that 'the champagne tasted a little flatter that evening – though not by the end of the night', while Nick Faldo felt that come the climax, the European side 'were simply running on empty'.

At the closing ceremony, Ray Floyd was magnanimous but keen to stress that Europe had not won the match, merely tied it. 'When they heard Floyd's comment, some players wanted a play-off to decide the match. They felt there was no point in just retaining it,' says Howard Clark. 'There was a little bit of sour grapes, with the speeches and stuff... but there were a few of us who let the team down on the last day and I wasn't the only one.'

To this day, Ray Floyd remains proud of his team's dedication in clawing back the four-point deficit and emerging with a tie, even though history has tended to mark it down as another European victory. That said, there is one regret that he still harbours. 'Looking back,' he says. 'I would take everyone that lost and I would put 'em with other people, no question.'

Curiously, in his autobiography some seventeen years later, Tony Jacklin referred repeatedly to the 1989 Ryder Cup as another victory for his team, despite the 14–14 final scoreline. It was 'three in a row' he wrote, adding that 'they'd have put you in a straitjacket if you'd walked into a bookie's in 1981 and put a hundred pounds on Europe winning three Ryder Cups before the decade was out.'

Later, in the European team room, a not-so-supergroup had been formed with lifelong golf fan and international singing star Chris De Burgh on piano, the American Payne Stewart on his harmonica and Ireland's Christy O'Connor Jr providing impromptu percussion with his spoons. 'Payne was wearing a red cap and a red bow tie,' recalls Gordon Brand Jr. 'He loved it over here – the European attitude to golf, and he just wanted to come in and join the party.'

Party or not, there was no denying that the unlikeliest of ties had tarnished the lustre of Tony Jacklin's swansong, even if he was still cradling Sam Ryder's trophy like a newborn baby. Nobody, it seemed, was going to prise it from him.

Patriot Games

PETE Dye had, at various times in his long and illustrious career in golf course design, been called everything from 'Dyeabolical' to the 'Marquis de Sod'. As an architect, his resumé read like the rap sheet of an incurable sadist. There were Harbour Town at Hilton Head, South Carolina, Whistling Straits in Mosel, Wisconsin, and Crooked Stick in Carmel, Indianapolis, Indiana, to name but three of his evil masterpieces.

Part golf visionary, part Bond villain, Dye had long regarded it as his *raison d'être* not merely to populate the planet with classic golf courses, but in doing so provide the very best players in the world with as stern a test as possible. 'Unless a few golf professionals are belly-aching about my course design,' he told the author in 2005, 'I wonder whether I've done enough to challenge them.'

Certainly, Dye knew how to get under the skin of the professionals. The Australian Greg Norman once described Dye as 'the man golfers love to hate', while Ray Floyd labelled his PGA West course at La Quinta, California, 'spiteful' and 'hateful'. Lee Trevino, meanwhile, said he knew 'some courses that were easier than the practice ground' at La Quinta.

But it was his Stadium Course design at Sawgrass at the PGA Tour's

HQ in Ponte Vedra Beach, Florida, that had most players mewling and puking. Renowned for its fearsome 17th hole with its island green, it had proved more than problematic for the field. At the inaugural Players Championship held there in 1982, a shell-shocked Ben Crenshaw had walked off 18 in search of a calculator, with a second-round 74 just a shot better than his first-round effort, and nowhere near good enough to make the cut. At the press conference later, his anger at the layout got the better of him. 'This,' he fumed, 'is *Star Wars* golf. This place was designed by Darth Vader.'

Darth Vader, Marquis de Sod. Dyeabolical. It was the kind of criticism that Pete Dye thrived on. 'Truth is,' he says, 'I just like to see the best players tested. You know, there may be one guy in the field who breaks 70 but that one player has shown that it can be done. I just want players to think, that's all.'

The venue for the 1991 Ryder Cup matches would be another of Dye's creations. Carved out of a three-mile stretch of coastal dunes, the Ocean Course at Kiawah Island's Golf Resort was finished just weeks before the 1991 competition was due to be staged. At 7,303 yards, it was, as ever, a typically tough test but this time it was compounded by the unpredictable winds blowing in from the Atlantic. As a public course, the club made great play of the fact that players could experience as much as an eight-club difference on the same shot, all depending on the direction of the wind. In short, it was like playing on a British links course, only worse.

When Jim Awtrey had taken over as CEO of the PGA of America in 1987, the 1991 Ryder Cup was scheduled to be played at PGA West in Palm Springs, California. However, Awtrey was worried by the extreme temperatures there (it often exceeded 100 degrees Fahrenheit in September), the time difference (which would eat into TV ratings back in Europe) and the fact that Concorde couldn't reach California without refuelling, and he therefore set about persuading the contracted course owners, Landmark, to move the venue. 'I asked them if they would move the Ryder Cup or if they would allow it to go to some other entity and they said no but they said we are building a course with Pete Dye on the ocean in Charleston and we could hold it there,' explains Awtrey. '[But] it all came together, the golf course was finished, the matches were highly competitive and it really launched America's and television's view of the Ryder Cup.'

Not everyone was taken with the decision to host it at Kiawah, not merely because it was a new course but also because it was one that seemed to play right into the hands of the opposition. 'It's a links course, long and wide open, and you're gonna get a lot of wind,' said the 1985 US skipper Lee Trevino. 'That's the kind of course they've played on all their lives'. Team member, Lanny Wadkins, took the view that 'the Cup should be played on some of our great old courses, and the same over there.' He added, 'The last two matches in England were played at The Belfry, and that's not exactly a work of art.'

It wasn't just the US players who had their concerns. Ireland's David Feherty, making his Ryder Cup debut, remarked that the course was 'not like something from Scotland or Ireland; it's like something from Mars'. He went on to say that it was so difficult you could 'drop a shot between the locker room and the 1st tee'.

A lifelong admirer of the classic British links course, Dye had taken his inspiration for the new course at Kiawah from some of the windswept coastal courses in Scotland. Prior to the event, he walked his new track with the new European captain Bernard Gallacher and the man who would soon become the new Chief Executive of the PGA, Sandy Jones, explaining how the course had taken shape. 'Pete would create these sand banks and then let the wind blow them for a few weeks,' explains Jones. 'He was telling us how he was trying to achieve the same look as Royal Aberdeen, a club myself and Bernard knew quite well. He said, "You must see the similarities with Royal Aberdeen," at which point an alligator walked across the course and Bernard said, "Yeah, Pete, we see a lot of alligators in Aberdeen".'

Kiawah Island and the 29th Ryder Cup couldn't have come quickly enough for the USA. After two defeats and the tie that felt like a defeat at The Belfry in 1989, the competition was in grave danger of losing its lustre in the US. The event needed a shot in the arm, something to make it seem like a proper contest once more.

Enter Dave Stockton. The PGA champion of 1970 and 1976, the 49-year-old Californian had played in the successful US Ryder Cup teams of 1971 and 1977, and boasted a record of three wins, one half and one defeat in the five matches he had played. More important-ly, Stockton was a different kind of captain. Patriotic, passionate and forthright, here was a man who was utterly committed to wrenching the Ryder Cup back for the US. If his methods upset a few people along the way, then hell – he could live with that.

Nineteen ninety-one had been a good year for Uncle Sam. Operation Desert Storm, launched in January 1991 in the wake of an Iraqi invasion of neighbouring Kuwait some five months earlier, had seen troops from a US-led coalition of thirty-four nations descend on the Persian Gulf to liberate the Arab state. And though it was never going to be an equal fight – the US-led Allied forces lost 379 lives, the Iraqis more than 100,000 – the eventual victory, which came with the Iraqi surrender in March 1991, caused Republican President George H. W. Bush's popularity ratings to soar. Moreover, with the ending of Soviet Communist domination of Eastern Europe, and the dissolution of the USSR (together with the fact that China was yet to really impose its economic hegemony on the Western world), the USA stood proudly as the sole, unchallenged superpower on the planet. A wave of patriotism had washed over the United States and it would be one the American captain Dave Stockton would ride with vigour. Even respected magazines like *Golf Digest* fell into the trap, labelling the match 'The War on the Shore'. It was as though they already knew what kind of Ryder Cup this was destined to be.

The man tasked with taking the fight to Stockton's pumped-up Americans was the new European captain Bernard Gallacher. Like the GB and Ireland skipper of 1969 and 1971, Eric Brown, Gallacher was a member of the Bathgate Golf Club in West Lothian, Scotland. Having played in eight Ryder Cups and acted as Tony Jacklin's assistant, he seemed a natural successor. Gallacher had made his debut in the Ryder Cup at the age of just twenty, in 1969, when he became the youngest ever Briton to play in the event. He also claimed a notable scalp by beating Lee Trevino 4&3 in the singles.

While Great Britain and Ireland claimed a tie in the 1969 Ryder Cup, the remainder of Gallacher's Cup career would see nothing but defeat compounded by miserable defeat. 'The Americans had such strength in depth, with Nicklaus, Trevino, Weiskopf, Watson, Larry Nelson and Lanny Wadkins. We were quite far behind as a team,' he reflects. 'The British public was always very interested, they would always turn up and think we could win but looking back, it wasn't realistic.'

Bernard Gallacher's run of thirty-one games in eight consecutive matches would finally come to an end in 1983, with just the shared cup on his debut to show for his efforts. 'Eight Ryder Cups and the first time I didn't play was 1985 and, of course, we went out and whupped them,' he shrugs.

That Gallacher, forty-two, was an obvious choice for captain was irrefutable, especially as he had a score, or eight, to settle. The problem for the Ryder Cup, however, was that it was now becoming almost too big. Gone were the days when it was run at a loss and where the begging bowl went round in a bid to lure sponsors and patrons. Now that it had become a genuine contest and TV contracts were in place, it had started to make money, serious money, and the questions as to how that revenue was split and distributed would prove vexatious.

With the PGA European Tour responsible for providing the players for the event and the PGA, the body representing club professionals, charged with organizing the Ryder Cup match, there was a crack in the relationship that was threatening to develop into one almighty chasm. It was, in many ways, the same club-versus-country debate that football often finds itself confronting. To his credit, Gallacher, as captain, felt he could do something to bring the parties together and help find a way forward, especially as he had the ear of the man who acted as President of both organizations, Lord Derby.

The European Tour had come into life in the early 1970s when the players had effectively broken away from the PGA to form a Tour of their own, much like the PGA Tour had done with the PGA of America in the late 1960s. While that, in itself, was inevitable, it had serious implications for the Ryder Cup in that the players whose bread and butter was the week-in, week-out schedule of the European Tour were now required to play in an event controlled by the organization they had just extricated themselves from.

But it was the Ryder Cup revenues that now seemed to be the issue. An ugly contretemps would ensue, with demands and counter-demands being made. Eventually, the Tour would offer the PGA a deal. While they would retain the television revenues, they would not take their share of the profits until the PGA had made £750,000 from the event. It would be an offer that sat unsigned on the table for months, long after Lord Derby had resigned as President of the Tour in the summer of 1990 after another dispute, this time over the potential venue for the 1993 contest.

With the Tour and the PGA at loggerheads on one side of the Atlantic, the mood was markedly different on the other. As far as Stockton was concerned, the US had been wounded one too many times. Like a golfing version of 'Stormin' Norman' Schwarzkopf, he had plans to restore the pride to golf across the pond. There would be videotaped motivational messages from the President, and communal prayer. There would even be a dedicated 'team song' that Stockton would play each day to rally his troops – 'Point of Light' by the country singer Randy Travis. And so what if it had nothing to do with golf – the US team liked it.

The bonding was going well, perhaps too well, and at times, it would be difficult for Dave Stockton to keep his team's emotions in check. 'I have a couple of players who have been talking like they really want to kill the Europeans,' he told the Associated Press, 'but I think our team as a whole has their heads where they want them. They are trying to cool it and keep calm and relaxed until Friday.'

On the Wednesday evening, three limousines chauffeuring the US team to the Gala Dinner in Charleston collided. Travelling with Wayne Levi, Steve Pate was thrown backwards when the first car containing Ray Floyd and Fred Couples stopped abruptly as it tried to avoid three police vehicles that had joined the escort, the net result being that the second car – Pate's car – smashed into the back of it, while the third car, containing Paul Azinger and Chip Beck then rear-ended that vehicle.

It was a minor accident, but for Pate it was but one of what would become an increasingly long list of freak injuries (he would even get knocked off his bicycle by a deer in his own driveway) to afflict the man they called 'the Volcano'. Rushed to nearby St Francis Xavier Hospital for X-rays, Pate was eventually released, but not before some urgent treatment on a bruised rib and damaged hip from a microcurrent machine.

It was doubly disappointing for the US team as Pate had not only been in terrific form during Tuesday's practice round, coming home in 6 under par over the treacherous Ocean Course, but was, arguably, their best current player. Indeed, his liking for Pete Dye's new track was such that Dave Stockton would choose not to replace him with his first reserve Tim Simpson (as was his right), but hold out and hope for the best.

Later, with the teams seated for the Gala Dinner, Stockton introduced his team and proceeded to present a fifteen-minute video, made by NBC Television, entitled *The History of the Ryder Cup* for the guests to enjoy. Halfway through the tape, however, it became clear that the film wasn't exactly the most impartial piece of documentary-making. There were shots from the 1950s, 1960s and 1970s, with one US victory followed by another. There were American players fist-pumping and high-fiving, trophy presentations and scenes of mass celebration. In short, the European wins of the 1980s and those players who helped make the event into the success it was had largely been airbrushed from 'history'. 'As far as I recall,' said Bernard Gallacher, 'it ended in 1983, the last time the Americans had won the match, and then only by a point... We were all disappointed and it highlighted a curious naivety in the Cup arrangements.'

Welcome to America. Disgusted, the European Tour's Executive Director and chairman of the Ryder Cup Selection Committee Ken Schofield nearly walked out but was persuaded to stay by Bernard Gallacher. Nick Faldo, meanwhile, was incredulous. 'It was unbeliev-able. You would think players like Seve Ballesteros were there just to make up the numbers,' he said.

The television commentator Bruce Critchley was also there. 'It was very one-sided and even the head of the PGA of America, Jim Awtrey, stood up and apologized at the end of it.'

Intentional insult or poor research and editing, it was the first of many things that would get under the skin of the European team during the week at Kiawah. On the eve of the matches, for instance, a DJ at a local radio station decided to broadcast the hotel and room numbers of the European side, urging his listeners to call their hotel and 'Wake Up the Enemy!' That night, as the European team slept, their phones began to ring. Nick Faldo's wife Gill took several calls, while Mark James was also one of the players who found his night disturbed, albeit briefly. 'I just turned over and went back to sleep,' he laughs. '[But] It's amazing to think it happened and ever since then you can't ring a player's room without going through the main switchboard.'

It was, essentially, the coward's way of playing knock-a-door-run, but – juvenile pranks and interrupted nights aside – there should have been little for Bernard Gallacher and his European team to fear. Though they included five Ryder Cup rookies in their team (in the shape of David Gilford, Steven Richardson, Paul Broadhurst, David Feherty and the man for whom the Ryder Cup would become a career-defining event, Colin Montgomerie), they also boasted four of the five best players in the world in Ian Woosnam, Nick Faldo, Seve Ballesteros and José María Olazábal, and, however you looked at it, the Ocean Course, with its howling, unpredictable wind, was about as European a golf course as they were going to get in the Ryder Cup in the United States.

When the draw for the opening Friday foursomes was announced, it was a given that Gallacher would send out his strongest pairing first and in Ballesteros and Olazábal he had two golfers who were beautifully and naturally attuned to each other's games, who trusted each other implicitly and had forged one of the most destructive partnerships in Ryder Cup history. Indeed, Gallacher's belief in the pairing was so complete that he had already announced that he intended to play them together in every session up to Sunday's singles.

While it was a relatively simple choice for Gallacher, it was less so for Stockton, especially as Steve Pate was still unavailable. His choice of opening pairing – Paul Azinger and Chip Beck – created one of those mouth-watering draws that every golf fan, regardless of nationality, wanted to see, purely because there was history with Ballesteros and Azinger.

Chip Beck was making his second appearance in the Ryder Cup. A captain's pick along with Raymond Floyd, he had been selected ahead of the people's favourite, the newly crowned PGA Champion John Daly. Nicknamed the 'Wild Thing', Daly had arrived for the PGA Championship at the Crooked Stick course in Carmel, Indianapolis, in August as the ninth reserve for the tournament, but, thanks to a series of freak injuries and withdrawals – Lee Trevino pulled out because he simply couldn't hit the ball far enough – Daly got a place in the starting field. Then, with a caddie borrowed from Nick Price and without so much as a practice round, the twenty-five-year-old from Dardanelle, Arkansas, decimated the field in an astonishing display of power hitting and rare subtlety around the greens.

Not getting the call from Stockton had been especially hard on Daly. A change in the qualification rules for the US team that year had meant that the PGA champion no longer received an automatic place in the side and as Daly had finished only 17th on the money list, he missed out. Stockton, realizing it had been the toughest of calls, invited Daly to attend the event as an unofficial team member, but the Wild Thing declined, choosing, instead, to send a fax to the US team. It read: 'Good luck. Now go kick butt!'

But, in the nicest possible way, nobody really wanted to see Beck or, for that matter, Olazábal. Two years had passed since the spat between Ballesteros and Azinger over the dropped ball at The Belfry, but time had done little to heal the rift.

The opening exchanges went the Americans' way and by the 7th hole the Spaniards were 3-down. At the 7th tee, though, Ballesteros had noticed that Chip Beck had teed off using a 100 compression ball rather than the 90 compression ball that they had begun the match with, a move which contravened the rule agreed at the teams' rules meeting (and also applied on both the PGA Tour and European Tour). He said nothing but discussed the matter with Olazábal and the caddies.

Two holes later, Azinger and Beck were 3-up on the Spaniards and closing in on a key win and the first point towards bringing the Ryder Cup back home when Ballesteros decided to send for Bernard Gallacher. The European captain arrived as the players made their way to the 10th tee and discussions ensued. Fifteen minutes later, the Americans admitted they had switched balls, but as Ballesteros and Olazábal had failed to say anything at the 7th hole, they were no longer in a position to lodge a complaint. 'We made a mistake,' Azinger admitted to his opponents, 'But we certainly weren't cheating.'

Ballesteros barked back. 'We don't say that, Paul,' he said. 'It has nothing to do with cheating. Cheating and breaking the rules are two different things.'

Though they had escaped reprimand, the controversy had rattled the Americans. From coasting to victory, they began to stutter, three-putting the 10th to take it back to 2-up. At the 12th Ballesteros tapped in after a laser-like approach from Olazábal to reduce the lead to one and by the 13th it was all-square, a 6-foot putt from Ballesteros taking the hole.

At the 15th, Europe, improbably, moved into the lead with yet more magic from Olazábal, and when Seve Ballesteros dropped a 25-footer at the 17th, the turnaround was complete and a five-shot swing in just eight holes had given the Spanish duo a 2&1 triumph.

Deliciously, the draw for the afternoon fourballs also paired the same duos and while the result was the same – a 2&1 victory for Ballesteros and Olazábal – so too was the residual tension. Again, Azinger and Beck became irritated by what they regarded as gamesmanship from Ballesteros, whose cough only ever seemed to surface in the middle of the backswings of his opponents and never during his partner's.

Later that day, Ballesteros would describe the US team as 'eleven nice guys… and Paul Azinger', prompting the kind of response from Azinger that would serve only to keep the tension simmering. 'The king of gamesmanship doesn't like me?' he laughed. 'Good. A feather in my cap.'

The truth, though it may have seemed implausible, was that Azinger was as close as the US team had to their own Ballesteros. Though he was never the player the Spaniard was or had been, he, too, possessed that drive, that innate belief that when you stepped on to the tee, losing was not an option. In *Golf Digest* magazine in February 2005, the Ryder Cup veteran and 2002 captain Curtis Strange revealed just how much Ballesteros had irritated the American team over the years he played in the Ryder Cup.

To say he was difficult is an understatement. To a man, every player who went up against him in the Ryder Cup had a run-in with him. His gamesmanship was irritating, and he never let up. He'd do outrageous, childish things like coughing as you got set to swing, and if you objected he'd act wounded and escalate the situation. When he put himself into the role of victim, that's when he'd play his best. Just knowing he'd use a nasty incident to play well made me so mad that I'd play worse. There was only one Seve, and a little of him went a long way. But I'll tell you this, he could back it up. If you were 0–5 against a guy, that stuff would hack you off, too.

Lanny Wadkins agrees. 'He was a gamesman and I loved it,' he says. 'I loved someone who played with that kind of fire. I loved competing against him and I wasn't always successful, but it was always a challenge. You knew you were going to be in for an eventful day when you played him.'

For the US team, Ballesteros had been and continued to be a pain in pretty much any body part you could name. For his own team, however, he was influential, inspirational and irreplaceable, one of those players whose character and charisma always put you one up on the 1st tee. 'Seve was always fantastic,' says Mark James. 'He could have played with my Mum in the Ryder Cup and been quite happy and it wouldn't have surprised me if they had got half a point – and she doesn't even play.'

No other player could have behaved like Ballesteros without censure. But then no other player was quite like Seve Ballesteros. Somehow, some way, Seve, especially in the Ryder Cup, would always make things happen. If he was down, he would find a way to reverse his fortunes. If he was up, he would merely pile on the agony for his opponent, as Peter Jacobsen, who played against the Spaniard in the 1985 and 1995 competitions, explains:

Seve goes into an almost trance-like state. Seriously, he comes out and he has got that lower lip jutted out, his eyes are darting around and he will literally look past everything, look past the other team, look past the crowd, and only if it could help him would he include the crowd. And in the Ryder Cup's case, interacting with the other team didn't benefit him so he wouldn't do it. Interacting with his teammates, with the caddies, with his playing partner and with the crowd benefited him. It played to his strength so he used that. It is an incredible motivation to everybody.

While Ballesteros and Olazábal had emerged victorious, it would prove to be a frustrating morning for the European side. Despite the fillip of the first point of the day, the US would win the other three games, with Bernhard Langer and Mark James losing to Ray Floyd and Freddie Couples 2&1, the rookie duo of David Gilford and Colin Montgomerie gunned down by the old hands of Lanny Wadkins and Hale Irwin 4&2 and Faldo and Woosnam losing at the last to Payne Stewart and Mark Calcavecchia.

It was hardly the start that another of the rookies needed to fill him with confidence ahead of his bow in the event. If you've ever wondered how the Ryder Cup differs from the routine of Tour golf, you need only look at David Feherty's first hole in the event. Paired with the old hand and his closest friend in the game, Sam Torrance, and playing the veterans Lanny Wadkins and Mark O'Meara, the petrified and pallid Northern Irishman played the hole as though he had never picked up a club before, yet alone swung one.

The enormity of the Ryder Cup had suddenly hit Feherty like a right hook and when he reached the opening green, his first putt in the competition, a relatively simple 15-footer, came up three feet short and four feet wide of the hole. On the way to the second tee, Torrance decided to dispense with the friendly advice and encouragement and try a different and decidedly more direct tack. 'This only happens to a few people, so you'd better be up to enjoying it,' said Torrance. 'So don't be a prick or I'll join Wadkins and O'Meara, and you can play the three of us.' Fortunately for Feherty's safety and Torrance's blood pressure, the Irishman soon rediscovered the form that had got him in the team, holing a seven-foot par putt on the 18th hole to secure a half point for Europe.

With Ballesteros and Olazábal's second win over Azinger and Beck and Mark James and Steven Richardson's impressive 5&4 triumph over Corey Pavin and Mark Calcavecchia, Europe seemed poised to right the wrongs of the opening foursomes, but another defeat for the flagging partnership of Ian Woosnam and Nick Faldo, this time to Ray Floyd and Fred Couples, would mean not just a 4½–3½ lead at the end of day one but the end for the Woosnam–Faldo pairing.

Faldo would return in Saturday morning's foursomes, with a new partner, the rookie David Gilford. It was a strange collaboration. Faldo was notoriously insular, a picture of introspection and concentration when he was on the golf course. Gilford, meanwhile, was the balding farmer from Staffordshire who wouldn't say boo to a goose, or any of his livestock for that matter. If you wanted fireworks, it was best to look elsewhere on the Ocean Course.

Drawn against the ever-present Paul Azinger and Mark O'Meara, it was a terrible mismatch. Faldo and Gilford looked more like a couple who had rowed that morning and spent the rest of the day giving each other the coldest of shoulders. It was a strange, surreal sight. Faldo doing his own thing, playing his own game, and Gilford wandering along looking for some crumb of comfort or the occasional word of encouragement from his partner. But no. Faldo seemed so distant and so distracted that he even accidently smacked his caddie, Fanny Sunesson, in the chin with a club he was swinging as he was walking the course, prompting her to burst into tears. If it was possible, the 7&6 mauling was a flattering scoreline.

In his 2004 autobiography, *Life Swings*, Faldo still seemed bemused by the reaction to that game. 'I am castigated to this day for that one miserable match. To me that is baloney,' he wrote. 'We were an untried and unproven partnership thrown together by circumstances and the chemistry just was not there.'

For David Gilford, however, it was a perplexing state of affairs. After all, he hadn't, as far as he was aware, done anything to offend Faldo and even if he had, the very fact that this was a team event meant they shouldn't have carried any residual bad feeling on to the 1st tee with them. Years later, in the *Guardian* newspaper, Gilford spoke of his feelings about Faldo. 'I am a big fan of what he has achieved,' he said, 'but he's not a wonderful man.'

Gilford wouldn't be the first or the last to be flummoxed by Faldo's ways. When Sandy Lyle was once told that he had been drawn with Faldo in a tournament at Wentworth, he shrugged, 'I guess I'll take my Walkman with me, then.'

Despite another win for Ballesteros and Olazábal against Ray Floyd and Fred Couples in the concluding morning foursomes game, preventing the shut-out, it had been a bleak start for Bernard Gallacher's team, as they trailed 7½–4½. 'Our butts certainly had been kicked in the foursomes,' said Gallacher later. '[But] we had clawed our way back on the first day with a good performance in the foursomes and there was no reason why we should not do the same again on the second afternoon.'

It didn't help that the US's form player, Steve Pate, had, thanks to the miracle of modern microcurrent technology, recovered sufficiently from his car accident to now warrant inclusion in the afternoon fourballs as well. Pate and his partner, the debutant Corey Pavin, had been drawn against Bernhard Langer and Colin Montgomerie, and with the US in control of the match, were intent on hammering home their advantage.

Small in stature but with the kind of patriotic, passionate appetite for the game that any US captain would want in his side, Pavin was what an American would look like if scientists set about creating one in a laboratory. With his fulsome moustache and slender frame, he looked like an angry version of Charlie Chaplin, only one that had swapped his cane for a club and his derby hat for a baseball cap. That said, he had just enjoyed the best year of his pro career to date, winning two events, the Bob Hope Chrysler Classic and the BellSouth Atlanta Golf Classic, and, with a few bucks short of a million dollars, topping the end-of-year money list on the PGA Tour.

When the pair turned up at the 1st tee, though, they were both sporting camouflaged 'Desert Storm' caps, in honour, they explained later, of the US troops who had served in the Gulf War. It was an error of judgement on Pavin's and Pate's part, not least because European troops were also being killed in the conflict. Showing solidarity with the US forces in the Gulf was one thing, but doing so in the middle of a golf competition where nothing save for some national pride and a little gold trophy were at stake, was ill-conceived and irresponsible. But were they really to blame? 'Heck,' said Dave Stockton in an interview with *Golf Digest* in September 2006, 'the camouflage hats, that was my idea.'

Nearly eighteen years later, when Pavin attended his first press conference as the newly appointed Ryder Cup captain for the 2010 event in Wales, he sought to defuse what, potentially, was still an embarrassment to him and his team, even though it wasn't his idea. 'That was misconstrued,' he shrugged. 'It was just a show of support for our troops over in Iraq. I think a lot of people took it the wrong way. I was showing patriotism to the guys out there putting their lives on the line for our freedom. If that's wrong then so be it, but I don't think that's wrong.'

Stoked by Stockton and with Pate and Pavin pumping the home crowd, an air of menace was soon sweeping over the Ocean Course. The noise was unremitting, the passion undeniable. And as Lanny Wadkins recalls, the Ryder Cup suddenly became an altogether spicier proposition.

It wasn't a normal golf course that you would see even in the British Open that had places for galleries. It was all sand hills, so what happened was the Europeans would congregate on one dune and the American galleries on another and it ended up like a big soccer match. It was like one side of the stadium yelling at the other. And they would almost go to these sand dunes and plant their flag, plant the Euro flag or plant the American flag so it became a different spectacle than I had ever seen in golf anywhere any time. I have heard a lot of people say that they didn't like that. Personally I loved it.

Hats or no hats, the US action men duo of Pavin and Pate may have been past masters at whipping up a crowd, but on the golf course they had met their match in a partnership that would form the bedrock of European success over the coming years. Thrown together by Bernard Gallacher on the back on one of those clever hunches that seem to come with decades of experience, Bernhard Langer and Colin Montgomerie would prove to be a formidable team and their victory – 2&1 – would bring the Americans back to within a single point. Later, after Mark

James and Steven Richardson had beaten Lanny Wadkins and Wayne Levi 3&1, it was left to José María Olazábal to hole a six-footer in the fading light for a half point in his and Ballesteros's game against Payne Stewart and Fred Couples.

All-square at eight points apiece. It had been a stirring comeback from the European team and the best possible retort to the ceaseless, brain-aching chants of 'U-S-A' that reverberated endlessly around the Ocean Course.

That night, the captains finalized their singles order but there would be more controversy waiting in the dunes. Despite being fit enough to participate in the afternoon fourballs on Saturday, Steve Pate, the player injured in the limo crash, would be withdrawn from the singles. It was a decision that not only meant he missed out, conveniently, on a head-to-head with Seve Ballesteros, but also that one of the European players would also have to withdraw, with a half point going to each team.

Traditionally, it is the job of that player's captain to inform his opposite number of the decision, out of courtesy if nothing else. Bernard Gallacher, however, would learn of Pate's withdrawal not from Stockton, but from BBC television – and not until as late as 8.30 a.m. on Sunday morning. Having finished breakfast with Ian McLaurin, Gallacher walked over to meet the BBC's Steve Rider for a television interview prior to the singles. As he chatted to Rider, the BBC anchorman received news in his earpiece that Steve Pate, the man who had been hitting it a country mile on Saturday and had been hitting balls on the range just fifteen minutes earlier, had been withdrawn from the US singles line-up because of his injuries. 'They had all night to look at the draw and they pulled him out next day,' Gallacher explains. 'Usually, it's a matter of courtesy to alert the opposing captain that there's a possibility that one of their players would be pulled out, but they didn't.'

With Pate now absent from the Sunday singles line-up, it meant that everyone in the European team would drop down a game in the playing order. Now, Ballesteros would be playing their weakest player, Wayne Levi, and not one of their strongest. 'They saw that David Gilford was playing Wayne Levi which meant that Seve would come down the draw and actually play their worst player. But I wanted Seve to play their best player because anyone could beat Wayne Levi. He was having a terrible week.'

It was as though Levi, through no fault of his own, had been sacrificed at the altar of Seve Ballesteros, but if Levi felt bad about getting the worst possible draw, then Europe's David Gilford, in his first Ryder Cup and yet to register a point, was beside himself. With each captain obliged to put a name 'in the envelope' that they would withdraw in the event of any circumstance requiring an opposition player to stand down during the match, Gallacher was torn between Gilford and fellow rookie Paul Broadhurst. He decided on Gilford because not only had he already lost twice that week but Broadhurst had only played once – and won.

When Gallacher told Gilford of his decision, the part-time cattle farmer broke down. 'He [Gilford] was distraught, because he had a poor Ryder Cup until then,' recalls Gallacher. 'I didn't think he had played badly and I was absolutely convinced he would win his singles because I had a lot of confidence in him that he would have got his Ryder Cup point but you know, that's just how things are.'

It wasn't as though this Ryder Cup needed any added spice but now it had it. The European team, sensing something untoward, had developed a siege mentality. Gallacher rallied his troops while Seve Ballesteros took it upon himself to prepare the rookies for the drama that lay ahead. 'Before the match Seve took me aside,' recalls David Feherty. '"They put you out early because they think you will lose",' he said, then grabbed me by my shirt and chest hair and pulled me close. '"But I know you have this heart". I got chills. I thought, "Wow! He believes I can win — and so do I".'

As the teams went through their final preparations, a visitor arrived in the European team room (or rather the portable trailer that passed for the team room) to wish them well. It was the US Vice President Dan Quayle. 'He came in and said hello,' recalls Mark James. 'Not many of us knew who he was.'

Dave Stockton, meanwhile, was banking on getting some fast points early in the day and then hanging on. His singles strategy therefore involved his strongest players going out first and last, with Raymond Floyd and Payne Stewart leading off and Lanny Wadkins and Hale Irwin tasked with the job of handling the pressure at the business end of proceedings. Curiously, though, Gallacher would send his most reliable men out in the middle of the draw, the only exception being Nick Faldo, who would play first against Floyd.

For the few neutrals watching the matches, there couldn't have been a more enticing day ahead. For the partisan crowd at Kiawah, though, it would be a day that ran the entire gamut of emotions from joy to despair, agony to ecstasy.

Initially, it seemed as though the US, as ever, was taking command of the singles. But this day would be different. Totally, sense-sappingly different. Take Mark Calcavecchia. Third out, he was 5-up at the turn against Colin Montgomerie and on the verge of completing what Americans like to call a 'whuppin'. But with victory in sight, cracks began to appear in the Nebraskan's game. With four holes to play he was 4-up, but the 1989 Open champion would play his last four holes in triple bogey, bogey, triple bogey and bogey, with a near shank at the par-three 17th that found the water. It wasn't as though Montgomerie was in full flight, more that Calcavecchia was collapsing spectacularly.

Here was a golfer in meltdown in full view of the watching world and with nobody but his caddie to help him through. Not only did it allow the steady Montgomerie to salvage a half point when he should have been back in the locker room licking his wounds, it also put America's chance of winning in real jeopardy.

Calcavecchia's total for the back nine was 9 over par. It was the kind of score that most weekend hackers might have been happy with but for Calcavecchia it was too much on several levels. After shaking hands with his opponent, he was hyperventilating so badly that he needed treatment from the on-course paramedics. Soon after, he skipped his press interviews and fled the course, heading to the beach in tears, believing he had perhaps cost the USA the Ryder Cup. 'If you play golf at a high level you will experience losses but nothing that traumatic,' says his teammate Lanny Wadkins. 'To Mark's credit he has come back – he did a lot of destroying. [But] you kind of forget about it and that has always been the thing in the Ryder Cup. You have failures but if the team wins that is what matters.'

First, Faldo defeated the stubborn Ray Floyd 2-up, while Ireland's David Feherty had now conquered his crippling nerves sufficiently to account for the reigning US Open champion Payne Stewart in the second match. Elsewhere, Paul Azinger took Olazábal to the last, beating him 2-up, while Corey Pavin nicked the point against the gallant Steven Richardson and Chip Beck upset Ian Woosnam.

But as the tide seemed to be turning red, the predicted victory for Seve Ballesteros against Wayne Levi duly occurred, while the under-utilized Paul Broadhurst maintained his 100 per cent record with an impressive win over Mark O'Meara, to bring Europe right back into it.

It was difficult to pick a winner, but when Freddie Couples defeated Sam Torrance and Mark James lost 'fairly promptly' to the terrier of the US side, Lanny Wadkins, it seemed that Stockton's side stood on the verge of victory. And all the time, David Gilford stood on the sidelines watching, wondering what might have been.

With the scores standing at 14–13 to the home side, the outcome of the 29th Ryder Cup would be settled by the last match out on the golf course, between Bernhard Langer and Hale Irwin. 'Dave Stockton had asked me where I might want to play and I said, "Dave, you are the captain, I'll play wherever you want me to play",' recalls Irwin. 'Then when he put me last and I saw the draw, I told my wife, "I have a distinct feeling that this is going to come down to our last match". I didn't know that I was being so prophetic.'

Certainly, Irwin has his strategy down pat. 'I thought if I can go out those first four or five holes and stay even and then win some of the downwind holes I'd have a chance because once you go back into the wind for those finishing holes, Bernhard was going to have the advantage because of the way he hits the ball. That's exactly what happened because I was 2-up with four to play.'

But with the crowd moving ever inward, suffocating the players, and the pressure, the sickening pressure, ever increasing, Irwin gave up 'a couple of silly shots', allowing Langer back into the game. When he then three-putted the 17th, the game was all-square going down the last.

What made Irwin's capitulation all the more spectacular was that the three-time US Open champion had been in total control of the game, standing 2-up with just four to play, and 1-up with two to play. Come the final two holes, though, and Irwin, like so many of the other players that Sunday, was falling apart quicker than flat-pack furniture. After his three-putting at 17, Irwin stood on the last tee, knowing the result hinged on him. 'I kept seeing more and more team members show up, which meant that this meant something,' recalls Irwin. 'So I was just really trying to keep my head down, and keep the ball in play and hit the ball as best I could.'

Theoretically, it seemed like a sound plan. But this was the final hole of the Ryder Cup, with just four hundred or so yards ahead of Irwin and Langer that would determine whether Europe retained the trophy or the USA won it back for the first time since Lee Trevino grasped it in 1983. Both men stood on the tee, knowing the fate of the Ryder Cup lay in their clammy, trembling hands.

Down the fairway, 25,000 pairs of eyes stared back at the pair. Ten deep they stood, lining the dunes all the way to the green. In an atmosphere of gut-wrenching tension, Langer found the fairway while Irwin pulled his tee shot badly left towards the dunes. Somehow, though, his ball ended up on the fairway. Some commentators suggested that the only way the ball could have found its way on to the short stuff was either divine intervention or that a spectator had rerouted it. Most observers favoured the latter view. 'I was in the scrum, I was in amongst the crowd, and it was such a mess,' says Sandy Jones. 'I don't know if anybody will ever know what really happened. Maybe one man in the world does. The rest of us can all assume what happened.'

Irwin, by his own admission, was gone ('I couldn't breathe, I couldn't swallow'). His approach flew way right, he then fluffed his chip, putted up to a couple of feet before Langer gave him the five. After a confident start, he, like so many before him, had imploded, taking 41 shots for the back nine. Langer too was struggling. His second shot had followed Irwin's but landed nearer, not much, but on the edge of the green, some 30 feet away from the hole.

Two putts to win the game and retain – not win – the Ryder Cup for Europe. The first attempt, downhill and quick, would be a nervy jab that streaked five or six feet past the hole, leaving Langer a shortish putt to complete an unlikely comeback. Ordinarily, a six-footer to win a tournament is sufficient enough to make knees knock and mere mortals crumble, but at the Ryder Cup, the third-most watched sporting event in the world, it was all or nothing for Bernhard Langer.

The pressure on the German would also be compounded by his recent problems with the putter. Known throughout the game as 'the yips', Langer's problems, like Vardon, Hogan and Snead before him, were those supposedly simple short putts that many players took for granted, but that he found himself twitching over and, invariably, missing. Indeed, that he had carved out such a staggeringly successful career despite his problems was testament to the character and determination of the man.

As much psychological as it is technical, the yips is a constant battle to get the putter and the mind to work in unison and see short putts for what they really are. It was easier said than done. In a bid to address his predicament, Langer had changed his putting grip on several occasions and had now resorted to a new, extraordinarily awkward and unconventional-looking one where his left hand was below his right and then held in place by the fingers of his right hand.

Indeed, it looked less like a putting grip and more like he was nursing a broken wrist.

To further complicate matters, now there was not only a six-foot putt to land one of the biggest prizes in world sport facing Langer but a dirty great spike mark right on the line of his putt. There was nothing he could do about it. Instead, Langer and his caddie Pete Coleman decided that their best option was to hit the putt firm inside the spike mark and take a little of the left to right break out of it. 'About a foot from the hole was this big spike mark which stood up quite high,' recalled Coleman in *How We Won the Ryder Cup – The Caddies' Stories.* 'So he said to me "Do you see that?" and I said, "Yes. You can't help but see it. Just hit it inside and hit it hard".'

Looking on was Langer's captain, Bernard Gallacher. 'I was very, very, very confident that he would hole that putt at the last,' he recalls. 'I didn't think it was a difficult putt; it was uphill and on the right level. But we had struggled on the new greens all week and the dwarf Bermuda grass they used had made them very difficult for our players.'

Langer's putt flirted with the hole, touching the lip, but stayed above ground and slipped by on the right. Hale Irwin and the USA had their half point. Crucially, they also had the Ryder Cup back in their hands. As the ball came to a halt, Langer's face collapsed in agony and his knees buckled.

Crouching by the greenside, Hale Irwin kept a lid on his emotions, while all those around him burst into life. Ever the gentleman, he then strolled over to Langer to offer his commiserations. 'I knew what he was going through and if it was me I would have been devastated so I wanted to temper my enthusiasm for a later time,' he explains. 'I didn't think it was appropriate at that time to be jovial, simply because that was a lot to ask of one man in one putt.'

Amid the hullabaloo, Bernhard Langer was joined by his teammate Seve Ballesteros. 'Nobody in the world would have made that putt,' he told the German, 'nobody'.

Not all the players were as gracious. Later, Paul Azinger expressed his delight, in his own unique way. 'American pride is back,' he beamed, adding, 'we went over there and thumped the Iraqis. Now we've taken the cup back. I'm proud to be an American.'

The trouble for Bernhard Langer is that history doesn't remember the winning or the losing team as such. Captains maybe, but not the teams. Instead, they remember the player who holed the winning putt or, more likely, fluffed the losing one. Men like Sam Torrance, Seve Ballesteros or Costantino Rocca. For Langer, it had been the kind of harrowing moment that could have done for him and his career. Indeed, few players recover from such trauma. Famously, the American Doug Sanders missed a 30-inch putt to win the 1970 Open Championship at St Andrews and then lost the resulting play-off to Jack Nicklaus. When he called time on his career he had finished second four times in major championships but never won. Instead, he's known as the man who blew it big time. 'Do I ever think about that putt?' he said twenty-five years later. 'Only once every four or five minutes.'

And what of Peter Alliss? In his first Ryder Cup in 1953, the Englishman had the chance to win the trophy for Great Britain and Ireland but finished 5–6–6, taking four from the edge of the green at the 18th, allowing his opponent, the New Yorker Jim Turnesa, to claim an invaluable point. 'People said it was unfair for him [Langer] to be put under so much pressure, but that's what sport's all about: holing an important putt, not missing a penalty, getting a serve in at match point,' says Alliss. 'It seems to me that his mistake was very quickly forgotten. Nobody mentions it now. But mine was mentioned for at least the next fifteen years.'

The following week Bernhard Langer and Hale Irwin travelled to Germany to play in the Mercedes German Masters in Stuttgart. While many players could have been forgiven for taking a raincheck given the drama of Kiawah, Langer, ever the professional, not only turned up but won the event, holing a crucial short putt at the final hole to make the play-off before beating the Australian Rodger Davis. 'He just shook off what would have been probably a devastating loss to most people,' reflects Irwin. 'How Bernhard came back and just kind of put it all behind him, and won in his home country... that's the kind of player and man he is.'

President Bush being otherwise engaged, the presentation of the Cup was made by the US Vice President and one-time scratch golfer Dan Quayle. With the trophy safely back in Dave Stockton's hands, the US team, resplendent in bright blue blazers perhaps stolen from a British holiday camp, repaired to the beach for a photo-call, complete with the regulation oversized Stars and Stripes. The pictures taken, Mark O'Meara, ably assisted by the rest of the team, carried Dave Stockton to the water and dunked him in. As the team piled into the brine, though, Chip Beck left them to it. 'One thing I remember is those boys going and jumping in the ocean and I was running because I didn't want to get wet and ruin that good suit we had on that day.'

For Ian Woosnam, Sam Torrance and Mark James, there was only one place to be – and it wasn't the beach. 'We were all down, some of the lads were in tears,' says Woosnam. 'So I grabbed a few of the team – I remember Sam and Jesse James came with me – and we walked over to the big beer tent where all the European fans had gathered and sank a few beers and sang a few songs with them.'

Regardless of his unconventional methods and his all-American kick-ass attitude, it had been mission accomplished for Dave Stockton. Yes, he had been abrasive and yes, he had tweaked the noses of the opposition, but he, unlike Floyd and Nicklaus before him, had got the job done. 'We wanted to win and we had been pushed to win and Stockton was kind of a fiery captain,' explains Lanny Wadkins. 'But we also had a good team, and the team played with a lot of emotion.'

Hailed as a hero at home, he was held in lesser regard by some of his opponents that week, who viewed him as responsible for stoking the fire of an often tempestuous contest. 'I think Stockton was completely out of order,' says Ian Woosnam. 'He went out to win and he didn't care how he did it. When the British lost in the 1940s, 50s and 60s they did it with grace; when the Americans began losing they didn't like it and Stockton got the crowds too aggressively wound up. It almost turned into a riot. It wasn't golf and it wasn't a fair match. When the Americans hit it into the trees or deep rough their balls would mysteriously reappear on the fairway. I didn't enjoy that week at all.'

The commentator Bruce Critchley agrees. 'The Americans don't understand being the underdog, they don't like it and they don't really know how to rally without it becoming offensive,' he says. 'And they don't really like or know how to handle the sort of rough and tumble of a really good tight match without going over the top.'

The bottom line, however, was that Stockton, unlike so many American captains, used the continuing failures of the USA to his and his team's advantage, creating the same kind of priceless team spirit that had carried the Europeans so far in previous contests. Nearly twenty years on, meanwhile, Bernard Gallacher's view of the match has mellowed. 'It was a very tough match and I always thought we could win but it really did go down to the wire. I would probably say a drawn match would have been a fairer result but we lost on the last green,' he reflects. 'In some ways, it was probably a good thing that America won in 1991 as it gave a new impetus to the event. We had won for so many years before that it needed a change.'

Much has been written about the so-called 'War on the Shore'. Some of it even makes sense. The truth was Kiawah 1991 was rowdier and more raucous than almost any other Ryder Cup that had gone before it, but it was hardly the riot that most reports suggested it was. 'Kiawah was never really an issue,' reflects Sandy Jones.

Sure, it had been unruly on either side of the ropes and yes, there had been some gamesmanship – on both sides – but it was just another passionate, fiercely contested Ryder Cup, which, given that the USA had won for the first time in four attempts and on home soil too, was hardly likely to be all handshakes and polite applause. 'They say that the crowd was bad but I played and I didn't think the crowd were all that bad, certainly not compared to '99 [at Brookline],' insists Mark James. '[But] in Kiawah there was an awful lot of space around so a lot of the time as players we were not that close to any crowd problems. I certainly didn't notice anything playing and I played every session.'

Sam Torrance agrees. 'I know things went on in a fairly hostile atmosphere,' he said in his autobiography *Sam*, 'but I'd take the rather unfashionable view that there was nothing too untoward.'

And if proof were needed that the 29th Ryder Cup was little more than a more boisterous, marginally more animated version of itself, it came as the teams made their way to the closing dinner. With two buses laid on to carry them to the hall, it was Ian Woosnam who suggested the teams share a bus instead, and with Dave Stockton's consent, the USA and Europe did what they always did after the Ryder Cup. They shared a beer.

War... then Peace

THE BELFRY, SUTTON COLDFIELD, WARWICKSHIRE

24–26 September 1993

Tom Watson had watched the events at Kiawah Island with a mixture of embarrassment and sadness. As a player and a man for whom integrity, tradition and honour meant everything, the gradual diminution of standards in the Ryder Cup represented a very real threat to the game he so adored. Something, he decided, had to change.

On his appointment as US captain, Watson, through a statement circulated by the PGA of America, spoke of his intention to restore some much-needed sanity and decorum to the Ryder Cup:

I love the spirit of the Ryder Cup, but I think some of that spirit has been lost because of the competitive nature of the players. I'd like to see less of the `War on the Shore' mentality. I don't want negative things to pop up that could detract from the spirit of the event. I want the event to win, and for that to happen, everyone has to understand that the spirit of the game is to do what's fair rather than whatever it takes to win.

It was a release that both irritated and angered the previous US captain, Dave Stockton, who later told *Golf Digest* that he had been 'offended by that, because that Ryder Cup, unlike any other, before or since, elevated the level of public interest tremendously'.

Lanny Wadkins agrees: 'I thought it [1991] was great. It really kind of put the Ryder Cup totally on the map,' he says. 'A little antagonism is not a bad thing. If everyone is sweet and pats each other on the back all the time what the hell good does that do? Why even play? If you don't want to beat the crap out of someone let's not go out there.'

By publicly declaring his desire and intention to make the 30th Ryder Cup a more sporting, more deferential affair, Watson's tack was already markedly different to that of his predecessor Dave Stockton. There were no butts to be kicked, no wars to be fought. Just a determination to see the traditions of the game upheld and the purest form of golf returned to something that didn't resemble a football match. 'We wanted the crowds to treat the matches with a little bit more respect than the American crowds did two years previously,' he explains. 'I would hate to see the game evolve into something that it shouldn't evolve into. I think everybody who loves the game, they didn't like to see that behaviour, that yelling and screaming – there is a limit.'

After his baptism of fire in 1991, Bernard Gallacher was also only too aware that things needed to change and a tacit agreement between the two skippers, where they said and did the right thing, developed. 'We didn't talk about it,' explains Gallacher. 'Tom came across and you would expect him to do all the right things before the match, you know? [He said] this isn't life or death, this is a competition and just do the right thing.'

Watson had made it known to the PGA of America several years earlier that he wished to be considered for the position of US captain, but with the caveat that with five Open Championship titles under his belt, it was, in his opinion at least, wiser for him to take charge of the team when they played in England, not only because of his playing success in the UK but because he had a natural affinity with the British galleries as well.

For Watson, the role of Ryder Cup captain, while a great honour, was not, perhaps, the critical position that some commentators and former captains maintained. Part ambassador, part listening post, it was more of a ceremonial responsibility than any great tactical or coaching job.

'The main thing is that a captain really doesn't do much,' he says. '[You] try and relieve some of their [the players'] anxieties and you do that with as much humour as possible, and frankly Payne Stewart, he was the one who carried the ball there, he helped keep everybody loose.'

If it seemed as though Tom Watson's approach to the job of US captain was perhaps more laissez-faire than those before him, this was simply because of his easy-going nature. Rarely prone to tub-thumping like, say, Stockton, Watson was a quiet, considered captain, more concerned with making the event as smooth and stress-free for his team as possible, than with delivering long, impassioned monologues or rallying-cries. 'How do you inspire people to play? If they are not already inspired to play they are in the wrong match, they are in the wrong profession,' he says.

A nice, easy-going guy, undoubtedly, but that said, not one who shied away from making the few tough decisions that a Ryder Cup captain was required to make. He may have had the innocent, freckled, grinning face of Huckleberry Finn, but they didn't call him 'Huckleberry Dillinger' for nothing. On the Sunday night after the PGA Championship at the Inverness Club, Toledo, Ohio, for example, Watson had called all those under consideration for a captain's pick, one of whom was Curtis Strange, who relived their phone conversation in *Sports Illustrated* magazine in August 2001.

'Tom?' said Strange who had been expecting the call.

'Yeah,' replied Watson, adding. 'You're out.'

'OK. So how is everything else going?'

Watson would settle instead for two of the Ryder Cup's most battle-hardened competitors, Raymond Floyd and Lanny Wadkins, presumably because not even the toughest of team captains would have the nerve to tell them they weren't playing. 'They gave the players who hadn't played there before stability,' says Watson.

Plucked from the pipes and slippers of the Seniors Tour (now known as the Champions Tour), Ray Floyd would become the oldest player to play in the Ryder Cup, at fifty-one years and twenty days when the event started. Later, Watson would defend his selection, maintaining that he was looking for 'heart and guts', two qualities that go a very long way in sport – and especially in the Ryder Cup – and of which Floyd and Wadkins possessed vast, deep reservoirs.

They weren't the only attributes that won Floyd a call-up. In 1992, he had won on the regular PGA Tour, aged forty-nine, taking the Doral-Ryder Open over the Blue Monster course at Doral, Florida, just a few weeks after his family home in Miami's Biscayne Bay had burned down, taking with it a lifetime of awards, mementos and memories. Then, having jumped ship to the calmer waters of the Seniors Tour after his fiftieth birthday, he also won the GTE North Classic, becoming the first player in history to win on the PGA Tour and the Seniors Tour in the same calendar year. When he was later awarded *Golf World* magazine's Man of the Year, it seemed that there was nothing Ray Floyd couldn't do, irrespective of his advancing years.

It helped, of course, that Floyd's record in the Ryder Cup was so strong and that his appetite for the fight remained as voracious as ever. This, then, would be his eighth appearance as a player, some four years after he had captained the team. Indeed, only three Americans had played more Ryder Cup matches than Floyd (Billy Casper, Lanny Wadkins and Arnold Palmer). Not that Floyd cared about records. 'You know what?' he says. 'I am the last one to tell you... In my mind [it] is wins and losses as a team. To me the Ryder Cup is a team effort. It is not about individual things.'

The week before they were due to depart for England, the American team was scheduled to attend the White House for the now traditional send-off by the President. On this occasion, for the first time in twelve years, the White House had a Democrat incumbent. William Jefferson Clinton had become the 42nd President of the United States in January of 1993, having defeated George H. W. Bush, a leader thought to be unbeatable during the aftermath of the Gulf War in 1991.

Like his predecessor, Clinton would join an increasingly long line of golfing Presidents. With a handicap he said was '12, 13, something like that' he had honed his game as Governor of Arkansas, slipping out of his office in Little Rock to squeeze in eighteen holes whenever he could. Indeed, one of Clinton's first decrees when he reached the White House was to have Dwight D. Eisenhower's famous putting green moved to its current location to the southeast of the Oval Office, facilitating quicker access and more practice time.

For many of the exclusively Republican American Ryder Cup team, while visiting the White House may have been a great honour, having to shake the hand of a Democrat, even if it was one who loved golf, was a team trip too far, especially when that self-same Democrat had just passed a new tax bill increasing income tax for the wealthiest Americans.

When the ceremonial send-off was announced in June, John Cook, for example, felt 'it would be hypocritical' to attend. Lee Janzen said he would love to see the White House, but only if Clinton was 'out of town', while Paul Azinger, who had tried to handle the issue with curiously uncharacteristic diplomacy, found himself undone by his friend and teammate Payne Stewart who said, 'Azinger doesn't want to go. His dad fought in Vietnam, and he doesn't want to shake hands with a draft dodger. That's what he told me.'

Though there was still no evidence that Clinton had actively avoided military service in Vietnam – he maintained his conscription notice arrived too late while he was studying in Britain, at Oxford University – the story had gained credence among Clinton's opponents, which, in the case of the 1993 US Ryder Cup team was pretty much each and every one of them.

Still, the idea that the US team could leave for the UK pursued by the kind of unpleasant headlines that could only inspire Bernard Gallacher's side, would be too much for Tom Watson and the PGA of America. Apologies and retractions would be offered. The players trawled out the misquoted excuse or maintained that their words had been taken out of context. One by one, the US team fell into line as Watson urged them to put politics to one side and concentrate on the more pressing matter of the Ryder Cup. After all, the competition was less than a week away while Bill Clinton, it would transpire, had another seven years of putting practice in the Oval Office.

At the meeting at the White House's Rose Garden on Sunday, 19 September, captain Tom Watson and eleven of his team – Freddie Couples was otherwise engaged in Spain – stood in line to shake the hand of the man who had just hit them where it hurt the most. The pleasantries over, Watson and the President talked golf, with the US skipper giving the US President a lesson in gripping the golf club. 'You know, Mr President,' said Watson, 'the golf grip is a lot like politics. If you hold the club too far to the right, you're going to get in trouble on the left. If you hold it too far to the left, you're going to have trouble from the right. But if you hold it in the middle...'

As was the leader of the free world's inalienable right, Clinton butted in: '...you'll get it just right!'

That evening, with a personal, political and potentially awkward crisis averted, the US team left for the UK, with Concorde once more carrying the bags.

Back at The Belfry, the final preparations were being made for the arrival of the opposition. Even in the autumnal Warwickshire weather, The Belfry was looking better than ever. A £2.5 million remodelling of the Brabazon course had also seen ten of the holes overhauled, with improved hotel facilities and better viewing for spectators too. Eight years after hosting its first Ryder Cup, the Brabazon had grown, gradually, into its own skin and already made more memories than most courses make in a lifetime. No longer did commentators query the location of the club or question the logic of playing the Ryder Cup on a course supposedly more suited to the opposition. The facts spoke for themselves: two Ryder Cups, one European win, one tie.

The British PGA also had a new Chief Executive at the helm. As the head of the Scottish region of the PGA, doubling the size of the sport in the country, Sandy Jones had been to every Ryder Cup, either as a spectator, referee or official since the massacre at Walton Heath in

1981. He had seen it grow from a competition, unloved and unnoticed, into one of the world's major sporting events. 'The 1983 match cost the PGA about fifty grand,' he recalls. 'There was no profit in the match up until 1985. That was the match that kind of broke even. In America, they never sold tickets until 1987 – that was the first match in America they got any sort of gallery.'

Born just outside Glasgow in December 1946, Alexander Martin Jones had taken up the game of golf aged twelve, fitting in rounds between trips to Ibrox to see his beloved Glasgow Rangers play football. 'Golf is my business,' he says today. 'Football is my passion.' Though he had trained as a structural engineer, Jones had sent in a speculative application to the Scottish PGA and having landed the position, set about developing the game in its spiritual home. It wasn't easy, but with the help of some like-minded compatriots, he began to make progress.

My first job was to put on a Scottish Championship because they had just lost the sponsor. So I had no sponsor and I had six months to put this thing on and I had no experience because I had just come in. In the end I managed to get East Kilbride's shopping centre to sponsor it. Imagine, a shopping centre. Then we needed a player, a star player, and I phoned Sam Torrance and he said he would come and play. And I thought the world of him for that and he never asked me for a penny. He never even asked me for a hotel room. He said I will come and play for you Sandy, and that was the first time that I had met him. [But] we were so short on cash we couldn't afford all the bannering [around the course] so we had this banner on the 18th to promote the East Kilbride Shopping Centre, the idea being the players would play their second shots near it and get the banner on TV. But the problem was that Scottish television only had one camera on a tower and when the wind changed all the players were driving way past the banner. So I had to get four guys to go and move the banner and it was really heavy. It was like a Benny Hill sketch. You had these poor guys carrying this banner around trying to judge the wind and get it in the right place. The East Kilbride Shopping Centre marketing department weren't too happy.

When he had succeeded John Lindsey at the end of 1991, the events at Kiawah Island were of little concern to Sandy Jones. Instead, Jones would turn his attention to getting the PGA back on track and to fostering better relations with the European Tour. 'The PGA had kind of lost its way as an organization when I came in and we were trying to get ourselves reorganized,' says Jones. 'John Lindsey had been our previous chief executive and, for right or wrong, it hadn't been a good spell, so my job was to rebuild the PGA really.'

Bernard Gallacher's team, meanwhile, appeared robust and well equipped to wrest the Ryder Cup back from the States, even if a few of the team had a few niggles to contend with. Bernhard Langer, for example, was still nursing a neck injury that had prevented him from playing properly for some six weeks, while Sam Torrance, playing in his seventh Ryder Cup, was suffering with a sore toe which rather than improving with rest, seemed to be getting worse. And so what if Seve Ballesteros was playing like a half-cut plumber hacking his way round the local municipal course at the weekend, there was no way the Ryder Cup could go ahead without him. 'The start of Seve's downturn was in 1992, and I picked him in '93 because he is such a great team player and he was still putting in a few good performances,' explains Bernard Gallacher. 'But he wasn't quite the same Seve.'

Injuries, ailments and suspect swings aside, there was plenty for Bernard Gallacher to be positive about. Team Europe was finally beginning to look truly continental in its make-up, rather than just a combined Great Britain, Ireland and Spain side, as the first Swede, Joakim Haeggman, and the first Italian, Costantino Rocca, entered the fray. 'I think when I played the Ryder Cup it didn't show [on television] in Italy, but it is the most important thing for me,' says Rocca. 'I know a lot of people want to see it but they don't show [it] in Italy.'

There would also be debuts for two Englishmen, Barry Lane, the journeyman pro who was enjoying the most consistent spell of his career, and the Walker Cup player and local lad made good, Peter Baker. 'The Belfry was like a home ground for me,' he recalls. 'I had had a good five months where I had played really well and come from really nowhere, not even in contention for the Ryder Cup, and made the team.'

Tom Watson and Bernard Gallacher's show of unity seemed to be working and with peace in real danger of breaking out, the Ryder Cup week progressed smoothly and without incident. Practice rounds were had, functions attended and everyone made the right noises about making this Ryder Cup one to remember, only for all the right reasons. It was only at the black tie Gala Dinner on the Wednesday evening that the first real sign of any hostility raised its head, not because the soup was cold or the disco was below par, but over the apparently vexatious issue of autographs, or, as it transpired, the lack of them.

Over the years, it had become customary for the teams to sign their menus at the Gala Dinner as a memento of their week spent trying to crush another continent. Indeed, on his Ryder Cup debut in 1977, Tom Watson himself had described the tradition as 'a nice thing to have and save' from the week. But when Sam Torrance sauntered across the empty dance floor and over to Watson's table, the Scot was rebuffed by the US skipper, with Watson arguing that if he were to sign one autograph, then soon every one of the 800 guests, who had each paid £150 for their ticket, would be lining up by his table for the same. Angry and embarrassed, a seething Torrance had returned to his table, his pride hurt, his menu unsigned.

The following day, however, the incident was reported by a media clearly desperate for some fuel for the embers of bitterness carried over from Kiawah. The *Boston Globe* ran the headline 'Watson Causes Ryder Flap' while the *Chicago Sun-Times* called it an 'An Autograph Snub Bogey'. Although Watson soon apologized, and Torrance tried to play down the incident, it was clear that the episode had spiced things up. Bernard Gallacher, meanwhile, had found a solution to the problem. 'Actually I know Tom Watson's signature, so I gave it to Sam,' he said. 'He was quite happy.'

Today, Tom Watson maintains that he was within his rights to refuse Torrance's request, even if it may have seemed rude or petty. 'How would you like to go to dinner and you never could eat?' he inquires. 'There are times and places for autographs and I said "please not at the dinner" and of course that got played a different way in the press. That did hurt a little bit, but I took one for the team, I guess you might say.'

Thick fog would delay the start of the 30th Ryder Cup matches by two and a half hours. When the games finally got underway, it would be a session notable for some sizeable victories on both sides, culminating in a share of the spoils. In the opening game, Sam Torrance and Mark James fell to Lanny Wadkins and Corey Pavin 4&3 while in the next, the scores were levelled by Ian Woosnam and Bernhard Langer's thumping 7&5 victory over Paul Azinger and Payne Stewart.

For rookies like Peter Baker, paired with Ian Woosnam in the first Friday afternoon fourballs, it was a terrifying experience, and this despite enjoying overwhelming local support and being as familiar with the Brabazon course as he was with his slippers. 'It was like an out of body experience,' explains Baker, now head professional at South Staffordshire Golf Club. 'You get on there and all the things that you have done all of your life just seem to evaporate and you say a few prayers and hopefully your shot resembles a golf shot and it's not too embarrassing.'

Getting on to the tee was one thing, but getting that first shot away was a different, more taxing dilemma.

I had played at The Belfry a hell of a lot before but I got on the tee with Woosie in the fourballs and I looked down the fairway and all of a sudden there's this big tree in the way, which is on the right hand side about fifty yards off the tee. I had never noticed it before in my life and all of a sudden this big tree seems to come in to play. It was quite mind-blowing, I was thinking, 'Bloody hell, I have never noticed that before'. Everything is exaggerated a hundredfold. Your senses are so on alert and this great big bloody tree seemed to be in the way. Of course if you went there now, you'd say what tree is that?

Fortunately, Baker would avoid the tree with his first Ryder Cup shot, although he did pull his tee shot into the rough on the left. From then

on, though, Baker and Woosnam would form a formidable partnership, defeating Jim Gallagher Jr and Lee Janzen by one hole, and then
crushing Fred Couples and Paul Azinger the following afternoon 6&5.
'It was a winning formula,' adds Baker. 'I played tremendously well.
Woosie carried me the first two or three holes [but] then I absolutely
smashed them. All Woosie kept saying was "keep going, keep going".'

While Baker's Ryder Cup was going swimmingly, he would soon
discover at first hand some of the more unorthodox tactics employed
by the opposition. In the Saturday morning foursomes against
Raymond Floyd and Payne Stewart, Peter Baker and Barry Lane had
been forewarned to expect some unsavoury treatment, but when it
happened they were still taken aback. 'On the 15th hole I had to hole a
six-footer to win the hole,' Baker explained. 'As Floyd picked up his ball
he backed away right along our line. I just stood there open-mouthed,
but Barry got stuck into Floyd. "What the **** do you think you're
doing?" Lane asked. "Oh, did I?" Floyd said with a smirk. Great golfer, not
a nice guy.'

The first day would end in the fading light, with the last match out
between Nick Faldo and Colin Montgomerie and Paul Azinger and Fred
Couples called off after Faldo had squared the match with a birdie at
the 17th, primarily because nobody could actually see what they were
doing any more. At 8 o'clock on Saturday, with their breakfasts still
swilling round their stomachs, the four men played their final hole in
what was, effectively, a one-hole shoot-out. Still, though, they couldn't
be separated and pars for Faldo and Azinger saw the game halved.

Where once Ballesteros and Olazábal had been the key weapon
in Europe's arsenal, now it was Faldo and Montgomerie's turn to
assume the mantle. The couple would play every session, taking 2½
points from their three games, an unbeaten stretch they were fully
expected to continue against the low-key duo of Chip Beck and John
Cook in the Saturday afternoon fourballs. A permanent fixture in the
world's top ten in 1992 and 1993, Cook sat kicking his heels for three
sessions wondering when his first taste of Ryder Cup would come and,

moreover, what all the fuss was about. When he finally got the call from Watson, though, he wasn't to be found wanting. Cook and Beck would answer every question asked by Europe's illustrious partnership, and in pulling off a one-hole win, gave the US a foothold back in the game, just as it threatened to get away from them. 'That match right there was one of those matches that you love in a Ryder Cup where a really strong team gets beaten unexpectedly, and it changed the course of our match, I believe,' says Tom Watson. 'Even though we were one point down that afternoon was a real uplift for our team. I think that inspired us.'

The session ended 3–1 in the visitors' favour, leaving Bernard Gallacher's team with a one-point lead (8½–7½). While Cook's and Beck's win over Faldo and Montgomerie gave the US team a point that they might not have expected, Cook's opinion of the event itself, as revealed in an interview with *Golf Digest* magazine six years later, was in stark contrast to the default reverential line taken by most players.

I can honestly say that my experience at the Ryder Cup wasn't one of my highlights. Making the team was wonderful. I enjoyed being with the guys. But I didn't play a match until Saturday afternoon. Even then there was hesitancy on Tom Watson's part to even put Chip Beck and me out. There was a chance I wasn't going to play until Sunday and then a chance I wasn't going to play at all. And I had earned my way on that team through points. I wasn't a captain's choice and I felt that I should have at least played once on Friday and again on Saturday. Fortunately we won a big match on Saturday, Chip and me. Maybe Tom didn't think I was playing that well, I don't know. But I don't think that should have had a bearing on my not being able to play. Like I said, I was a point-earner.

On Saturday evening, Bernard Gallacher and Torrance discussed the Scot's troubled toe before sending for Tom Watson to inform him of the problem and the likely outcome. After Dave Stockton's failure to tell Gallacher of Steve Pate's omission at Kiawah, it would have been understandable if Gallacher had chosen to keep a lid on it and then drop his bombshell at the very last moment. But this was the new Ryder Cup, where an entente cordiale – autograph-hunters aside – had broken out, where civility had made a rare and welcome appearance and where the two captains were publicly committed to contesting the Cup in the most sporting manner, with no untoward, underhand tactics.

Watson arrived to be greeted by Torrance whipping off his shoe to reveal his foot covered in a pus-stained bandage, as Bernard Gallacher recalls. '[I said,] "He can only play if he gets a painkiller on the 1st tee and on the 10th tee," and I said that might not be a very fair thing to do because it was on his right toe, which is crucial in golf, crucial in balancing.'

The pair agreed to sleep on it and reassess in the morning, but the prognosis wasn't good. Suspecting the worst, Watson went away and thought about which of his players should go in the envelope and step aside for the singles. But that delicate, difficult decision would be taken out of his hands by captain's pick Lanny Wadkins. 'He said, "Tom, I don't deserve to be on the team, I don't deserve to be playing, put me in the envelope because someone else deserves it more than I do",' explains Watson. 'Typical Lanny. He understands.'

That evening, Watson sat with his team at dinner and explained the situation as he saw it. 'Tom looked at the guys [and said,] "We are going to win tomorrow, and I can tell you why we are going to win because I am the luckiest son of a bitch that has ever played golf",' recalls Wadkins. 'When he said that I looked at Raymond [Floyd] and he looked at me… We were the only two people around who were old enough to get that, to understand the things that Tom had done and we looked at each other like, no shit Tom, we have known that forever.'

Two years earlier, at Kiawah Island, Bernard Gallacher had harboured thoughts that Steve Pate's injury may not have been all it seemed and that by pulling him out of the singles, it had given the US a half point that, in all likelihood, they may not have won otherwise. Two years on, though, and the spikes were on the other foot. 'I think we always felt that if it was an individual tournament, he [Torrance] would have done whatever it took to play the match,' reflects Lanny Wadkins. 'But smart thinking on their part – a half point at that point in time was a big half point.'

The following morning, Torrance's toe had shown no improvement. He was out of the singles and so too, then, was Lanny Wadkins. For the American, who had the experience and the form to play a pivotal part on Sunday, not to mention a passion for the Ryder Cup that was second to none, it had been a massive, magnanimous gesture to volunteer. 'The only downside,' he says, 'was when the draw came out and I was drawn against Seve… I would have loved to play Seve.'

And Torrance's injury? 'I still don't know what a septic toe is,' says Wadkins, '[but] next time I see him I am going to ask him what the hell a septic toe is. Never had one of those!'

The singles began promptly at midday, with 30,000 fans sandwiched into a chilly Belfry and Europe entering the fray with their slender one-point advantage. The initial exchanges suggested that it was destined to be another famous day for Team Europe. Ian Woosnam took a creditable half from Fred Couples while Colin Montgomerie defeated Lee Janzen at the last.

But that early optimism would soon turn to anxiety, as the US strengthened their hold in the majority of the other games. For Peter Baker, there had been more pressing concerns. On the Saturday afternoon, the 25-year-old had walked off the course after his and Ian Woosnam's emphatic victory over Fred Couples and Paul Azinger to learn that his baby daughter, Georgina, had been rushed to hospital with suspected meningitis. Without time to change, Baker fought his way through heavy traffic to be with his daughter, the emotion of what was turning into a memorable Ryder Cup for him personally, suddenly replaced by the kind of anxiety that any parent would feel when confronted by such news.

Later that night, Georgina Baker's condition would improve and a diagnosis of an unusually high temperature, rather than meningitis, was given. At 10.30 p.m., Baker returned to The Belfry, still wearing the same clothes he had played in that afternoon. As he walked into the team room, Ian Woosnam approached him. 'Do you want the good news or the bad news?' he said. Baker looked puzzled. 'The good news is if you really don't want to play tomorrow then certain players in the American team have said they will drop out too.'

'And the bad news?' asked Baker.

'The bad news,' added Woosnam, 'is if you want to play you have got Corey Pavin.'

Having been cast as one of the villains of the piece at Kiawah Island two years earlier, Corey Pavin was the US team's player of the week, a tough, obdurate performer who thrived on the cut and thrust of the Ryder Cup. For a rookie like Baker, it was a formidable proposition. At breakfast the following morning, Seve Ballesteros took it upon himself to offer the Englishman some advice over the tea and toast. 'He said, "Peter, you have got a very, very tough game today. This guy is a tricky customer".'

Tricky, though, would be no match for Baker. Despite the stresses of Saturday, both on and off the course, and little sleep, Baker would once more find his finest form, and a 2-up victory would send the galleries, Baker's home galleries, into raptures. It had been a remarkable week for Baker, a week where, despite his baby daughter's illness, he had proved himself to be one of the key members of the European team, winning three points from his four games, culminating in arguably the best win of his career. 'It was an incredible game and the best scoring of the day,' recalls Baker. 'That night we had to go to dinner which was the last thing he [Pavin] wanted to do. He was chatting away and he said, "Do you know, you had 23 putts today". After I got back home and thought about it I realized that he had had 26 putts; so between us we had had 49 putts, which was some sort of record.'

Not everyone enjoyed the same success as Baker, not least his partner from his sole defeat in the Saturday morning foursomes, Barry Lane. Out second, Lane had eased into a commanding lead against his opponent, Chip Beck, and with five holes to play was 3-up

Right: Samuel Ryder – the man (and the moustache) behind the Ryder Cup.

Below: The British team (with Samuel Ryder second on the left) set sail for the inaugural Ryder Cup at the Worcester Country Club, Massachusetts in 1927.

After twenty-four years and seven contests without a victory, Dai Rees celebrates a rare British win at Lindrick in 1957.

'I don't think you would have missed that putt Tony, but in the circumstances I would never give you the opportunity.' Jack Nicklaus concedes Tony Jacklin's putt and the 1969 match at Royal Birkdale ends in a tie.

The US team in 1981 – the strongest American side ever assembled for the Ryder Cup – steamrollered Europe at Walton Heath by 18½ points to 9½.

Having sat out the 1981 contest, Seve Ballesteros was persuaded by Tony Jacklin to rejoin the team in 1983. Eavesdropping on their conversation is Brian Waites.

Europe's monobrowed magician, Seve Ballesteros, plays that 3-wood out of the bunker at West Palm Beach, 1983.

Victory at last: members of the European team salute the crowd after victory at The Belfry in 1985. Left to right: Seve Ballesteros, captain Tony Jacklin, Sam Torrance, Paul Way and Bernhard Langer.

After the breakthrough success of 1985, Tony Jacklin's Europe went one better in 1987, beating the USA on their captain Jack Nicklaus's home course at Muirfield Village, Ohio.

Europe's Seve Ballesteros and José-María Olazábal in 1989 – arguably the greatest partnership in Ryder Cup history.

Rival captains Bernard Gallacher of Europe and Dave Stockton of America before the start of hostilities at Kiawah Island, South Carolina, 1991. Gallacher would have to wait until 1995 to win the Cup.

Kiawah Island hosted the most dramatic of finishes in 1991, with Bernhard Langer missing a short putt at the final green to hand victory to the home side.

and seemingly coasting home. At the Masters in April, Beck had been criticized for laying up short of the water at the par-five 15th in the final round as he chased down the leader Bernhard Langer, eventually settling for second place. Now, though, he was in the same kind of rich scoring form that had taken him to a record-breaking round of 59 at the Las Vegas Invitational two years earlier. Hole by hole, Beck began pegging Lane back as the anxiety of the home crowd finally, and fatally, got to the Englishman as he lost at the last.

Though it was only the second singles game, European skipper Bernard Gallacher sensed that it had been a critical reverse in his attempt to wrestle the Ryder Cup back. 'I knew at the time that it was crucial,' he says. 'I could see the board and it looked crucial that Barry had to hang on, but Beck was inspired.'

Chip Beck's remarkable turnaround helped shift the momentum of a compelling contest as the US team began to take control. Soon, the US began to rack up the points at a rate of knots. Victories for Payne Stewart over Mark James, Tom Kite over Bernhard Langer and Jim Gallagher Jr over an out-of-sorts Seve Ballesteros brought the scores level at 12½ points each. With Ray Floyd dormie-three against José María Olazábal in a game he would go on to win, the game between Costantino Rocca and Davis Love III would become key.

In the run-up to the singles, Costantino Rocca had played just once, partnering Mark James in a 5&4 drubbing at the hands of the ever-dependable Corey Pavin and Jim Gallagher Jr in the Saturday afternoon fourballs, but as his game neared its climax, it began to show. With two to play, the Italian was 1-up, and all set to record a debut win when it seemed that the importance of what he was doing suddenly smacked him in the face like a wet fish. On the 17th green, the Italian erred on the side of caution, but in endeavouring to two-putt for his par and maintain his slender advantage going down the last, only succeeded in knocking his first putt four feet past, and then, to the horror of the home crowd, missing the return putt.

All-square, it would go from bad to worse for Rocca and Europe at the final hole. Now with the honour, Love drew his driver out of his bag but was stopped short by his captain Tom Watson, who suggested the safer shot would be the three-wood. Love concurred and proceeded to split the fairway with his drive. Rocca, meanwhile, ditched his tee shot in the rough, leaving himself 200 yards to the green over the famous lake guarding The Belfry's final green. To his credit, Rocca would clear the water, but come up short of the green. The Italian wasn't the only one collapsing under the pressure. Later, Davis Love would admit that as he stood over his approach into the final green, it was as much as he could do to stop himself from kneeling down and vomiting on the fairway. Still, he found the putting surface, some 25 feet away from the hole.

Rocca, meanwhile, would tickle a nervy effort 20 feet past the cup, before taking another two putts to hole out. His clumsy, edgy effort had given Love the opportunity to sink a 6-foot right to left putt to take the point and effectively put the match beyond the home team. When he drilled his putt home, Watson knew that even though the scoreboard said otherwise, the US had won the Ryder Cup once more. Moments later, José María Olazábal hooked his drive into the water at the 18th, gifting the rejuvenated Ray Floyd a 2-hole victory and taking the US team to the magical 14½ points barrier. All that was left was for Paul Azinger, obstinate as ever, to deprive Nick Faldo, who himself had made only the second Ryder Cup hole-in-one at the 14th hole, of his win, a fiddly putt at the last halving the game. 'Beating them on their home turf,' reflects Watson, 'is a little sweeter than beating them on your own turf.'

While Rocca was singled out as the man who had cost Europe the Ryder Cup, it was obvious that any number of players could have filled the role. From Barry Lane to Mark James, even Sam Torrance, there were plenty of Europeans who hadn't contributed any points but, as ever, there had to be one man for the media to vilify and it wasn't going to be anybody British. 'Oh yes, I lost the Ryder Cup – it said so on the front page of *The Daily Telegraph*,' laughs Rocca today. 'But you know, sometimes being on the front page can make you famous. I got a lot of invites to go and play in Japan, everywhere, after that.'

Sports Illustrated's Rick Reilly went further than most, suggesting that Rocca looked 'less like a golfer than like the guy who carves the pork at the Rome Hilton buffet'.

For the captains, it was a tough way for the match to finish, but the Ryder Cup thrives on creating heroes of the hour and villains of the piece. In Bernard Gallacher's mind, though, nobody was at fault for the loss, especially Rocca. 'Costantino had given us great hope because against the run of play he went 1-up with two to play,' says Bernard Gallacher. 'He'd hit three good shots into the 17th, went for the match and knocked it four foot past and then lost the last and that was that.'

Tom Watson, meanwhile, certainly felt for Rocca as his touch deserted him at the critical point in the match. 'That is the tragedy of sport,' he adds. 'Missing that putt at the 17th against Davis turned the match.'

Worried that Costantino Rocca was shouldering the burden of Europe's second successive defeat, Bernard Gallacher dispatched Seve Ballesteros to find the Italian and do whatever it took to console him. The two would talk at length, playing over the dramatic denouement again and trying to take away some positives from the experience. Later, Rocca would recall the Spaniard's intervention. 'It was okay,' he said. 'I managed to stop him crying after a while.'

With four wins and a tie to his name, Watson's Ryder Cup record as player and captain remained unbeaten. Mission duly completed, Watson addressed his team – his winning team – choosing to recite an extract from Theodore Roosevelt's 'Citizenship in a Republic' speech that the US President had given at the Sorbonne in Paris in April 1910:

It is not the critic who counts, not the one who points out how the strong man stumbled or how the doer of deeds might have done them better. The credit belongs to the man who is actually in the arena; whose face is marred with sweat and dust and blood; who strives valiantly; who errs and comes short again and again; who knows the great enthusiasms, the great devotions and spends himself in a worthy cause and who, if he fails, at least fails while bearing greatly so that his place shall never be with those cold and timid souls who know neither victory nor defeat.

It was a fitting tribute not just to his men, but to the efforts of Bernard Gallacher and his team too, beaten but unbowed after another defeat. After the petty squabbles of Kiawah, Ryder Cup order, according to Tom Watson, had been restored.

I think Roosevelt's speech was one of the great thoughts about competition and about human behaviour and he put it very succinctly that it is the man in the arena who understands what it is like. People outside truly don't understand what it is like. I wanted to make the point to the players on both sides that they had achieved something great, even though one side had lost and one side had won, it was a battle that really mattered that you were there and through your blood and your sweat, even though you might have lost, it was still worth the effort.

Third Time Lucky

OAK HILL COUNTRY CLUB, ROCHESTER, NEW YORK

22–24 September 1995

TEN times Bernard Gallacher had played or captained in the Ryder Cup and ten times he had been a runner-up. It was a disappointing, dispiriting record for such a keen proponent of the competition and one that he patently didn't deserve.

Oak Hill, however, would prove to be the last roll of the Ryder Cup dice for Gallacher. Having been the youngest ever player to represent Great Britain and Ireland in the event in 1969, aged twenty, now successive defeats as captain had left the proud Scot on the verge of calling it a day as the leader of the European team. Despite a side loaded with the likes of Faldo and Ballesteros, Olazábal and Woosnam, the Jacklin-inspired successes of the 1980s had been undone by two stubborn, gutsy US performances at Kiawah Island and The Belfry and now it was Europe, once more, that was faced with the quandary of how best to win back a trophy they had, finally, become accustomed to winning. 'I was quite happy to stand down after the second defeat but there were people who thought maybe I should get another crack,' recalls Gallacher. 'It's not as if we have been heavily defeated. It's not as if the tactics were all that wrong. They seemed to be a happy camp.'

In Gallacher's favour was not merely the manner of the defeats – he was right, they could have gone either way – but some high-profile support from some senior members of his team. Not only did Seve Ballesteros and Nick Faldo pledge their public backing for Gallacher but so too did the man who came so close to retaining the Ryder Cup for Europe in that dramatic denouement at Kiawah, Bernhard Langer. In the days before email and the internet, the German had sent Gallacher a letter, imploring him not to stand down. It would be a gesture that would convince the Scot to have one final crack at the captaincy. 'He said, "we hope you don't stand down [because] we need someone who has the experience going to America",' adds Gallacher. 'That's what really clinched it for me… if people like Langer and Seve and Faldo had got the confidence in my captaincy then I was very happy to go across there again.'

For the Ryder Cup committee, Gallacher certainly warranted another try, not least as there was a dearth of able candidates lining up to replace him. 'Because of the evolution of the players I think we had got such a stock coming through that these were all captains going down the line in the future,' says the PGA's Sandy Jones. 'At that time we didn't have lots of choices and I was pleased for Bernard that he took the third match. I thought he was brave.'

While the Americans were content to change their captain for each and every Ryder Cup, the European team's success had largely been built on continuity and that inestimable team spirit, and after Tony Jacklin's four attempts, the idea that Gallacher could stay on for another, even though he had lost two already, was not as harebrained as it may seem today. Experience, it seemed, counted for a great deal.

Few players, of course, had more Ryder Cup experience than America's Lanny Wadkins. As dogged a competitor as had ever trod the sod, the 1977 PGA champion epitomized the spirit that the American team had, with the exception of 1991 and 1993, seemed to lack in some of the recent events. A veteran of the Ryder Cup, the tough-nut Virginian had already scrapped his way through eight previous events, winning five, losing two and tying one, and had the scars to prove it. 'The Ryder Cup has always meant a lot to me. From the time

I did my very first one in '77 I just found it exhilarating,' he explains. 'I felt the idea of having all these great players as my teammates was pretty neat. Golf is sometimes a very lonely sport. You are out there just you against everyone else, so it is nice to have great players on your side.'

Wadkins, undeniably, had been one of the players of the American Ryder Cup. With 21½ points, he was the third-highest scorer in US team history, second only to Billy Casper in the number of matches played (thirty-four) and to Arnold Palmer in the number of games won (twenty). With such an impressive record, it had long been a matter of when Wadkins would be appointed captain of the US team, not if. 'It wasn't something I was surprised about,' he says today of his appointment. 'They had always talked about me being captain at some point down the line, so it didn't come as a shock – it came as a great honour.'

The concluding event in the two-year qualification process for the US team, the PGA Championship at the Riviera Country Club at Pacific Palisades, had seen a dramatic last-gasp shake-up of the US team with strong finishes for the likes of Jeff Maggert and Brad Faxon propelling them into the team while pushing Mark Calcavecchia, who fell from 9th to 11th in the standings, out of the reckoning.

Faxon, especially, had come from nowhere to take his spot. Needing a 5th place finish at the PGA to make the team, he had shot a 63 in the final round on Sunday – including a record 28 on the front nine – and as he romped around Riviera, the fans followed his charge, shouting 'Ryder Cup' as each birdie putt dropped and the prospect of playing at Oak Hill grew ever closer. Come the end of the round, Faxon had posted the lowest round in the seventy-seven-year history of the PGA Championship, securing his Ryder Cup berth in the most sensational manner imaginable. 'I'll be playing with the best in the world,' said Faxon. 'It means as much as anything I've ever done.'

It would be Wadkins's picks, however, that would cause most consternation. Opting for Freddie Couples and the veteran (and fellow Wake Forest graduate) Curtis Strange, the US skipper had overlooked some high-profile names for the team, most notably Lee Janzen, arguably the hottest player on the PGA Tour. With three wins under his belt in 1995 and standing second on the PGA Tour money list with $1.3 million, Janzen had failed to make the team automatically on account of his performances in 1994, the net result being that, despite three wins, he could still only finish 15th on the final points list.

In an edition of *Sports Illustrated* magazine in 2001, Janzen recalled just how he had discovered that he had not been selected. 'At the start of the week [of the PGA Championship] Lanny asked for the phone number of the house where we were staying,' he said. 'By a certain time on Sunday night he hadn't called, and I simply had to know. So I called him. He said that he had lost our phone number.'

Once more, there would also be no place for John Daly, and this despite winning his second major title at the Open Championship at St Andrews a month or so earlier. In Daly's case, there seemed to be some tacit suggestion that with his myriad problems on and off the golf course (drinking, divorces, discipline, hairstyle, etc.) he wasn't exactly a team player. Faced with a choice between Daly and Strange turning out for the US team, however, there would be little doubt whom the galleries would rather root for. This time, though, there would be no good luck fax from Daly and, to date, he remains the only two-time major winner in history never to play Ryder Cup golf.

Perhaps the most interesting new member of Wadkins's team was the young Californian, Phil Mickelson. A psychology graduate from Arizona State University, Mickelson had played golf since he was a toddler, grappling with his kiddie clubs almost as soon as he had mastered walking. He had even run away from home, aged 3½, telling his neighbours that he was heading for the golf course. Later, aged nine, he had watched the 1980 Masters at Augusta on television and as the champion-elect Seve Ballesteros strode up the 18th fairway, told his mother that that was exactly what he wanted to do as well.

That passion would never wane. Mickelson would go on to win thirty-four San Diegan junior golf titles, three consecutive AJGA

Player of the Year titles and a scholarship to Arizona State. He would even win a PGA Tour title before he turned professional – only the fourth man in history to do so – taking the 1991 Northern Telecom Open in Tucson.

Aged twenty-one, Mickelson would turn professional on the eve of the 1992 US Open at Pebble Beach, bypassing the terror of Q-school thanks to his win in Tucson and hitting the ground running. By the time the Ryder Cup at Oak Hill arrived, Mickelson had already banked another four PGA Tour titles and there appeared to be little in the way of preventing his childhood dream of achieving golfing greatness from becoming a glorious reality.

Another rookie in the US team, albeit one the wrong side of forty, would be Loren Roberts. One of the finest putters in modern golf, the man they called 'The Boss of the Moss' had been on Tour since 1981 but, by his own admission, had not started winning golf tournaments until 1994. 'I was a late bloomer, I guess,' he says.

Despite securing his place in the US team with a top-ten finish at the Byron Nelson Classic in May, Roberts would suffer a back injury during that year's US Open at Shinnecock Hills and not return to action until the Open Championship at St Andrews in mid-July. 'It was nice to be able to get on the team because obviously that had been a goal I really wanted to achieve,' he explains. 'But I was basically out for five weeks and Lanny kept asking me, "Are you going to be able to go? You have got to tell me!" Well, there was no way I was going to tell him that I wouldn't be there. No way.'

While Wadkins was tasked with blooding five rookies in his team, (Brad Faxon, Tom Lehman and Jeff Maggert being the others), Bernard Gallacher's team, meanwhile, had just two new boys to look out for. One was the Swede Per-Ulrik Johansson, who played alongside Phil Mickelson on Arizona State University's NCAA Championship winning team, while the other was the Irishman Philip Walton, who had enjoyed a career year in 1995, winning the Catalonia Open, the English Open and his own nation's PGA Championship for the fourth time in eight years. For Walton, it had been a close call, as a last-gasp campaign to give Gallacher three rather than two picks had gathered pace which, if it had been successful, would have seen the tenth-placed qualifier – Walton – jettisoned in favour of a wild card.

There would also be a last minute call-up for Ian Woosnam. Though he was long since past his best and languished at 57 in the world rankings, Gallacher had drafted the Welshman in when José María Olazábal was forced to pull out with a mysterious foot injury that would keep him out of golf for eighteen months. Gallacher's other pick was Nick Faldo and it had been a torrid time for the Englishman. With a little over six months to go until the Ryder Cup, he had won just $40,000 for his season's efforts on the PGA Tour, or around ten times less than the PGA Tour money-list leader, Peter Jacobsen. He was playing less like a five-time-major winner and more, as he later conceded, 'like an old trout'.

It was fortunate, then, that he had the kind of Ryder Cup record and experience that made his omission from the 1995 European team almost impossible. Selected by Bernard Gallacher as a captain's pick, Oak Hill would be Faldo's tenth successive appearance in the Ryder Cup, equalling the record of Ireland's Christy O'Connor Sr.

Yet his form, or lack of it, would be the least of Faldo's worries. Back in the UK, the European team was packed and ready to leave for Heathrow Airport. As they waited at the Radisson Edwardian Hotel on the Monday morning, their wives, partners and caddies in tow, the daily papers were passed round to help pass the time. Among the group was Gill Faldo, who was planning to meet up with her husband when the party reached Rochester. Splashed across the tabloids, though, was the news that Faldo had been conducting an affair with Brenna Cepelak, a college golfer whom he had met at a tournament in Arizona. Cepelak was twenty years old. Faldo was thirty-eight – and a father of three young children.

The flight to the US would be awkward and uncomfortable. The only consolation, for Gill Faldo at least, was that it was supersonic.

In the seat behind her on Concorde was the PGA's Chief Executive, Sandy Jones. 'I just sat there thinking, "God, what is she thinking".' he recalls. '[But] she was fantastic. What went on between her and Nick I've got no idea... but publicly you'd never for a moment think there was anything wrong. She was unbelievable. Most women would have just belted him. She was class.' Within a month, the pair, with almost a decade of marriage behind them, would announce their intention to separate.

Oak Hill Country Club was one of those fabled venues that seemed to have been around as long as the United States itself. Opened in 1901 on an eighty-five-acre plot next to the Genesee River in upstate New York, it began life as a simple 9-holer but thanks to a land-swap deal with the nearby University of Rochester in 1921, found itself with enough room for two 18-hole courses, the East and the West, both designed by the pre-eminent golf course architect of his time, Donald Ross, and later tweaked by another legendary designer, Robert Trent Jones Jr.

With six major championships under its belt, including three US Opens, Oak Hill was a course designed for drama, or as the acclaimed sports journalist Hugh McIlvanney said, one that had been 'calculatingly prepared to provide a butcher's slab on which the Europeans can be dismembered'. Clearly, the US captain Lanny Wadkins knew full well what it would take to win the contest and, as such, was intent on making the most of any advantage he could muster, setting the course up much like a typical US Open track or perhaps a PGA Championship, with tight, narrow fairways, thick collars of rough and viciously quick greens. 'I worked a lot with Kerry Haigh who is a Scotsman who works for the PGA of America and does all their course set-up,' recalls Wadkins. 'He is spectacular. I really didn't know what to do and I just said, "Kerry, just set it up like you would for a PGA Championship" and that is what he did.'

When play got underway on Friday morning, there was rain in the air. It was a blessing for Bernard Gallacher. Faced with a tough, brutal golf course, it was at least one way to level the playing field.

Where the greens were, ordinarily, slick and inaccessible, now they were slower and more receptive and less of a problem for both teams. Lanny Wadkins could control the course, the crowd and the choice of players, it seemed, but controlling the weather was one task that was beyond him.

With honours even after the morning foursomes, Bernard Gallacher decided to keep what looked to be a winning partnership together for the afternoon, leaving Ian Woosnam and Philip Walton on the sidelines for both sessions of the opening day. Wadkins, meanwhile, ensured that all of his twelve players would play on the opening day by resting his three oldest players, Jay Haas, Curtis Strange and Ben Crenshaw, in the afternoon, and sending out the all-rookie pairing of Loren Roberts and Jeff Maggert for the fourballs.

Roberts, in particular, had impressed in practice, with Jay Haas reporting back to Wadkins that he more than merited considera-tion for the opening day. 'Jay and Lanny were both at Wake Forest University, North Carolina, and they knew and trusted each other,' explains Roberts. 'I thought I was probably going to sit out the first day but Jay went to Lanny and said Loren has been hitting the ball great and so Lanny put me in on Friday afternoon.'

It was a ploy that paid handsome dividends, with Roberts and Maggert streaking home against Sam Torrance and Costantino Rocca by 6&5. 'We both played really well,' recalls Roberts. 'I think I was maybe five or six under through thirteen holes.'

If the Roberts/Maggert gamble had worked, so too had Wadkins's decision to get all of his team out as quickly as possible. Fred Couples and Davis Love III put paid to a tiring Faldo and Montgomerie 3&2 while the debutant Phil Mickelson partnered Corey Pavin to a rapid 6&4 win over Langer and Johansson. Indeed, the only shaft of light for Europe among the afternoon gloom at Oak Hill would be a win for the unlikely pairing of Seve Ballesteros and David Gilford.

Seve Ballesteros, clearly, wasn't the player he once was. Without a win in 1993, the Spaniard had turned to the American coach Mac

O'Grady to help change his fortunes. With a reputation for being eccentric, O'Grady had taken ten years to complete his research paper into the golf swing which he had called Mankind's Objective Research and Development; or 'MORAD' to give it its marginally less unwieldy name. Among the five 250-page volumes was an entire section devoted to a shot that Ballesteros had dumped in the water at the Masters at Augusta in 1986. Before long, the pair had convened in the desert near Palm Springs, where O'Grady worked with Ballesteros on his swing plane and his shoulder turn and, curiously, got him to cut his hair.

Still, O'Grady's unorthodox methods – he had his new pupil burn a box of photos of his former glories – transformed Ballesteros's fortunes with dramatic effect. In 1994, Seve would win both the Benson and Hedges International Open at St Mellion and the Mercedes German Masters in Berlin, propelling him, briefly, to the top of the Ryder Cup points table and into Bernard Gallacher's Ryder Cup team.

Come the Ryder Cup, though, and the ageing Ballesteros had reverted to type, much to Bernard Gallacher's chagrin. 'Seve knew he was a passenger and he felt bad all week. He was trying to do his best and he was trying to encourage the players but his game had completely gone off and from a playing point of view he shouldn't have been there; but everybody still wanted him there.'

To his credit, Ballesteros was only too aware of his limitations. 'Seve was as honest as the day was long,' adds Gallacher. 'He said, "I am not the player I was and it is going to be a tough week," and I said, "You know that doesn't matter, Seve, I am glad you're here and the team want you here".'

The decision to partner David Gilford with a personality as all-encompassing as that of Ballesteros was a brave one from Bernard Gallacher, especially after the experience Gilford had had with the other great player of the era, Nick Faldo, at Kiawah in 1991. But there was method behind what some perceived as madness. 'David Gilford was the perfect player for him [Ballesteros] because, first of all, he is very, very straight, he never misses a green, and he was not going to be put off by all the hullaballoo round about him,' says Bernard Gallacher.

US skipper Lanny Wadkins agrees:

The thing about Seve, even though he wasn't playing his best, was that he always managed to have a putt that would matter. You know, he would have an eight-footer for a par to save the hole and I saw him do that on several occasions when he needed to. In that respect, he would cover Gilford so he was a very good partner. The other thing about Seve was that he never quit trying. He always thought, 'I am going to hole this next shot'. He didn't care if it was from 200 yards and behind three trees, he thought 'I am going to hole it' and that was the way he played. He never took himself out of a hole mentally and that's a great thing in a partner. You want your partner to be part of it and always be in there. Even in foursomes, Seve did what I always did and went to the back of the tee when my partner was hitting it, and acted like I hit the shot. You have to do that to be a good partner.

Peter Jacobsen, who partnered Brad Faxon against Ballesteros and Gilford on the opening day, agrees. 'David Gilford played as well as Seve played poorly but Seve was still inspirational,' he recalls. 'Seve was literally on his shoulder the entire time, helping him, which just goes to show you how much impact a player like Ballesteros can have not only on one player but on an entire team and in the Ryder Cup's case on an entire continent. There has never been a player like Seve Ballesteros in the Ryder Cup. Never.'

For David Gilford, it would be a Ryder Cup that went some way to erasing the bad memories of 1991. With a return of three points from his four matches – including a 4&3 win over Jacobsen and Faxon – he would be one of the stars of the European side, and proved, if proof were really needed, that while he was hardly the court jester of the European team, he was, nevertheless, a gritty performer, and that was all any Ryder Cup captain could ever ask for.

With a two-point lead, Wadkins declared himself more than happy with the day's play. For Bernard Gallacher, whose teams had, traditionally, performed better over the fourballs and foursomes, it was a worrying deficit, not least because no team from either side of the Atlantic, since Bernard Hunt's GB and Ireland side in 1973, had ever lost the Ryder Cup having scored five points or more on the first day.

Saturday would bring renewed optimism for Europe, with an emphatic 3–1 session win in the foursomes, the highlight of which was only the third hole-in-one in Ryder Cup history. For the Italian Costantino Rocca, Oak Hill would be the earliest opportunity to erase the memories of The Belfry in 1993, and a chance also to impress a sizeable Italian-American contingent in the galleries. 'You know,' he says, 'the Ryder Cup is always different every time. There are different players. Different opponents. But for me, being in America for the first time in the Ryder Cup was really important.' From the disappointment of being the player who inherited the label of the man who lost the Ryder Cup, Rocca had bounced back in admirable fashion, coming tantalizingly close to winning the Open Championship at St Andrews that year, losing in a play-off to John Daly, but only after holing a 65-foot putt from the Valley of Sin at the Old Course's 18th to force the extra holes.

Clearly, Bernard Gallacher didn't hold Rocca responsible for what happened two years earlier as the Italian, along with Faldo, Langer and Montgomerie, would play every session, forging a successful partnership with Sam Torrance and justifying his captain's faith in him. The pair's 6&5 thrashing of Love and Maggert was a case in point. Having holed a 10-footer to win the 5th hole, Rocca and Torrance moved on to the tee at the short 6th. With a cross wind swirling over the hole, Rocca turned to his partner: 'What club are you thinking, Sam?' he asked.

'Six,' replied Torrance. 'Maybe seven.'

Rocca checked the wind again and promptly ignored Torrance's suggestion. 'I chose to punch a 5-iron and it felt fantastic. When I saw the ball going, I said, "just give me a chance" and the wind didn't take it too much. When it went in, it was the most fantastic moment.'

With the scores level going into Saturday afternoon, the fourballs session was going the way of the US, as they led 2–1. The final game between Nick Faldo and Bernhard Langer and Corey Pavin and Loren Roberts, then, would prove crucial. Despite some initial nerves, the rookie Roberts had found the Ryder Cup to his liking, playing exceptionally well all week. Indeed, as the teams had practised on Tuesday, he had arrived at the 1st tee and soon discovered precisely why his fellow players were so enthusiastic about the event. 'There were five thousand people around the 1st tee and this was just a practice round on Tuesday,' he recalls. 'Was I nervous? Sure, I was nervous'.

With a 100 per cent record from his two games so far, Roberts had gelled well with Pavin, but the resistance from Faldo and Langer had been stubborn. When they reached the 18th the match was all-square. As the group got to the green, Roberts managed to lag his long putt up to the hole, securing a par. Faldo and Langer could do no better than par the hole also, which left Corey Pavin with a chip from the fringe that could win the game. Taking his wedge, the diminutive Californian flipped his ball towards the hole and watched as it meandered, right to left, before catching the side of the hole, spinning round like water going down a plughole, and dropping into the cup. That shot not only handed Pavin a 1-hole win, but gave the US a two-point lead – something that Europe had never managed to overturn in the history of the event. 'When Corey made the chip on the 18th to beat them 1-up it was really my crowning achievement,' says Loren Roberts. 'It was what the Ryder Cup is all about.'

At the press conference that evening, Lanny Wadkins declared himself 'real confident' ahead of Sunday's singles, while Europe's Ian Woosnam was busy telling reporters that it was 'time to catch the Concorde home'. That evening the American team gathered in their locker room. After Pavin's miraculous chip-in had stolen the advantage for the home side, Lanny Wadkins wanted the singles to take place there and then, so keen was he to get the job done. 'He was just really excited and ready to go,' says Loren Roberts.

Wadkins's enthusiasm was infectious and US morale couldn't have been higher. At dinner that night, an air of quiet confidence permeated the team. Each player took turns to stand up and say a little something about the day's play, what they were looking forward to come Sunday, and what victory in the Ryder Cup would mean to them personally.

Choosing the singles order is, as any Ryder Cup captain will concede, an exercise fraught with difficulty. As the week develops and the tension tightens every muscle, every sinew, suddenly players who had seemed impervious to pressure reveal cracks in their usually immaculate make-up. As Bernard Gallacher weighed up his options, the Swede Per-Ulrik Johansson, for example, expressed his reservations about being the final man in the line-up. 'He was a bit nervous about playing the last match out, and he took a bit of persuading,' says Gallacher, 'but eventually he went along with it.'

With the help of an inner circle of friends and confidants such as Ken Schofield, Tommy Horton and John Jacobs, as well as the senior players in his team, Gallacher settled on his order. 'We thought long and hard about the singles,' he says. 'But luckily I did have people I could bounce ideas off because it was crucial how we put people out.'

With a two-point deficit to overhaul, Gallacher loaded his top and middle order with his strongest, most confident players. The exception, of course, was Seve Ballesteros, whom Gallacher opted to send out first. Yes, he was unlikely to beat Tom Lehman but having him, the living, breathing epitome of European team spirit, leading the side into the final day, regardless of the result, was an inspired piece of tactical thinking by Bernard Gallacher. Or was it? 'We had to put Seve out first in order to take the pressure off him,' conceded Gallacher. 'We couldn't have him in the deciding match, at the middle of the draw or at the end of the draw, so he went off first, and although he lost to Tom Lehman he did miraculously well.'

Despite his game being in pieces, Ballesteros managed to stay in the game longer than anyone anticipated, giving the players behind him, such as Howard Clark, a real fillip. 'I got to the 7th and I had seen Seve out of the corner of my eye so I said to one of the marshals, "How is Seve doing?" and he said, "He's all-square". I said, "You are kidding me, that is amazing". He had been all over the joint, I had just seen him at the 7th and he had hit it right, left of the green, and it had gone miles away and yet he had halved the 7th and he's all-square. I just thought, that's good news [because] he could end up winning this against Lehman. I kind of thought I have got to try and back him up, because if he is going to win I have got to win too.'

And, as ever, there was more than a little controversy during his game with Tom Lehman. At the 3rd hole, for instance, Ballesteros had insisted his opponent make a 1-foot putt rather than conceding it. Then, at the 8th, when he was already out of the hole, he had hesitated before conceding Lehman's putt to win the hole. Two holes later, Ballesteros was at it again, refusing to give Lehman an 18-inch putt.

By the 12th hole, Lehman had had enough and when Ballesteros pulled him up for knocking in a 6-inch tap-in, without asking to putt out of turn, the two became embroiled in an altercation that needed the match referee to step in. At the side of the green was Ballesteros's old enemy, Paul Azinger, who was working for NBC television. As the dispute threatened to get out of hand, it seemed as though Azinger was on the verge of ditching his microphone and launching himself into the fray as well. Mercifully, it never came to that.

To his credit, Lehman successfully circumnavigated the gamesman-ship of Ballesteros and cruised to a 4&3 victory. Now the USA had a three-point lead with eleven matches out on the golf course. It was a healthy lead for Wadkins and the USA and the kind of advantage that Gallacher, whose previous sides had both lost the singles and then the match on the Sunday, would have done time for.

Gallacher, however, was banking on two of his northern stalwarts, Howard Clark and Mark James, to claw Europe back into the game. Blond and brash, Clark was another of those Ryder Cup veterans who had enjoyed a successful professional career but had never really chal-lenged for anything like major glory. Indeed, by 1995, the best years of Clark's golfing life were largely behind him and it had been some seven years since he last won a tournament when he took the English Open title in 1988. In the Ryder Cup, however, Clark – like his friend Sam Torrance – became a different player. Resolute, dogged and proud, he had a knack of toughing out a result when it mattered most and in his singles match against Peter Jacobsen, he showed his mettle once more. Though he had been sat on the sidelines since the opening morning's fourballs when he and Mark James had lost heavily to Davis Love III and Jeff Maggert, Clark was still champing at the bit to play. Other players might have bristled or thrown their clubs out of the buggy. But Clark was from Yorkshire.

With Jacobsen making a birdie at the 10th to move into the lead, the pair moved on to the par-3 11th. Both men remember what happened next – only differently. The outcome, however, is always the same. Howard Clark takes up the story:

I still felt a little bit shaky on certain shots and the 11th tee was one of the shakiest because there was water just right at the green and you don't come back from water – you have lost the hole, almost a dead cert. Anyway, I hit my tee shot at the 11th and I thought it was on line so I looked away to find my tee and then I thought, I haven't used my tee. When I looked back up to the hole the ball had pitched and trickled into the cup. It shocked me to such a state that it took me two or three holes to calm down.

Jacobsen, however, remembers it differently. 'He had pulled it and he looked away but the ball bounced off the left hand of the green, off the edge of a bunker and it rolled towards the hole and it went in for a hole-in-one. I remember turning round and coming back and giving him a high-five and we both laughed about how crazy a game it is.'

So who was right? 'Watch the video,' says Clark. 'He is in the bunker. I am in the middle of the green. None of that rubbish!'

In his last-ever Ryder Cup game, and with the second European ace of the week, Howard Clark would go on to win 1-up, pocketing his special ball, rather than lobbing it into the crowd. It was a fitting way to end an impressive Ryder Cup career that had spanned some eighteen years and six events. His partner from that first morning's drubbing, Mark James, meanwhile, would be out straight after him and, like Clark, had been busy doing, well, nothing much since Friday morning. He too, however, would deliver in style, romping home against Jeff Maggert, 4&3. 'They got us off to a great start,' explains Gallacher, 'because they beat some very strong players right behind Seve and they got us back right in the match. Tactically, it was great.'

Buoyed by the efforts of Clark and James, the European players bullied their way back into the singles matches, quickly overturning the two-point deficit before fashioning a lead of their own. Woosnam took a half from Fred Couples, David Gilford pipped Davis Love III at the last and Colin Montgomerie emerged triumphant after a tight tussle with Ben Crenshaw.

In the eighth match, meanwhile, Nick Faldo was embroiled in another epic struggle with Curtis Strange. As ever, there was little to separate these two titans but, like the US Open play-off at Brookline in 1988, it seemed to be going Strange's way again. By the 16th, the American wild card was 1-up and stood in the heart of the fairway with his opponent foraging around in the undergrowth. Hit the green and he would be dormie. Hit it horribly wide and to the right and there would be a chance for Faldo. Fortunately for Faldo, he did the latter.

To compound his misery, Colin Montgomerie and David Gilford had also recorded victories over Ben Crenshaw and Brad Faxon respective-ly and, Lehman aside, the only other American player to have won his singles was Davis Love, who had beaten Costantino Rocca 3&2. The tide was turning, the heat increasing.

Clearly shaken, Strange then gifted the 17th to Faldo, missing a rela-tively straightforward par putt and taking the game down the 445-yard final hole. Now it was Faldo's turn to feel the overwhelming pressure of the Ryder Cup. He pulled his tee shot into the trees, while Strange, his bones rattling and his nerves eating him up, somehow found the perfect drive at the perfect time.

When Faldo reached his ball, he found himself with a dog of a lie and little option other than to chip his ball out as far as he could muster. It was advantage Strange. Hit the green and he would almost certainly win. But Strange's approach would turn out to be the kind of shot to keep him awake night after sleepless night. He slapped his 3-iron woefully short and to the left of the raised green, leaving him with an almost impossible chip to get it close. Later, he admitted that he 'couldn't have imagined hitting a worse shot' and that the approach was 'the shot that killed me'.

Bizarrely, it was now Faldo who was the better placed. With a little under 100 yards to the pin, the thirty-eight-year-old then, conversely, managed to conjure up what he would later describe as 'one of the best shots I've ever played' as the ball skipped and stopped just six feet from the hole. It was the shot of a man who had been there before, a man intent on revenge, for him personally and, collectively, for his team.

Strange, meanwhile, now stood over an improbably difficult chip from out of the rough. To his credit, however, he flipped it up on to the raised green, bringing the ball to a halt within eight feet of the hole and leaving this most crucial of matches in the hands of their putters. Strange would go first but his par putt would stay up, prompting shrieks of horror from the home crowd.

Now it was Nick Faldo's turn. Faced with a four-foot, left-to-right par putt, the kind that he had holed so many, many times in his long career and which, in most other situations, would scarcely warrant a second look. But this was on another scale altogether: while the Ryder Cup couldn't be won in this game, it was, with the game poised at 12½–12½ points apiece, absolutely pivotal.

Even Faldo, the coldest, most ruthless golfing machine of his generation, was feeling the heat, but with admirable fortitude, he kept his nerve and rolled the putt home for an improbable win and a barely believable point.

It was a par. Just a simple par, yet it felt like the greatest shot of all time. Faldo's win had brought Europe to the verge of a wondrous victory and, holding back the tears – he was always one to blub – the

Englishman found himself mobbed by his fellow players, many of whom were also crying.

Curtis Strange, meanwhile, stood shell-shocked, his bogey-bogey-bogey finish eating away at him as the USA's Ryder Cup hopes ebbed away. In truth, though, there was still some life left in the match, not least because there were still two matches left out on the course. If the Americans could win both of them (or even win one and halve the other) they would retain the Ryder Cup and render Faldo's true grit largely pointless. Not that that was any consolation to Lanny Wadkins. 'When you get down to those final stages you feel completely helpless,' he explains. 'You have done all you can do.'

Before the Ryder Cup had started, the unassuming Irishman Philip Walton could have strolled through Oak Hill without anyone stopping him for an autograph or strong-arming him in front of a camera for a photo-opportunity. Now, after Per-Ulrik Johansson had lost in the final game against Phil Mickelson, he stood charged with the task of claiming the point that would win the Ryder Cup for Europe. But, inevitably, it wouldn't be easy. Haas was 3-down with three to play, but would take the 16th, holing out from the bunker, and then won the 17th with a par as Walton's match-winning putt lipped out. 'After winning the 16th and 17th I felt I had the momentum to get the half point we needed,' said Haas. 'Everything was going to plan.'

As they stood on the 18th tee, the feeling began to drain from Walton's legs, and his drive, an ugly push into the rough, was proof, if it were needed, of the huge pressure of the situation. Fortunately for Walton, Haas too was feeling the heat and hooked his tee shot behind a tree, leaving him with no option but to punch his next shot back onto the fairway. Walton, meanwhile, would go for the green with his second, leaving it short of the green in thick rough. Eyeing an opportunity, Haas found the green with his third shot but watched, aghast, as it span back on to the fringe, from where he could only chip eight feet past the hole. Walton's chip from the ugly stuff would come to rest just ten feet from the hole, leaving him a simple two-putt with his trademark broomhandle putter to take victory for him and for Europe. In one fleeting, fabulous moment, Philip Walton had become the hero of the hour and the face of the world's back pages. He'd also become a little better-off too, having had a £1,000 bet on his team to win at odds of 5/2. 'Maybe the Americans know me now,' he beamed. 'Tell 'em I'm related to all those Waltons on that TV show.'

At the eleventh time of asking, Bernard Gallacher finally discovered what it felt like to be a winner of the Ryder Cup. 'I can't tell you what this means to me,' said Gallacher, his tears spilling into his two glasses of champagne. 'It's just… I can't.' He had said all along he had the best players, and he may have been right. Every European team member, after all, had won a point.

While Gallacher finally had his hands on the Ryder Cup, the US team led by Lanny Wadkins sat in their team room in a state of shock. Wadkins, as ever, did his best to rally his troops, but it was hard. A three-point lead had disappeared and the expectation of Saturday evening had been replaced by despondency. As the team consoled each other, a face appeared at the door. It was Paul Azinger. The 1993 PGA Champion was still recovering from radiation treatment for his cancer and had spent the week working as an analyst for the American broadcaster NBC. With permission from Wadkins, Azinger summoned the team together, as Peter Jacobsen recalls. 'He said, "Two years ago I was dying with cancer and I didn't know if I would ever see another Ryder Cup but here I am now, I am cancer-free. I can't tell you how happy I am to be here watching this match. I know it wasn't the outcome you wanted, or any Americans wanted, but I must tell you that I am proud of each and every one of you… there is no guarantee that any team is going to win, but the most important thing is you handled yourselves as gentlemen, as true professionals".'

It was a speech that, momentarily at least, held the American squad spellbound. With his hair still growing back from his chemotherapy, Azinger's address had seen the return of that age-old absentee from the Ryder Cup – perspective. 'Everybody jumped up, we all shook his hand, we gave him a hug and the party began,' adds Jacobsen. 'Not only celebrating the fact that we all made the team and we all had a great competition, but we all celebrated with the Europeans on their victory as well.'

Not everyone could brush off the defeat quite so readily. For Curtis Strange, as proud a player as ever picked up a putter, it was agony. Though he safely negotiated the press conference, flat-batting the questions back to the media ('No matter how bad you beat me up,' he said, 'it's not gonna hurt as much as what I'm gonna do to myself'), he cracked during the closing ceremony when he saw his wife Sarah crying in the crowd. As he buried his head in his hands, the image was flashed across the TV networks and on the giant video screens around Oak Hill, prompting Strange's brother and agent, Allen Strange, to storm off the course.

Soon after, the magazine *Sports Illustrated* ran a review of the Ryder Cup under the headline 'WRONG MAN, WRONG TIME' as if those three bogeys had somehow rendered Strange's myriad other achievements invalid. It was tough on Strange. Certainly, he wasn't the player he had been in the late 1980s, but when he was asked by his friend Lanny Wadkins to step up he had done so without hesitation – only to emerge as another in the long list of players cast as The Man Who Lost The Ryder Cup. Eight days later, Wadkins finally contacted Curtis Strange to see how his old college buddy was dealing with the fallout from Oak Hill. 'Turns out he was concerned about *me*,' Wadkins said.

The flight home on Concorde would be delayed. The European team left Rochester late because of a technical problem, but nobody seemed overly concerned, even though the hangovers were kicking in. As the team boarded the plane, Bernard Gallacher called into the cockpit and handed the Ryder Cup to the plane's pilot, Captain Jock Lowe. 'You can be the captain that brings the Ryder Cup home,' he smiled.

The Reign in Spain

VALDERRAMA, SPAIN

26–28 September 1997

IT'S difficult, if not impossible, to picture a Ryder Cup without the genius of Severiano Ballesteros. Imagine if, back in 1983, he had met Tony Jacklin over breakfast at Southport's Prince of Wales Hotel and having listened to what he had to say, simply polished off his toast, glugged down his coffee and then gone on his way, leaving the European captain to pick up the tab. What then for the European team? What then for the Ryder Cup?

Fortunately for Jacklin, Europe and the competition itself, he didn't. Instead, Ballesteros threw himself into the task at hand with boundless energy and typical ingenuity. Brash and brilliant on the one hand, pig-headed and a pain in the arse on the other, he was the perfect figurehead to take the Ryder Cup into a new era. But Ballesteros wasn't alone in making things happen. Aided and abetted by a battalion of able compatriots like Garrido and Cañizares, Rivero and Piñero, and, of course, José María Olazábal, the Spanish, more than any other nation had given all they could to help transform the Ryder Cup.

When the Ryder Cup committee announced that the Ryder Cup would be taken abroad for the 1997 matches, Spain was the clear and obvious choice. No other nation from continental Europe had contributed quite so much to the transformation of the Ryder Cup. 'There was an inevitability about the fact that when you started to introduce the European players there had to be a moment in time when the match actually went somewhere else,' explains the PGA Chief Executive Sandy Jones. 'If you look at the influence of Spain over that twenty years from '77 to '97, as well as the number of tournaments on the Tour [in Spain], there was a clear need for Spain to be recognized. So it was right that the match when it moved outside the UK for the first time went to Spain. There is no doubt in my mind about that.'

While there could be little dispute as to Spain's right to be awarded the 1997 Ryder Cup, the actual venue was still open to debate. One course, however, stood head and shoulders above its rivals. As the host of the Volvo Masters since 1988, Club de Golf Valderrama on the Sotogrande Estate near San Roque in southern Spain not only had experience of staging one of the bigger events on the Tour schedule but, in Jaime Ortiz-Patiño, an owner with the determination and, crucially, the wherewithal to make a successful Ryder Cup a likelihood rather than a possibility.

Valderrama was the pet project of 'Jimmy' Patiño. A Bolivian multi-millionaire who had made his money in the family's tin mines, he had long been obsessed with the game of golf after Dai Rees had given him a couple of tickets for the 1957 Ryder Cup match at Lindrick.

That match, which saw a rare win for the Great Britain and Ireland team, proved to be the start of a lifelong fascination for Patiño and in Valderrama, he had the opportunity to write his very own chapter in the history of Ryder Cup. The course had been designed by the renowned Robert Trent Jones Sr and was called, in the first instance, Sotogrande New and then latterly Las Aves. Patiño purchased the club in 1985 with the intention not just of turning it into Europe's answer to the Augusta National but in doing whatever it took to bring the Ryder Cup to his club. He reversed the two nines, rebuilt tee boxes and relaid greens. He built a new practice ground, installed a new 12,000 square foot practice green and a new drainage system across the course, complete with 3km of new subterranean pipes. Money was no object.

No effort was too great. 'I have a golden rule here,' said Patiño. 'I have the gold. I make the rules.'

While Patiño invested his 'gold' into making Valderrama the irresistible choice, not everyone was taken with its position as the front runner. Seve Ballesteros, earmarked but yet to be confirmed as captain of the European team, was the most vocal opponent, describing Valderrama as 'the most elitist club in the world – even more elitist than Augusta'. Instead, Ballesteros had championed the cause of a course he had designed, Novo Sancti Petri in Cadiz. Indeed, as the rival clubs jockeyed for position in a bid to win the nomination for the 1997 Ryder Cup, Ballesteros went out of his way to rubbish the claims made by Valderrama, arguing that it didn't possess the minimum facilities required to host the event. During the Spanish Open in Madrid in 1994, he even issued a statement alleging that he had been offered $1 million to support Valderrama's candidature and promote their bid.

Ballesteros's allegation was, according to Patiño, a question of interpretation. In 1993, Ballesteros had redesigned Valderrama's signature hole, the 17th, refusing to accept a fee for his work. Later, Patiño had written to Ballesteros, offering him a percentage of the club's green fees in lieu of payment and for his 'agreement to support our candidacy for the Ryder Cup'. The green fees alone were calculated to be worth at least £675,000, but as Ballesteros had yet to be appointed to the Ryder Cup committee, Patiño failed to see how such an offer could be construed as a bribe. 'I knew that we had the best course and if we had Seve on my side there would be no opposition,' Patiño told the *Guardian*. 'You want Jack Nicklaus on your side you give him $2 million. There's nothing wrong with making someone a business proposal.'

Correspondence would continue between Patiño and Ballesteros throughout 1993, but by October, Ballesteros had decided not to accept Patiño's 'business proposal' which, given that he was appointed as Tony Jacklin's replacement on the Ryder Cup committee just two months later, was a wise decision.

But with someone as free-thinking and idiosyncratic as Seve Ballesteros things were never clear-cut. After just one meeting as a member of the Ryder Cup committee, Ballesteros resigned on the grounds that his public backing for the Novo Sancti Petri bid made his position untenable. 'In retrospect I should not have been invited or accepted the position when I had already declared my support for one of the candidates,' he said. 'I do not think there is any member of the committee that loves the Ryder Cup more than I, or knows my country and my people better than I do. But I find myself in a very difficult position because I have stated clearly and strongly that in my opinion Novo Sancti Petri is the best venue for the Ryder Cup.'

Ballesteros's resignation from the Ryder Cup committee did little to halt the momentum behind Valderrama's bid, and on 25 May 1994 Valderrama was announced as the venue for the 32nd Ryder Cup matches. Suddenly, magically, peace broke out. Even Seve Ballesteros conceded defeat and began to toe the party line – and he hadn't even been confirmed as captain yet – offering his 'heartfelt best wishes to Valderrama and Mr Patiño who has worked long and hard and I'm sure the American team will enjoy Valderrama'.

For the Ryder Cup committee, Valderrama had always been the outstanding candidate for the match. And, as Sandy Jones adds, there was never any doubt it was the right choice. 'I remember going around all the courses in Spain and... Valderrama was the best venue by miles,' he says. 'It was the best prepared venue as a golf course and Patiño, the owner and operator of Valderrama, could really support the match in its entirety.'

Seve Ballesteros was duly appointed European Ryder Cup captain, though he would have to wait until January 1996 for final ratification. Given that Spain's first Ryder Cup demanded a Spanish captain, Ballesteros was the only realistic candidate for the job. 'He was a captain of an entirely different style,' says the PGA's Sandy Jones. 'He was inspirational but probably from an administrative point of view he was a bit of a nightmare for us to control... But from a point of view of having a vision and a feel for the game I don't think I have met anybody better. And for being disorganized and chaotic I don't think I have met anyone better either.'

Faced with Europe's Mr Ryder Cup in charge on his home turf, the Americans opted for a captain with a Ryder Cup pedigree every bit as impressive as that of Ballesteros. In late November 1995, the PGA of America had given the job to a man who lay sixth in the US list of most Ryder Cup games won, a player who had become synonymous with handing out some of the most brutal batterings in the history of the event – Tom Kite. 'An event of this nature requires a strong and an experienced leader that has a special love for the game of golf,' said the PGA of America President Tom Addis. The US media agreed. Describing his appointment as 'a perfect fit', the *New York Times* said, 'when it comes to Kite, substance is everything'.

Kite had substance by the moatful. A veteran of seven Ryder Cups (second only to the eight of Billy Casper, Raymond Floyd and Lanny Wadkins) the forty-five-year-old Texan had emerged triumphant from a shortlist that included Larry Nelson, Curtis Strange and Ben Crenshaw, and with 19 wins since he joined the PGA Tour in 1972, including the 1992 US Open at Pebble Beach, was second only to the Australian Greg Norman on the career money-winning list. 'Being named the Captain by the PGA is one of the highest honours I have ever received,' says Kite today. 'The entire experience from the time I was named the captain in late 1995 to the departure of our team back to the US the Monday after the matches were over was one I will long treasure.'

Tom Kite's team for Valderrama had certainly presented him with the best possible opportunity to take the Ryder Cup back on Concorde. Out had gone Ben Crenshaw, Loren Roberts, Peter Jacobsen, Corey Pavin and the man hounded for losing at Oak Hill, Curtis Strange. In had come a handful of new names, the new Open champion Justin Leonard and Jim Furyk, a man with a swing so unorthodox that it had been likened to 'an octopus falling out of a tree' and 'a one-armed man trying to kill a snake in a phone box'. Whatever it resembled, it was brilliantly and idiosyncratically successful.

By far the most fascinating new recruit in Tom Kite's team, however, was the young phenomenon Tiger Woods. Aged just twenty-one, Woods was already well known in the golfing world, having rewritten the record books in the amateur game, winning a glut of titles, including three consecutive US Amateur Championships. Indeed, Woods's record was so unprecedented, so outstanding, that when he turned professional in August 1996, having decided to leave his studies at Stanford University prematurely, he immediately signed multi-million dollar contracts with the likes of Nike and Titleist.

Woods could have been created in a marketing laboratory. An African-American in the whitest game imaginable, he was not only the most gifted player of his generation but a young man who had in his hands the power to revolutionize a game so often criticized for being elitist, inaccessible and out of touch. *Sports Illustrated* even made him their Sportsman of the Year, declaring that Woods was 'not just a promising young Tour pro any more, he's an era.'

True to form and despite the almost indecent expectation that surrounded his every move, Woods had gone from strength to strength and in April 1997, in his first major tournament as a professional, won the Masters at Augusta with a record low total of 270 and by a record 12-stroke margin, becoming the youngest winner of the Green Jacket in history and the first player of African-American heritage to win a major title.

By the start of the Ryder Cup at Valderrama, the Tiger effect was in full, irrepressible flow. Where once the US team could convene and prepare, fulfilling their duties for the media and the organizers, now every press conference, every interview centred on the world's newest sports superstar. The press simply couldn't get enough. 'I think the Woods thing had a disruptive effect,' argues Sandy Jones, 'because he is so strong as an individual and the media want to talk about him all the time. If you put twelve of the best players together to represent your country, they are all millionaires for a start [and if] eleven of them who have got pretty big egos themselves keep reading the paper everyday and keep reading about this guy and they start to think "hang on… I wonder why the rest of us have turned up". So it's a disadvantage.'

For the US captain Tom Kite, it was a difficult situation that he chose to manage by treating Woods as though he were just one of his team with an equal part to play in their bid to win back the Ryder Cup. 'I told the entire team to have some fun with the matches,' he says. 'I have always believed that players play their best when they are enjoying the competition, the course, and the interaction with the fans. So as much as we could, we tried to create an enjoyable attitude towards the matches.'

Woods aside, there would also be special attention paid to Tom Kite's captain's picks, especially after Lanny Wadkins's ultimately disastrous decision to pick Curtis Strange in 1995. Now, having been overlooked two years earlier, Lee Janzen found himself back in, alongside the ever-reliable Freddy Couples. 'I did not have any players make a strong move towards the end of the year to make my selections easier,' explains Kite. 'I had been hoping that one or two players would really come on strong late in the points race and move up the list. The closest anyone came to doing that was Lee Janzen, who had a top-three finish at the PGA at Winged Foot, hence his selection. Freddy has always been a good Ryder Cup team member, and at the time, he was as good a player when healthy and motivated as anyone in the world. He also brought some great chemistry to the team in that everyone loves to be around Freddy. Having that chemistry is important in the team room before and after the competition.'

Despite the home advantage and the ever-present Seve Ballesteros, Kite's team were nevertheless overwhelming favourites to win the match, quoted with odds as short as 4–9 on them regaining the Ryder Cup. It wasn't just the American feel of the course at Valderrama, which if you removed the cork trees and the caddies' language, could have been Florida or California, but also the stark reality of the world rankings. The US team's twelve players' official rankings stood at 2, 6, 7, 9, 10, 11, 12, 13, 16, 21, 28 and 40, with an average of 15. The Europeans, meanwhile, had just one player in the top ten, Colin Montgomerie, and had an average world ranking of 36. Lest there be any complacency in his team, however, Kite put up a huge, ten-foot by two-foot banner in his team room at Valderrama that read: LOSING IS WORSE THAN DEATH. YOU HAVE TO LIVE WITH LOSING.

For his part, Ballesteros had recognized that the opposition were, on paper at least, the stronger of the two sides and set about maximizing his own side's chances. His redesign of the par-five 17th hole, for example, showed just where he thought the threat would come from, narrowing the fairways at precisely the point where the Americans' biggest hitters, like Woods and Mickelson, Couples and Love, would land their drives, and even placing rough in the middle of the fairway to make them think twice about trying to reach the green in two. The putting surface was hardly the most receptive either. Guarded by a lake that Ballesteros had had built, and with a vicious slope at the front and to the sides, it required the perfect approach shot to prevent the ball from pitching and spinning back into the water. Not everybody was taken with Ballesteros's tinkerings at the hole they called 'Los Gabiones'. 'I never cared much for a par-5 where you hit driver, sand wedge, sand wedge,' said Tom Lehman, while Phil Mickelson declared that he wasn't 'a fan of rough in the middle of the fairway'. Even his own players hated it. Colin Montgomerie called it 'the worst hole we play all year – the worst in Europe'.

Not that Ballesteros cared. 'I designed the 17th hole and I know how it should be played strategically,' he mused. 'When my players are playing the 17th, I will use my experience and I can tell them the way it should be played, which will have some influence in favour of the Europeans.'

While Tom Kite found himself with a 'dream team' that was in form and brimming with confidence, Ballesteros's team came together in the most unseemly manner. Miguel Ángel Martín was a self-taught professional who having served his apprenticeship in the ranks of the bagmen and rake rats, had decided to give playing a go and made a terrific fist of it. In the twelve-month qualifying period for the Ryder Cup team, the twenty-five-year-old from Huelva had put in a string of solid showings on the European Tour, including a win in the co-sanctioned Heineken Classic in Australia in February, becoming one of the first players to bag a place on the European team, some time before the August deadline.

For Martín, it was a huge personal achievement, not least as the event was being held on his home soil, but a wrist injury sustained at the Scottish Open at Loch Lomond in the week prior to the Open Championship at Royal Troon in mid-July would throw his preparations into doubt. With his participation in the balance, Martín had opted for surgery on his wrist to give himself the best possible chance to be fit for the Ryder Cup.

Clearly, Martín wasn't wanted on Ballesteros's team, irrespective of the fact he had done all that was required in qualification. 'Seve didn't want him to play,' insists Sandy Jones. 'He [Martín] kept saying that he had recovered and Seve wasn't sure. But equally I don't think Seve rated him either.'

One month after an operation on his wrist, on 3 September, the Ryder Cup committee requested via fax that Martín play 18 holes not near his home in Madrid but nearly 400 miles away in Valderrama itself, just to prove his fitness. It was an unprecedented demand and one that looked extremely suspect, given that the player who stood to gain most from Martín's exclusion was not only the 11th placed player in the qualification points list but also the man who had been by Ballesteros's side through so many memorable matches, José María Olazábal.

Martín was, rightly, incensed and refused to play on the grounds that he could actually do more damage to his wrist by playing when he didn't need to. 'What did they want?' he asked. 'For me to break my arm also?'

With Martín standing his ground, the European Tour acted swiftly and issued a statement, announcing that as Martín could not prove his fitness, he had, therefore, been deselected from the 1997 European team.

The Ryder Cup committee and the captain are agreed that currently there is an indisputable presumption that even if Miguel Ángel was fit to play in the matches, which is in doubt, that he cannot be competitive at Ryder Cup level. The proposal of Miguel Ángel playing on Wednesday was intended to give him every opportunity of countering this presumption. As Miguel Ángel has not availed himself of this opportunity, the Ryder Cup committee and the captain have, with regret, informed him that he will be replaced on the European team.

At a press conference in Madrid soon after, Martín vented his spleen. 'The captain Ballesteros is responsible for this,' he said. 'If José María Olazábal had been number 17 this would not have happened. 'When he was then asked if he felt there was a plot to remove him and replace him with another player, Martín merely laughed and said, 'Yes.'

Certainly, Martín had the sympathy of his fellow professionals. His friend and compatriot, Ignacio Garrido, described it as 'the most unfair decision I have heard in the history of golf', adding that 'It's very unfair what they are doing, and I don't think it ends here. Maybe if he goes to court he can stop the Ryder Cup?'

Legal action was a very real possibility for Martín. To him, and most neutral observers for that matter, the 'plot' to oust him was little more than a thinly veiled attempt to placate Seve Ballesteros as part of some circuitous route around the qualification rules laid down years before. He even warned the European Tour's Ken Schofield of his intentions. 'He said to look for a good lawyer,' said Schofield. 'And I have one.'

In his defence, Seve Ballesteros maintained it was the Ryder Cup committee and not him that had made the decision to remove Martín. 'I asked the committee to give him some time. I don't make the rules here,' he said. 'I only have so much power. Please don't implicate me in this.'

As the issue threatened to overshadow this most historic of Ryder Cups, the matter was further complicated by a clause in one of Martín's contracts with his sponsors that guaranteed him a bonus if he made the Ryder Cup team. But thanks to some clever thinking from Ken Schofield and Sandy Jones an agreement, albeit an unlikely one, would eventually be struck. 'We managed to stop it going legal and we came up with a deal that Miguel Martín could come to the match knowing that he wouldn't play but he would be recognized as a player and someone that was in the Ryder Cup team.'

With Martín now the official, non-playing 13th man – he would even appear in all the team photographs – Seve Ballesteros was well placed to field what he saw as his strongest side and with Olazábal taking Martín's place, he had two captain's picks once more, and drafted in Nick Faldo, who was now a six-times major winner after overcoming Greg Norman to take the Masters in 1996, and the idiosyncratic Swede Jesper Parnevik, to complete a team that clearly demonstrated how truly cosmopolitan the European team had become. With six nations now represented, there were five British players (Colin Montgomerie, Darren Clarke, Lee Westwood, Ian Woosnam and Faldo), two Swedes (Per-Ulrik Johansson and Parnevik), two Spaniards (Ignacio Garrido and Olazábal), a Dane (Thomas Bjørn), a German (Bernhard Langer) and an Italian (Costantino Rocca).

Despite protesting his innocence in the Martín saga, it was apparent that Ballesteros's style of captaincy was already markedly different from the subtlety and tact preferred by his predecessor Bernard Gallacher. In short, Seve didn't do diplomacy. During the practice rounds, he would appear, as if by magic, and tell his players what club they should be hitting. At night, he would awake his assistant, Miguel Ángel Jiménez, to discuss potential pairings and strategy. Some reports even told of how an enraged Ballesteros had sent Colin Montgomerie, Nick Faldo, Lee Westwood and Darren Clarke back to the tee to play the 17th again when he saw just how poorly they were coping with it. Others spoke of how he had instructed his players to sandpaper the soles of their new dress shoes before the Gala Dinner, just in case they slipped over and did themselves some damage. His presence was everywhere, his control total. 'I will never forget when we all met with our wives in the team room on the Monday,' recalls Costantino Rocca. 'He [Seve] said, "OK, wives outside now" and all the wives had to go out.'

The Sky Sports television commentator Bruce Critchley agrees. 'I have not been into the team room but you get the impression [that] losing isn't an option,' he says. 'He was exceptional and I don't think he, or we, will ever fully understand what exactly he does or what he brings to the party.'

There seemed to be nothing Ballesteros wouldn't do to eke out an advantage for his team. When the US team arrived, for instance, Ballesteros greeted them as they stepped off Concorde, as Brad Faxon explained to Golf.com in October 2009.

'I had just been through a very public divorce, which wasn't really over, and Colin Montgomerie made some comments that I wouldn't be in the right frame of mind to play good golf. So, we're getting off the plane, and Seve was there to greet us. He shook [US Captain Tom] Kite's hand and Kite's wife's hand. And he looked at me and said, "Where's your wife?" To this day I believe he knew and was trying to get in my head. I said, "Look, I'm just getting divorced," and walked away. I was so pissed off. He apologized, but the damage was done. He'd put the dagger in. I respect him as a golfer, but that didn't go over too well.'

Ballesteros's 'greeting' soured an otherwise enjoyable flight over to Spain on Concorde. As the team left JFK Airport, British Airways pilot Captain Jock Lowe had invited Tiger Woods to join him on the flight deck for take-off. Then, when they were over the Atlantic, Lowe grabbed the old wooden putter and the rare Concorde-monogrammed ball he had with him in the cockpit and wandered back to see his illustrious passengers. 'I suggested to Tom Kite that we try the longest putt down the aisle and he said he'd ask Brad Faxon because he was the best putter,' says Lowe. 'From the front to the back it took Brad's putt twenty-three seconds to find the cup which, at the speed Concorde was going, made it an eight-and-a-half mile putt.'

But there was trouble ahead. When Lowe recovered his equipment, he realized that the ball that had been returned to him wasn't his prized Concorde ball. 'It was some old Maxfli,' he explains. 'So I told them I wasn't going to land the plane until I got my ball back. Sure enough, it turned up soon after.'

One of the many advantages of taking the Ryder Cup to Spain, away from the wild West Midlands, was the favourable weather. With its long, hot summers and the kind of mild winters that could easily pass for a British summer, the Costa del Sol had become a magnet for the continent's golfers, with thousands of happy hackers arriving each year to test their mettle on the scores of new courses springing up all along the southern coast.

The meteorologists had maintained that Sotogrande was only likely to get maybe 18mm and perhaps four days of rain in the whole of September. What they didn't predict, however, was that it would all arrive in Ryder Cup week. And it wasn't just the occasional shower or mild drizzle. These were epic, batten-down-the-hatches, almost British storms. In one week, Andalusia had been deluged by a year's worth of rain.

Each day, the teams would rise to find their practice rounds delayed as the ground-staff waited for the skies to clear so they could begin their mopping-up operation. After three days of stop-start practice, the rain held off for the opening ceremony. With the *QE2* anchored off the coast, Spain's King Juan Carlos and his family, former US President George Bush and Britain's Prince Andrew all in attendance, it was a show that set a new benchmark for Ryder Cup curtain-raisers, with its flamenco dancers and scores of Spanish horses. It was just a shame that it rained. Any other course in the region might have suffered given the extent of the deluge but Valderrama's owner Jaime Ortiz-Patiño had left nothing to chance, installing a new, state-of-the-art drainage system against the kind of Biblical weather that Sotogrande was now experiencing. What use, after all, was spending £1 million on the redesign of the 17th hole alone if the rest of the course was a boating lake?

Play would even be delayed on the first day as the rains continued to fall. As the 8 o'clock start time for the first match came and went there were now serious concerns as to whether there would be any play at all on the opening day. But with Patiño's much-vaunted drainage system coming into its own and the industrious efforts of the ground-staff and their squeegees, the course, miraculously, was ready to play a little over two hours after the rain ceased at 9 a.m. Every other club in the region, meanwhile, would be closed.

That first morning would once more reveal just how far Seve Ballesteros would to go to forge any kind of advantage for his team. Where it had long been traditional for the format to be a morning session of foursomes followed by an afternoon session of fourballs, Ballesteros had decided to switch them around, as was his prerogative, based on his belief that Europe always seemed to play better in the fourballs. Cue raised eyebrows in the American camp. 'I think I know why Seve wants to do that,' said Tom Kite. 'He thinks he'll get a better feel for how the players are playing by watching them in the morning play their own ball.'

Ironically, Ballesteros's tactic, while not exactly backfiring, failed to give Europe the lead going into the afternoon, with points being shared on a soggy, strength-sapping course, made all the longer by the rains. The highlight, undoubtedly, was the debut of Tiger Woods who, coupled with his close friend and Isleworth neighbour Mark O'Meara, eased to an impressive 3&2 win over Europe's strongest pairing, Colin Montgomerie and Bernhard Langer. The European pair would gain handsome revenge that afternoon, though, trumping Woods and O'Meara in the fourballs 5&3 and helping the hosts to a slender 4½–3½ lead at the end of the first day's rain-affected play.

What was instantly noticeable was the contrast between the two captains. Kite was considered, pensive and thoughtful. Ballesteros, meanwhile, was the polar opposite, careering around the golf course in his buggy, one hand on the wheel, a walkie-talkie in the other, endangering players and fans alike with his reckless driving. He was everywhere, playing every shot, offering advice when players patently didn't need it. 'I knew the Americans were always aware of my presence and I think it made them uncomfortable,' explained Ballesteros later.

For Tom Kite, a player who had become accustomed to the wiles of Ballesteros over decades of Ryder Cup play, it was predictable and pretty much par for the course. 'Were there some heated moments? Sure, it is competition. Was there some gamemanship? Sure, it is the Ryder Cup; but it came from both sides,' he reflects.

The rain would come again on Saturday, delaying proceedings once more, and with play commencing at 10.40 a.m. it would prove to be an undefeated session in the morning foursomes for Europe, with the USA's only half point coming from the dependable duo of Tom Lehman and Phil Mickelson against the home favourites José María Olazábal and Ignacio Garrido.

Ballesteros's team would stretch their lead still further in the afternoon fourballs, although only one game, the contest between Colin Montgomerie and Bernhard Langer and Lee Janzen and Jim Furyk, would finish on the Saturday, the remaining games falling victim to the weather delays.

That game, however, was not without incident. In a tense finish, the players had reached the final hole all-square, and, as Colin Montgomerie revealed recently, it was almost a point lost for the Europeans.

We were one up playing the last but I hit the tee shot into the trees and I remember saying to Bernhard on the way to the ball, 'Just focus and play your own game because Seve is bound to be there,' and, sure enough, when we walked down to the ball, Seve was there, with his hands on his knees, peering down to study the ball. Where he had come from, I don't know, he just appeared – but that was the way it was all that week. Anyway, he was at the ball, looking at the shot, but the ball was dead, absolutely dead. The only way to play it was to chip it out sideways and start again. But Bernhard and I could see Seve bending up and down, squinting, trying to visualize the shot with his hands, going round the trees, starting with a slice and then with a touch of fade before hooking, dipping and swerving it on to the green – honestly it was a shot you'd only make about one in every fifty attempts! As Seve was pacing up and down the fairway, Bernhard had already chipped out – believe me it was the fastest shot he ever played in his life!

As Montgomerie found the green, Lee Janzen faced a 12-foot putt to halve the match, but as he hit it he watched, incredulous, as it raced another 12 feet past the hole, handing the point to the Europeans. The pace of the putt had taken Janzen by surprise, so much so that a discussion with his partner ensued, as they pondered just how the greens could have quickened up quite so much. The Americans could only conclude that the green had just been double-cut ahead of the four players reaching it. With the light fading it's possible that the ground-staff assumed the game wouldn't reach the final green and so went about their routine as normal, cutting the green once more, but in a contest where suspicion often got the better of reason, the Americans began to suspect that the green had maybe been cut on orders. For his part, Furyk was gracious in defeat. 'It happened. It's over with,' he said. 'I don't look back at it bitterly, but it was something we were never made aware of... I'll accept it as human error.'

If the Americans were uncomfortable, so too were the Europeans. It was one thing to offer support and advice, but Ballesteros, it appeared, was going beyond that, all but playing the shots of some of his team, believing, presumably, that he should have been playing too. The debutant Thomas Bjørn found himself berated for three-putting, for instance, while Colin Montgomerie had to take a stronger line as his captain instructed him how to play his short approach to the 17th on Saturday morning. 'There's Seve at my side telling me, "Hit it in softly, feel it in",' he recalled. 'In the end I had to tell him to piss off.'

With a 10½–5½ lead after the fourballs and foursomes, the Ryder Cup was now Europe's to lose. With his team facing a comprehensive and humiliating defeat, US captain Tom Kite called on the former US President George Bush to drop by the team room and talk to his beleaguered troops on Saturday evening. 'Being able to pass on a word of encouragement was easy for me since I have been in tough situations in sports and in politics,' said Bush later.

Whatever one thought of his politics, Bush's pep talk seemed to produce immediate and unexpected results for the American team as they rallied in the singles. Drawn against Fred Couples in the opening exchange, the former world number one, Ian Woosnam, reached the 11th hole with his score level par for his round. It was solid if unspectacular golf. Couples, meanwhile, was busy devouring the golf course like a kid with a cookie tin and when he reached the 11th he was 8 underpar for his round. Moments later, another ludicrously long birdie putt from the American found its target and the match was over in a little over two whirlwind hours.

For Woosnam, bewitched, bothered and clearly bewildered by Couples's genius, it was a sorry, inauspicious way to conclude his playing career in the competition. It was, as he shrugged later, 'just one of those days'. Or, to be more precise, it was yet another one of those days. A record 8&7 defeat, matched only by Howard Clark's loss to Tom Kite at The Belfry in 1989, meant the Welshman had failed to taste victory in the Sunday singles in any of his appearances for Europe. Played eight, drawn two, lost six, won none.

As the US threatened the kind of comeback that would send Seve Ballesteros over the edge, Europe found some points from the unlikeliest of sources. Per-Ulrik Johansson, the Swedish debutant, defeated the PGA champion Davis Love III 3&2 while Thomas Bjørn fought back from 4-down after four holes to snatch a valuable half point. Of all the points Europe would win on Sunday, though, the most improbable came from Costantino Rocca. Drawn against Tiger Woods, it seemed for all the world like the most one-sided of contests.

Woods, after all, was a machine created purely for golf, a player who had won three US Amateur titles – a matchplay event – and who had just decimated the greatest field in golf at the Masters while barely breaking sweat.

His opponent, meanwhile, was a tubby, chain-smoking Italian who used to make boxes for a living. 'He's been playing since he was three, I'd been playing since I was twenty-seven,' laughs Costantino Rocca. It seemed like a mismatch – and it was. By the turn, Rocca was 4-up and even though Woods was hitting 6-iron approaches to Rocca's long irons, the Italian was in total control. Woods, meanwhile, was doing what he could to get back in the match but even when Rocca found trouble, such as at the 16th, he still had the measure of his much-lauded opponent. After carving his drive into the trees, the Italian, with victory in sight, made what he calls today 'the most beautiful shot of my life'. With his line to the green impaired by the cork trees, and with Ballesteros breathing down his neck, suggesting he chip it out sideways or aim for a bunker, Rocca whipped a low, fading 1-iron up and on to the green, leaving himself a 2-foot putt for a worthy 4&2 win. 'I think he is not too happy,' adds Rocca. 'He [Woods] didn't want to give me that one because he is thinking I am under pressure but even if I miss the putt I still win. I win 4&2 not 3&2.' The point secured, Rocca sought out his wife at greenside and proceeded to carry her around as though he was back in the factory hurling boxes about.

Rocca's win interrupted what was turning out to be another trademark US charge. Tom Lehman battered Ignacio Garrido 7&6, Mickelson pipped the debutant Darren Clarke and Mark O'Meara got off to a flyer against Jesper Parnevik, birdieing five of the first eight holes before easing to a 5&4 win. Lee Janzen beat Olazábal at the last, Lee Westwood fell to Jeff Maggert and Jim Furyk felled the captain's pick, Nick Faldo. Crucially, though, the ever-reliable Bernhard Langer had beaten Brad Faxon, gaining the point needed to ensure that Europe would, at the very least, retain the Ryder Cup.

A tie, though, was hardly the result the Spanish crowd, Jimmy Patiño and, more pertinently, Seve Ballesteros demanded. The last game on the course then, the encounter between Colin Montgomerie and Scott Hoch, would prove pivotal.

In a tight contest, Montgomerie had been 1-up with two to play but Hoch, as gutsy a player as they came, had manufactured a birdie to steal the 17th hole and send them to the 440-yard last hole all-square. With the honour, Hoch teed off but strayed left, leaving Montgomerie to step up and unleash what he would later call the 'best 3-wood of my life'. Given the pressure, not just from the crowd but from Ballesteros watching him over his shoulder, it was a perfect, peerless tee shot and one that fully warranted the award it received two months later as the European Tour Shot of the Year.

Advantage Europe. Hoch, his line to the green hampered by trees, would only find the green in three, while Montgomerie would cushion a 9-iron on to the green with his approach, leaving himself an 18-footer, some three feet longer than his opponent's. When Montgomerie edged his putt up to the hole, prompting a concession from Hoch, the American was left with a difficult putt he needed to make to win a half point. But with the odds against Hoch making his putt, Ballesteros ambled on to the green and simply picked up the American's ball, handing him his half. While the tie mattered little – Europe had still won 14½–13½ – it was also a concession which had not only denied Montgomerie the pleasure of another singles win but also cost a lot of punters who had bet on a final 15–13 scoreline, your author included, a lot of money. When he got home Montgomerie would find himself deluged with letters, most congratulating him but many asking why he had conceded Hoch's putt. Considerately, Montgomerie issued a letter of apology through his management company, IMG, in which he 'heaped the blame' on Ballesteros.

Briefly, Montgomerie felt 'cheated' by the intervention of his captain but, as time passed, the European number one realized that he had carried his team home and finally put paid to a gritty American fightback. It was, as he later admitted, the first time he had felt like a senior member of the European Ryder Cup side and that he had never 'felt as good as a golfer as I did that afternoon'.

For Tom Kite, always hoping against hope, it had been a commendable attempt from his side but one that had, agonizingly, been too much for them. 'Only when it was finally over and they had retained the Cup did I think it was over,' says Kite. 'For a lot, if not most, of the last day I was convinced that the US would take the Cup home. We jumped out to such a strong start the final day and every player was into the comeback. We came very close but just could not pull it off on the back nine.

'With 20/20 hindsight I'm sure I would do some things differently, but being a player, I have always tried not to second-guess any decision made as it does little good. I did my homework. I knew my team as well as the European team, and I studied the history of previous Ryder Cups so I could make the best decisions at that time. Ever since the final putt dropped I have made a special effort not to second-guess myself.'

Second-guessing yourself was one thing but second-guessing Seve Ballesteros was a dangerous and essentially futile game. Certainly, Ballesteros had Tom Kite's measure that week in a soggy San Roque. 'I don't think Tom knew what was going to happen next,' suggests Sandy Jones. 'And I would accept that because we didn't know what was going to happen next either.'

The rain continued to fall during the presentation but it could do little to dampen the European celebrations. In their soaking team suits and with their hair slicked back, the team took to the clubhouse terrace to greet their fans – Seve's fans. Ballesteros had made good on his promise to deliver success to his homeland – after twenty years of Ryder Cups, twenty years during which he had grabbed hold of a lifeless contest and injected it with endless energy, abundant talent and genuine competition. As Ballesteros stood on the terrace, surveying his kingdom, Bernhard Langer sidled over to him and whispered in his ear. 'Always remember that nobody in the world could have done more for this team,' he said. 'Nobody.'

The Battle of Brookline

BROOKLINE COUNTRY CLUB, MASSACHUSETTS

24–26 September 1999

SEPTEMBER 13, 1979. It's 3 p.m. and the opening ceremony for the 23rd Ryder Cup at The Greenbrier in White Sulphur Springs, West Virginia, is about to get underway in the gargantuan, hangar-like sports complex. With the great and the good of golf in attendance, the PGA's Executive Director Colin Snape carries out a quick head count of his team, only to find that he is a man short. It's the Englishman Mark James. Rushing to find a phone, Snape calls James at his hotel room to ask where he is, only to find that the twenty-five-year-old Mancunian is still in his room.

Incredulous, Snape informs one of his senior players, the man-mountain Brian Barnes, who decides to take matters into his own hands. Commandeering a buggy and driving through the rain to the team hotel nearby, Snape and Barnes arrive at James's room. 'Come on, Mark,' says Barnes. 'Open the door.' No reply. Barnes tries again but to no avail. 'The next minute,' recalls Snape, 'the door splintered – the best description is Barnes went through it – and all I will say is there was a degree of persuasion by Barnes on James. Anyhow, he [James] got up and waddled his way down and it started half an hour late.'

But it wouldn't be the only flashpoint with Mark James on the trip. Along with his partner in crime, the young Scot Ken Brown, James had reportedly turned up late at Heathrow Airport for the team's flight dressed in jeans and trainers when every other member of the party was decked out in official blazers, trousers and ties. The pair would miss a team meeting and appear almost deliberately uninterested in the official team photo-calls. And, with the game over and another cakewalk of a victory for the USA duly completed, James decided to put all his team clothing in a bag and shove it in a bin at Washington Dulles International Airport as their team awaited their flight home. 'He just said, "Well, I won't need these any more," and he just tipped the whole lot down into the trash can,' says Snape.

Over thirty years on, Tony Jacklin still can't talk about that week in West Virginia without feeling his blood pressure rise, describing James's antics as being 'very disruptive' and maintaining that the pair 'made it their business to sabotage any chances the team had'. The PGA agreed. On their return from The Greenbrier, James would be hit with a £1500 fine for unprofessional conduct while Brown would be fined £1000 and banned from international competition for twelve months. 'Only a psychiatrist could explain what he was up to [that week],' adds Snape.

The fact that some players, like Jacklin, found it hard to forgive and forget James's antics in 1979, failed to prevent James enjoying a long Ryder Cup career thereafter, spanning seven matches and eighteen years in which he more than atoned for his behaviour at The Greenbrier. Indeed, just two years after The Greenbrier, James had been chosen as a wild card pick by the captain John Jacobs ahead of Tony Jacklin, prompting Jacklin to all but call time on his association with the Ryder Cup.

After assisting Seve Ballesteros in Valderrama, James's appointment as Europe's new Ryder Cup captain in late August 1998 was an obvious one, even if it wasn't met with universal approval. As chairman of the European Tour's Tournament Players' Committee, he was well respected in the game, acting as a mouthpiece for the players in the corridors of power and always looking out for their interests. And, nearly twenty years after saying he would never want to be a Ryder Cup captain, the man they called 'Jesse' was now relishing the opportunity to lead the team in the USA. 'I think I said you would have to be mental to want the job,' said James. 'But that's what twenty years on the Tour will do to you.'

The Ryder Cup committee had left it comparatively late to appoint James as captain, not because they harboured doubts about his suitability, but because both James and the only other real contender for the position, Sam Torrance, were still intent on qualifying to play on the team. Ben Crenshaw, James's opposite number for the match at the fabled Brookline Country Club in Boston, Massachusetts, for example, had been selected some ten months earlier in October 1997. But by the summer of 1998, James was all but out of the running and as Torrance still had a chance to make it to Brookline as a player, James accepted the offer. Not that the delay really mattered. After all, the real work for the captains wasn't the smiles and handshakes of the pre-match press calls or photo-opportunities, it was when the teams had been finalized and the match itself about to begin.

The trouble for James was that while he had assumed he would not be a playing member of the European Ryder Cup team at Brookline, his form had improved to such an extent that after a tie for 43rd at the Open Championship at Carnoustie in July 1999, he was still occupying ninth position in the qualification points table, prompting reports that he was all set to resign his captaincy and hand it over to one of his assistants, Sam Torrance or Ken Brown.

There was no such uncertainty in the American camp. Captained by 'Gentle' Ben Crenshaw, the two-time Masters champion, there was now a sense of resolve in the team, fostered by the back-to-back defeats at Oak Hill and Valderrama. 'Quite frankly, we're due,' said Crenshaw. 'There's a sense of urgency, no question about that.'

With ten of the world's sixteen highest-ranked players in the team, it was, on first impressions, a supremely talented side, with household names by the hatful. Confidence, it seemed, was one trait the Americans always had in spades. 'Let's face it, we've got the twelve best players in the world,' said Jeff Maggert (world ranking 18). It was a view shared by the new US Open champion Payne Stewart. 'On paper,' he shrugged, 'they should be caddying for us.'

The build-up to the event, however, would be overshadowed by the simmering issue of the players, or rather the US players, being paid for playing in the Ryder Cup. Days before the Canon Greater Hartford Open, an interview with the American player David Duval appeared in the magazine *Golf Digest* wherein the leading money-winner on that year's PGA Tour suggested that the time was right for the players to withhold their services from the Ryder Cup until such time as a deal was struck to compensate them for their time and efforts.

Payment for playing wasn't a new notion, not in the United States. In 1997, Mark O'Meara had broached the subject ahead of the match at Valderrama. 'I think the whole thing needs to be looked at. It's not about greed – it's just the thing to do,' he had said. 'There is a lot of pressure at a Ryder Cup and there are a lot of functions. If the Ryder Cup has become big business and a lot of money is being generated, then maybe it's time to take a look. There could be some avenue to thank the players – maybe with money into a retirement fund.' Two years on and the Ryder Cup had grown still further to the point where Brookline had already sold all their corporate marquees for the match for over $15 million – and this *before* the match at Valderrama had even taken place. Certainly, the revenues involved in the Ryder Cup certainly suggested Duval had a point. *Golf Digest* magazine, for example, estimated that the total income from the 1999 Ryder Cup would be around $63 million, with $13 million from the sale of the television rights and with a net profit for the PGA of America of $17.5 million and $6 million for Brookline Country Club.

The controversy was still rumbling come the PGA Championship at Medinah Country Club, Illinois, in August, with Tiger Woods even suggesting that a player boycott of the Ryder Cup was just one of the options available to the players. 'Do I see it happening? Well, it could.

Will it happen? That's a different story,' said Woods. 'Will players get fed up to the point of where they will not play in a tournament? I presume that could be a yes.'

Faced with an issue that threatened to overshadow their flagship event, the PGA of America's CEO, Jim Awtrey, convened a meeting with the top players on the US team points list and the PGA Tour commissioner Tim Finchem, and assured them that a satisfactory settlement would be agreed before the end of the year. The issue would finally be resolved in December, nearly three months after the end of the Ryder Cup at Brookline, when, true to his word, Jim Awtrey announced that each player would receive $200,000 from the profits from the event, with half the amount going to a charity of the player's choosing and the other half going to developing golf programmes in that player's own community.

If the potentially divisive issue of compensation had come close to derailing Ben Crenshaw's preparations for the Ryder Cup, it was hardly happy families in the European camp either. As the qualification period came to an end at the BMW International in Munich, the six-times Major winner Nick Faldo had cornered Mark James in the course's hotel lobby to see if he was in the frame for a captain's pick. Faldo's recent form, however, had been dire, missing cut after cut on the PGA Tour and with just one top-ten finish in his last twelve events. While there could be little argument with his exceptional Ryder Cup record, captain Mark James was keen to field a team that was focused and, importantly, in form, telling Faldo, 'Even if you win [the BMW] it's unlikely I'll pick you.'

In his autobiography, *Life Swings*, Faldo declared himself 'devastated' by James's 'negative reaction', so much so that soon after he went straight back to James to make sure what he had heard was right. When James confirmed what he had said, Faldo was fuming. The following day, Faldo addressed the media, criticizing James for the way he had handled the issue. 'I'm gutted,' he said. 'I hope he [James] has got some more motivating lines for the rest of the team.'

James, though, was unperturbed. 'He's been complaining that I haven't talked to him all year and now he suddenly doesn't want to hear what I do have to say,' he shrugged. 'If I say nothing, he's not happy. If I say something, he's not happy.'

While it would be a better performance for Faldo at the BMW, claiming a tie for 21st, eleven shots off the eventual winner, Colin Montgomerie, it did nothing to alter Mark James's stance. Nick Faldo, holder of the record for the most matches won at the Ryder Cup, with twenty-three, was out of the 1999 competition and his hopes for a record twelfth consecutive appearance in the event had been crushed.

With the BMW finished, James's team was finalized and, on paper at least, it appeared to lack depth and experience, especially when compared to a US team that had just one rookie, David Duval, and a collective total of twenty-five appearances in the Ryder Cup. Now there was no Faldo or Ballesteros, no Woosnam or Langer. Only Colin Montgomerie and José María Olazábal had played more than one Ryder Cup, while Lee Westwood, Darren Clarke and the captain's pick, Jesper Parnevik, had just one appearance, at Valderrama in 1997, on their CVs. Moreover, other than Olazábal and Paul Lawrie, the surprise winner of the Open Championship at Carnoustie in July, beating another of his new teammates, the Frenchman Jean van de Velde, in a play-off, there wasn't a single major winner in the side, while the seven debutants had just fifteen Tour wins between them, with nine of those belonging to the Swede Jarmo Sandelin and the charismatic Spaniard Miguel Ángel Jiménez.

Even Olazábal had his problems and this time it was entirely self-inflicted. After the long struggle with the foot injury that had kept him out of the game for eighteen months and threatened to finish his career in the mid-'90s, the Spaniard had made an extraordinary return to action, culminating in his second victory at the Masters at Augusta in April. Two months later, however, Olazábal had another injury to contemplate. After a disappointing first-round 75 at the US Open at Pinehurst, he had returned to the course's old hotel and taken his frustrations out on the wall, punching it so hard he broke a bone in his hand and forcing his withdrawal from the event. 'I was upset with myself and made a mistake,' he said later. 'I was so disappointed at the way I played yesterday I punched the wall. I did something I should not have done and now I am paying the price.'

His friend and manager Sergio Gomez, meanwhile, had another explanation for the fracture. 'If we had been staying in a chain, like usual,' he suggested, 'the wall wouldn't have been so solid.'

Still, at least James had the hottest young player in world golf in his ranks. Touted as being the European answer to Tiger Woods, Olazábal's nineteen-year-old compatriot Sergio García had turned professional after shooting the lowest ever amateur score at the Masters in April 1999 and had won his first Tour title at the Irish Open just eleven weeks later. At the PGA Championship at Medinah, meanwhile, the man – or boy – they were calling 'El Niño' then pushed Tiger Woods all the way, finishing second by just a single stroke. Dashing and impetuous, García's youthful exuberance was never more evident than at the 16th hole where having stuck his drive right up against a tree trunk and with his line to the green obscured, the youngster had taken a blind thrash at his ball, hitting a massive fade, before hopping and skipping up the fairway as his ball curled viciously and bounced up on to the putting surface.

In need of some experience, Mark James had opted for the eccentric Swede Jesper Parnevik as one of his picks. With his drainpipe trousers, tight cardigans and his upturned peak cap, Parnevik was one of the most distinctive players in the game and had won on the European Tour and also on the PGA Tour, where he now played his golf. The son of Sweden's most famous stand-up comedian, Bo Parnevik, and known affectionately as 'Spaceman', Parnevik was a one-off, a player known as much for his more eccentric ways (like using volcanic sand and snake juice as dietary supplements, believing in reincarnation or having his metal fillings replaced with ceramic versions just to reduce his mercury levels) as he was for his golf. In 1997, the *Independent* newspaper had profiled the Swede, maintaining that 'there is a considerable body of evidence to suggest Jesper Parnevik is 100 per cent barking mad', adding that while 'Walter Hagen may have gone around smelling the roses, you get the impression this Swede would not only smell them and talk to them, but crush the petals into a juice to be taken at breakfast along with his volcanic dust and, maybe, a croissant'.

But while the selection of Parnevik made some sense, the decision to enlist the twenty-nine-year-old Scot Andrew Coltart baffled virtually everyone. 'In my experience,' shrugged James, 'experience is overrated.' Coltart was sat in the departure lounge at Munich airport with fellow Tour pro Richard Boxall, awaiting his flight back to Heathrow, when he learned the news. 'Boxall was on the phone home, and whoever he spoke to was watching the television and said he saw pictures of Andrew Coltart and Jesper Parnevik. I just thought, "This is awesome. I just can't wait to get going",' said the former Scottish Boys Champion.

The decision to pick Coltart was especially hard on the dashing Swede Robert Karlsson who had finished ahead of Coltart in the points table in 11th, and to a lesser extent, on Bernhard Langer, who, given the relative inexperience of the European side, may have expected to make the team. Not that Coltart was unduly concerned. 'I really do feel some sympathy for both Langer and Karlsson,' said Coltart. 'Probably more for Robert. Bernhard, I'm sure, will admit he hasn't played the way he's capable of playing, but Robert came on strong at the end and played really good golf. He had an equal claim to be picked.'

Once more, the European team would head across the Atlantic on Concorde and this time the honour of attempting the now customary world record putt fell to José María Olazábal. Borrowing a putter from the captain, Dave Studd, the Spaniard sent his ball 150-feet down the length of the cabin and a little over twenty-six seconds later it rolled dutifully into the cup. With the speed of the plane measured at 1,270 mph, Olazábal's ball had travelled some 9.2 miles by the time it found its target, beating the previous record set by Brad Faxon two years earlier. Olazábal, meanwhile, can rest easy that his record will remain intact. With Concorde now retired, it's going to take one almighty putt ever to beat his mark.

When Mark James and his team stepped off Concorde at Boston's Logan Airport, he spoke to the media, launching a charm offensive and making all the right noises about the upcoming match. 'We have come to one of the most beautiful cities in America… and we are playing one of the best golf courses,' he said. 'Although we are hoping to retain the trophy, the main thing is that we all have a good week.' Ben Crenshaw, too, was looking forward to a close contest, conducted in the right spirit. 'Golfers,' he mused, 'generally comport themselves very well.'

One of the oldest cities in the United States, Boston had a long-held obsession with sport, particularly with baseball and their success-starved Red Sox, and basketball with the Boston Celtics. It was also, as Sandy Jones explains, a town that liked a good drink. 'Boston is notorious,' he says. 'All the sporting occasions in Boston can be dominated by rowdiness and noise… It's a Bostonian-Irish sort of thing.'

If boorish behaviour went with the territory at the baseball, then at least the Ryder Cup never needed to worry about heckling or hooligans, especially when the match was being played at the famous Brookline Country Club. Set half an hour from the centre of Boston in the small town of Brookline and just a couple of miles from Lexington, where the American War of Independence began, The Country Club was one of the five charter clubs that formed the United States Golf Association in 1894. It famously hosted the 1913 US Open when a local twenty-year-old amateur, Francis Ouimet, turned up, having dashed across the road from his house on Clyde Street, to defeat the might of England's golfing superstars Ted Ray and Harry Vardon in a play-off and record one of the most thrilling and unpredictable victories in major championship golf. Ever since that day, no American team or individual had ever lost at The Country Club. At Brookline, good things, it seemed, always happened to the home favourites.

While its celebrated reputation preceded it, the trouble with

Brookline was that it was a club – and a golf course – never designed with huge numbers of spectators in mind. Yes, it was quaint and quirky, steeped in history and as pretty as a picture in the autumnal sunset, but it was ill-equipped to hold a sizeable crowd, as the Sky Sports commentator Bruce Critchley explains. 'Brookline was a beautiful little members' club, [but] it was like having the Ryder Cup at Swinley or somewhere along those lines.'

The first day of the 33rd Ryder Cup would merely confirm those concerns. With over 30,000 fans swarming into The Country Club, the atmosphere was claustrophobic and uncomfortable. On the 1st tee, the fans were closer than ever. As a personal friend of both of Europe's opening pairing, Colin Montgomerie and the new Open champion, Paul Lawrie, the PGA's Chief Executive Sandy Jones, accompanied by his partner Christine and Montgomerie's father Jim, had decided to walk round with them in their match against Phil Mickelson and the debutant David Duval. 'We were walking with the official armbands on, [for] the European team, and I remember getting spat on and thinking, how bad is this?' he says. 'Now I have done Rangers and Celtic matches my whole life and I have done Scotland and England at Wembley and Hampden, so I have been in some pretty emotional crowd situations [but] Christine only did nine holes and has never gone to watch a Ryder Cup match again inside the ropes because she said she never wanted to repeat that experience. Muggins here kept going.'

Despite the close attention of some of Boston's more boorish golf fans, the European team would forge ahead on the first day, with the madcap, seemingly carefree, new duo of Jesper Parnevik and Sergio García proving to be the stars of the day, winning both their games, against Woods and Lehman in the morning foursomes and Furyk and Mickelson in the afternoon's fourballs. The only victory the US team would secure, meanwhile, would be Jeff Maggert's and Hal Sutton's foursomes win over Darren Clarke and Lee Westwood.

At the close of play, the scoreboard read Europe 6 USA 2. It had been the worst start by an American team since the landmark defeat at Muirfield Village in 1987 and a day noticeable for the fact that none of the box-office names in the US team, like Woods and Duval, Love III and Mickelson, managed to win a single point. Suddenly, the '12 best players in the world' had a game on their hands.

It had been an implausibly strong start from Mark James's team and with Europe forging ahead, the captain decided to keep faith with the same four pairings that had begun the match for the Saturday foursomes. At lunch, after the teams had shared the points, James then played the same four that played on Friday afternoon, with Jiménez coming in for Harrington once more.

It was a gamble on James's part, not because his team weren't playing well – they were at their very best – but rather that he now had three players, and three rookies to boot, who wouldn't get a game until the pivotal singles on Sunday. But what could he do? Break up the successful partnerships that were out on the course and bringing home the points and risk allowing the USA back into a match they were so clearly losing?

James talked to Coltart, Sandelin and van de Velde and told them of his decision, explaining why he couldn't change things. Initially, they all seemed to understand. Only van de Velde seemed to be irked. 'It was as tough for him as it had been for me having to make the decision,' said James later. 'Without doubt it's far from easy to be on the sidelines for two days but van de Velde appeared at the time to be taking it well... I was hoping he realized that sometimes a player has to do exactly what his captain wants him to do.'

When Paul Lawrie and Colin Montgomerie sealed a 2&1 win over Steve Pate and Tiger Woods in the final fourballs game on Saturday afternoon, Europe had managed to maintain their four-point cushion, leading 10–6, and James's strategy, it seemed, had worked wonderfully. Now, just four and a half points were all that stood between Mark James's Europe upsetting the odds and winning the Ryder Cup.

That evening, with his team down and all but out, Ben Crenshaw pulled up a chair in front of the assembled media. Far from being dispirited, the Texan was surprisingly upbeat given his team's bleak position. 'I'm going to leave y'all with one thing: I'm a big believer in fate,' he said, wagging his finger like a parent admonishing an errant toddler. 'I have a good feeling about this. That's all I'm going to tell you.' While Crenshaw talked a good fight, history suggested that it was little more than rhetoric. No team had ever started the final day more than two points behind and ended it with the Cup in their possession. Moreover, in thirty-two previous Ryder Cups, only five teams had ever come back from being behind to win.

That evening, Crenshaw sat with his team and their partners at the Four Seasons Hotel, and as they dusted off a dinner from P. F. Chang's China Bistro, he talked about the mammoth task at hand, invoking the history and mystery of Brookline to try and rouse his men. Later, one by one, the team stood up and talked about their hopes and expectations for Sunday. When one of them began with an 'if we win' or a 'should we win', Crenshaw cut them short, rephrasing their words so they started their speech with a 'when we win'.

Also in attendance that evening was a surprise guest, the Governor of Texas and Republican presidential candidate, George W. Bush. A long-time friend of Crenshaw's and a fellow Texan, Bush was due to attend a debate sponsored by the California Republican Party and talk about tax reform with the businessman and fellow Republican Steve Forbes, but when the call came in from Crenshaw, he hopped on a plane to Massachusetts instead.

After his father had tried and failed to rally the US team at Valderrama two years earlier, it was now down to 'Dubya'. Recounting the story of the battle of the Alamo in 1836, Bush read the famous letter that the commander Colonel William Barret Travis wrote to the people of Texas as he defended his ground in the face of insurmountable odds: 'I have sustained a continual bombardment and a cannonade for twenty-four hours and have not lost a man. Our flag still waves from the wall. I shall never surrender or retreat... Victory or Death.'

The story stunned the players into silence, some even shed a tear.

It was left to David Duval, meanwhile, to stand up and shatter the peace. 'Let's go out and kill 'em,' he shouted, as his team roared their approval. Later, Phil Mickelson would explain the effect that Bush's contribution had had on his team. 'It was impressive,' he said. 'They were holding off a couple of thousand troops but [Travis] was going to fight to the end. It shows what a number of Americans have done for this country. We might not be soldiers who fight in wars, but this is something of its own, and we need to fight as if it were.'

For the record, the Texan army lost the battle at the Alamo (although they won the crucial rematch some six weeks later at San Jacinto). For Mark James, the man who would be Santa Anna, though, there was already a sense of foreboding about the day ahead. 'The draw didn't look great as it came out,' he reflects. 'It looked as though we could have problems... no question.'

Predictably, Crenshaw had gone for broke, loading the top half of his line-up with the very best he had available. James, meanwhile, was more circumspect, choosing, oddly, to put the untested trio of Sandelin, van de Velde and Coltart out one after another in third, fourth and fifth places, only to find that they would be facing the powerhouses of Phil Mickelson, Davis Love III and Tiger Woods respectively. It was difficult enough making your Ryder Cup debut but to be asked to do it in an atmosphere as hostile and unforgiving as Brookline and to do so against some of the finest players walking the earth simply served to make it all the more formidable.

It was only now that James's policy of playing his best players on the first two days began to unravel. Seven of his team had already played four rounds of golf in two days and were battle-weary, ill-prepared for the onslaught that was surely to come. For two days, Mark James had been one of the most successful European Ryder Cup captains in history, enjoying the kind of lead that only Jacklin had had before him. Now, when he needed one last superhuman effort from his men, he would be found wanting.

On Sunday morning, with the first pairing, Lee Westwood and Tom

Lehman, due on the tee in a little over an hour, the PGA of America's CEO Jim Awtrey stopped by at the US team room to wish his players and his captain Ben Crenshaw luck. 'I knew something was going to be totally different,' he recalls. 'The players were eating their breakfast and were not talking to one another. I picked up on it and every single player when I watched them warm up had the same serious focus.'

That they were so focused was a testament to their professionalism, especially given the shirts that Ben Crenshaw had designed for them for the final day. While Friday and Saturday's uniforms had been comparatively sober numbers, the players had now been presented with a burgundy polo shirt covered in a crazy-paving collage of photographs of past US Ryder Cup teams and players. 'A lot of thought went into the shirts,' said Ben Crenshaw, apparently oblivious to the fact that his team now looked like twelve giant slices of pepperoni pizza. 'Do you know even the Americans hated those shirts?' says Mark James. 'I think even Ben looks at them now with a mixture of awe and wonder. Or maybe shock and awe.'

Not all the American players. 'Those shirts at Brookline certainly divided opinion but I liked them,' says Tom Lehman. 'They were very Hollywood. Very American. People can say what they like about them but nobody can really say that they didn't work, can they?'

For James, there were no such sartorial concerns. 'You get a catalogue from Glenmuir and you pick the shirts to go with the trousers,' he says, matter of factly. 'You have to keep in mind that you have got to have navy blue for the last day. If Seve is playing he will suddenly switch it to the last day when we get there. I have played in matches where it is not navy blue on the last day and we have had to rejig it all. Which is fine because no one cares if it's Seve. That's the weird thing about Seve. He makes himself unpopular at times but everyone still loves him.'

One by one the players made their way to the 1st tee. Tom Lehman led the way for the US team, singing the 'Stars and Stripes' as the expectant galleries joined in. 'You saw all the American flags go up,' recalls Jim Awtrey. 'The fans were really loud, and you could hear it, they were totally behind the American team.'

Remarkably, as the games went through, not one American would miss the 1st fairway, while the Europeans, especially those who had yet to play, seemed to struggle. Jarmo Sandelin was a case in point. Drawn against Phil Mickelson, the Swede looked ill at ease on the 1st tee and despite getting his first shot away, shanked his approach.

Within a couple of hours, the scoreboard had become a mass of red as the US team powered into a significant and sizeable lead. If the din at the 1st tee had been ear-shattering, now somebody had turned it up still further. Despite the comfort blanket of a four-point lead, Mark James was already fearing the worst. 'I remember thinking the scoreboard has turned the wrong colour,' he explains, 'and you start to feel pretty powerless.'

Just before 2 p.m., the floodgates opened. Davis Love III, the only American to have played on a victorious US Ryder Cup team, crushed a disconsolate Jean van de Velde 6&5 triggering the kind of tidal wave that Mark James could never have anticipated. Ben Crenshaw, maybe, but not Jesse.

Moments later, Tom Lehman wrapped up a 3&2 victory over Lee Westwood in the opening game, followed soon after by Phil Mickelson's win over Jarmo Sandelin and Hal Sutton's over Darren Clarke. As each point was chalked up for the home team, so the roars went out across Brookline, filtering through to the other players still out on the course. In the course of one bewildering hour or so, the Americans had wiped out the healthy European advantage. The match was all-square at 10 points each.

Suddenly, the '*olés!*' from the European fans were conspicuous by their absence. That said, even another Concorde fly-by would probably have gone unnoticed, such was the wall of noise reverberating around the course. Now, when a putt dropped or rolled by you didn't need to witness it to know precisely what had just happened. 'You know if it's a loud roar with some depth to it, that it's an American one, whereas if it's a slightly lighter one with a few straggling bits at the end, you know it's probably a European one,' adds James. But there would be little for James and Europe to cheer. Further victories for Tiger Woods over Andrew Coltart and David Duval over Jesper Parnevik saw the US move ominously into a 12–10 lead, having won each of the first six singles matches.

It was loaves and fishes golf; the kind of unfathomable, unimaginable and unpredictable reverse that even the great prophet Ben Crenshaw couldn't really have foreseen. The manner and margin of the victories too was significant. Not one of the first six matches reached the final hole. They were all one-sided affairs, often embarrassingly so. 'It went wrong from the start [when] they got on a roll,' explains Mark James. 'You hope for a point in the afternoon when the momentum starts to shift a bit and your team holes a few putts but that never really happened. They got the momentum and fair play to them, they hung on to the momentum for pretty much the whole afternoon and that makes for a big swing.'

Now Europe went searching for miracles, but there would be no Seve on standby, no Faldo sat on the sidelines. While Paul Lawrie, Europe's star of the week, closed out a 4&3 win over Jeff Maggert, his point would be cancelled out by Jim Furyk's equally emphatic victory over a tiring Sergio García and then trumped by Steve Pate's 2&1 win over Miguel Ángel Jiménez.

In the seventh game out, meanwhile, Padraig Harrington and 1998's double-major winner Mark O'Meara stood all-square at the final hole. With the score at 14–11 to the hosts, a simple half would see the US win the Ryder Cup in the most resounding manner imaginable, but, charged with bringing it home, O'Meara pulled his tee shot into a bunker, hooked his second into another trap, made a bogey and handed the point to the resolute Irishman.

As the day wore on, the beer flowed and the scoreboard changed red, so the behaviour of the fans deteriorated. At the 9th hole, the par-5, Andrew Coltart had pulled his tee shot into the trees and having been given directions to it by officials went off to find it, with his assistant captain Sam Torrance in tow. With no joy, he walked back to the tee to hit another ball but as soon as he had played again, word reached him that his other ball had been found, only it was 50 yards away from where he had been looking and, bizarrely, was plugged or perhaps stamped, into the light rough.

At Kiawah Island, the players had been protected by ample space and elevated, sometimes isolated fairways. At Brookline, though, the course was heaving and the mood increasingly hostile. Now, players were being openly booed, missed putts were cheered, Mark James's wife, Jane, was spat at, while in the final game, Colin Montgomerie faced such unremitting abuse throughout his match against the US Open champion Payne Stewart that his father, Jim, walked off the course, unable to take any more. 'The crowd there scaled new heights of serious abuse... it was really not very nice at all,' says Mark James. 'The level of hatred was extremely high and the fact that the crowd was so close to a lot of tees and greens just made it more difficult.'

Montgomerie had long been the target of hecklers whenever he played in the States, not least because his 1991 Ryder Cup teammate David Feherty had once remarked on a perceived similarity to the Robin Williams film character Mrs Doubtfire and the name had stuck, at least with some of the more vocal and unimaginative fans. But this had gone way beyond ribbing. Now, it was vicious and verging on the violent. Time after time, he had to back away from putts as insult followed insult while at the 9th tee, for instance, he teed up his ball but as he shaped to swing, a drunken voice from the back of the tee box punctured the silence, screaming 'You cunt!' Swift action ensued with Montgomerie's brother, Douglas, and no less a figure than the Duke of Golf himself, Prince Andrew, locating the offender and having him removed from the course.

The USA still needed a half point to secure the Ryder Cup, and attention now turned to the match between José María Olazábal and Justin Leonard. With just eight holes to play, Leonard, the 1997 Open champion, had been 4-down, but, buoyed by the exploits of his team-mates and spurred on by the now rabid crowd, the twenty-four-year-old Texan won the 11th and the 12th and then made birdies at the next two holes to tie the match. To his credit, Olazábal composed himself to halve the next two holes and, at the 17th looked favourite to take the hole, hitting his approach to 20ft while his opponent found the front of the green, some 45ft away from the hole.

With only the Montgomerie–Stewart game left out on the course and with the Scot ahead, the hero of the hour would come from the Olazábal–Leonard game. If the Spaniard could restore his advantage and win his game and Montgomerie could hold on against Stewart, Europe would have a tie and retain the Ryder Cup. If Leonard could fashion a half point from what had seemed like a battle lost just an hour earlier, then the US team would complete an inconceivable comeback.

At the rear of the green sat both teams and their captains, joined by their partners and caddies and countless officials who looked like they should be doing something else. It was impossibly, painfully tense. Leonard would putt first. It was a difficult putt at the best of times, uphill before levelling out on the upper tier as it got nearer the hole. It was two-putt territory – if you were lucky.

Stood in the shadows on the very same green where Francis Ouimet famously holed clutch putts on his way to the US Open title, and in almost eerie silence, Leonard made his shot, watching intently as the ball scampered up the slope. On and on it went and as it drew ever nearer to the hole so the volume around the green increased. When it rattled into the hole, slapping the back of the cup, the mood of what had already been a raucous day suddenly turned into something never seen before in the Ryder Cup.

As Leonard raised both arms to the sky, his face contorted by both shock and elation, his teammates stampeded across the green like cattle (albeit ones with poor fashion sense), oblivious to the fact that Olazábal still had a putt to half the hole and deny the USA the half point they seemed to have assumed they had already won. The chief culprit, at least in the eyes of the European team, seemed to be Tom Lehman. A committed Christian, the 1996 Open champion had been a man on the edge all day, whipping up the crowd whenever he got the opportunity. When he made a long birdie putt at the 13th hole to go 4-up against Lee Westwood, for instance, he ran off to the next tee, jumping, skipping and high-fiving the fans on his way through, without even stopping to pick his ball out of the hole.

Now, though, Lehman was a man possessed, leading the line to Leonard, and, according to some reports, running right across the line of Olazábal's putt. The Spaniard, to his credit, was dignity personified as Massachusetts went into meltdown. The Ryder Cup, even golf, had never seen anything like it. Pitch invasions were commonplace in soccer games, but not at a golf course, and certainly not by the players.

As the melee eventually subsided, Olazábal made a gallant effort at halving the hole but his putt came up short. The USA had their half point and the Ryder Cup was theirs once more. As the two players made their way to the 18th (a hole that Olazábal would win, thereby claiming a half point), Mark James's assistant Sam Torrance sat by the green, apoplectic. Targeting Tom Lehman, the man he perceived to be the ringleader, he gave a brief interview to the Sky Sports presenter Andrew Castle. 'Tom Lehman calls himself a man of God,' he fumed, 'but his behaviour today has been disgusting.'

Yes, running on the green was plain wrong. Yes, the celebrations were wild, inappropriate and over the top, but given the heat and tension of the moment, it was perhaps understandable. This, after all, was an American team that had lost the previous two Ryder Cups, a team that had been heavily criticized for broaching the subject of being paid to play in the event and a team that had all but given up the fight after the first two days. The PGA of America's CEO, Jim Awtrey, watched the scene unfold from the back of the 17th green. 'It was such an unexpected event and a reaction there,' he recalls. 'I don't think anybody intended for that, nor considered it, but just got caught up in the moment... I think it just reflected the excitement that the players felt having come from having not much of a chance to being right there at the end and winning.'

Sandy Jones, Awtrey's British counterpart, agrees. 'Do you think if we had been in the same position and you reverse the situation at the 17th that one or two of us might not have run on the green?' he suggests. 'Did they run across his [Olazábal's] line? I have got no evidence to support that. I have looked at tapes and I can't really say that. Was it bad behaviour? Yeah, it was bad behaviour. The guy still had to putt, but would we have behaved the same? Possibly. Maybe.'

Even the player forced to wait as the Americans whooped and hollered, José María Olazábal, conceded that given the nature and the sheer unprecedented scale of the comeback, there was always going to be some particularly enthusiastic celebrations. 'I have to say if it would have been just the opposite, we might have reacted the same way,' he said. 'We're all human beings; we have our emotions. The Ryder Cup brings them to the highest level possible.'

Back in Britain, the media weren't quite as forgiving. The *Sun* labelled the scenes 'Disgusting', adding that 'American players and their fans belong in the gutter', while its rival the *Mirror* maintained that 'Football hooligans act better than the way the Americans have treated the Ryder Cup over the last three days' and that 'Sporting relations between the two nations have now slipped to an all-time low.'

In the London *Evening Standard*, the columnist Matthew Norman, meanwhile, upped the ante. 'Let us be painfully honest about it. Yes, they are repulsive people, charmless, rude, cocky, mercenary, humourless, ugly, full of nauseatingly fake religiosity, and as odious in victory as they are unsporting in defeat. The only good thing to be said in favour of the American golfers, in fact, is that, at golf if at nothing else, they are better than the Europeans.'

Even the American press seemed a little embarrassed. 'It seems an American team can't get through an international competition without acting like jackasses at some point,' suggested the *Washington Post*.

For some of America's older Ryder Cup guard too, the events at Brookline hadn't even resembled golf. It was new, uncharted and wholly unpleasant territory. 'Those peaks and valleys or emotions [you feel] in the Ryder Cup were brought to the front I think right there. And I was embarrassed about that personally,' says Hale Irwin. 'I think you should never put aside your pride, be it for your team, your country or yourself, but I think you always have to keep a tight rein on your emotions when it comes to how it affects another player's perform-ance, particularly in the Ryder Cup where you are out representing more than just yourself… I think that was lost in the scuffle.'

When the dust had settled, many questioned Mark James's strategy of leaving three of his players (and rookies to boot) out of the action until the singles on Sunday. Of course, if Europe had maintained its lead and gone on to win the Ryder Cup, nobody would have said anything. Indeed, James, like Jacklin, Gallacher or Ballesteros before him, would have become another in an increasingly long and illustri-ous line of European heroes. But his tactic of keeping Andrew Coltart, Jarmo Sandelin and Jean van de Velde on the sidelines, so that their first taste of Ryder Cup action came on the most important day of all, was a gamble that had failed to pay off.

Andrew Coltart's omission was the most curious. Selected as a captain's pick by Mark James, at the expense of Bernhard Langer, he, of all the rookies, could have expected to play. Instead, he sat out the early games and when he came to make his bow, he found himself facing the number one player in the world, Tiger Woods. 'Maybe in his mind he [Mark James] thought he would play him on the Saturday afternoon and when he got close to it he then thought, if I stick with what I have got we can probably win this, this afternoon,' suggests Sandy Jones. 'But the guys were knackered on the Sunday and that was a risk – he took the risk that he was putting out young guys who hadn't played.'

Jones's comment certainly reflects the reality of the match situation. For James to change a winning line-up with the Ryder Cup almost within his grasp would, in all likelihood, have attracted just as much controversy as his decision to leave the trio on the bench. It was, as James's predecessor Bernard Gallacher explains, an impossible predicament. 'I think Mark wanted to rotate the players but the players he was putting out were just winning every match,' he says. 'I always felt it was unfair for people never to play before the singles because it looks like you have no confidence in them. I always told the team on the eve of the Ryder Cup that everyone played before the singles and it kept everybody on their toes.' Certainly, James's singles strategy is one you will never see again in a Ryder Cup. After Brookline, it is now a given that, barring exceptional circumstances, captains will always play every member of their team at least once before the final-day singles.

The truth, however you choose to examine the events, is that the behaviour of the Brookline crowd and the shenanigans at the 17th, overblown and ridiculous though they were, overshadowed what was one of *the* greatest golf and, indeed, sporting performances of all time. In winning the singles 8½ points to 3½, the American team, collectively, was a staggering 38 under par for the day. The Europeans were just 10-under. 'Sometimes,' says Mark James, ten years on, 'one team plays extremely well and that certainly happened at Brookline.'

That evening, the American team celebrated long and hard into the night, giving Steve Pate what he would later describe as 'a massive hangover' the following day. As the team partied, Payne Stewart, so often the focal point of any get-together, started dancing on the top of a piano in the clubhouse, dressed in some old sweatpants and an orange T-shirt. When the team noticed that Tiger Woods had sloped off to his room, a press gang was dispatched to his room, whereupon he was bundled out of bed and summoned to join in.

American joy would soon turn to despair. On 25 October, a month to the day after the Ryder Cup win, a Learjet carrying Payne Stewart, his agents Robert Fraley and Van Arden, and the golf course architect

Bruce Borland, left Orlando, Florida, bound for Dallas, Texas. Shortly after take-off, the cabin lost pressure, starving the two pilots and passengers of oxygen and killing all on board. The pilotless plane would continue to fly across the country for over 1,000 miles before crashing into a field near Mina, South Dakota. Stewart, one of the most recognizable and most loved players in the game was dead, aged just forty-two. Suddenly and tragically, the events at Brookline seemed as petty, puerile and thoroughly inconsequential as they surely were.

Game Off...

PERSPECTIVE is often conspicuous by its absence in the wide and often misguided world of sport. A great player isn't just a great player, he's a 'genius'. Vital games are 'must win' matches played in the 'last chance saloon'. Fierce contests aren't just competitive encounters, they are 'wars', 'clashes' or, in the case of Brookline in 1999, 'battles'. It is, for the most part, tabloid talk that helps to ramp up the enthusiasm and interest and puts bums on seats.

But in golf, where tradition and dignity, honour and honesty are everything, Brookline had been a step too far, the moment when what was, after all, just a golf competition, crossed the line into something uglier, something angrier, with antagonism and jingoism, gamesmanship and a marked absence of gentlemanly conduct, from players and spectators alike.

Just one month after Brookline, the PGA of America announced their new team captain for the 34th staging of the event, once more to be held at The Belfry. Curtis Strange was a former shoe salesman from Norfolk, Virginia, who, years on from his past vocation, could still tell a person's shoe size just by looking at their feet. A veteran of five Ryder Cups, Strange had been one of the pre-eminent players of the 1980s, winning sixteen events on the PGA Tour in the decade and, in 1988, becoming the first player in history to win more than $1 million in prize money in one season. Memorably, he had also beaten Britain's Nick Faldo in an 18-hole play-off at the 1988 US Open at Brookline and, the following year, became the first golfer since Ben Hogan in 1951 to successfully defend the title. When asked just how he had accomplished this rare feat, Strange was unusually terse. 'Guts,' he said, 'and pars.'

At the announcement at the PGA's HQ in Palm Beach Gardens, Florida, Strange spoke of his pride at being made skipper, saying, 'You're chosen for your ability to lead, to prepare your players and to win back the Cup... It's truly an honour, but also a tough task.'

Soon after, Europe would also name their new leader, and it came as a surprise to nobody with even the faintest interest in the sport that Sam Torrance, the vice-captain at Brookline and a stalwart of European golf for nearly thirty years, had been handed the task of wrestling the Ryder Cup back from the Americans. After the catcalls and brickbats at Brookline, Torrance already had a couple of men in mind for his wild cards. 'My two picks,' he joked at his press conference, 'will be Lennox Lewis and Prince Naseem.'

The longest-serving player on the European Tour – he had made his debut in 1971 – Torrance would prove to be a popular choice. Not only did he have the respect of the players who would represent him, he was also well liked in the media and by golf fans alike. And so what if had never won a major (or even really contended in one), he was known throughout the game as the man (with the moustache) who won the Ryder Cup back for Europe after twenty-eight long and lonely years. That, more than anything, was qualification enough. 'Being on Tour for thirty years was my application form [for the captaincy],' explains Torrance. 'I'd been Mark James's assistant in 1999 and enjoyed the experience, but I only really decided that I wanted to do it when they asked me. You don't really want to think that you might be captain, especially when you're still playing because it's not good for your game.'

Torrance and Strange went back a long way, their career paths having criss-crossed over three decades as professional golfers, and while they weren't exactly drinking buddies the two shared an inherent respect for the traditions of the game and the Ryder Cup itself. Indeed, prior to their first official press conference together, the pair had spoken several times on the phone, agreeing that the scenes witnessed at Brookline should never be repeated, at least not on their watch. Yes, it should be a proper contest, uncompromising, passionate and fuelled by the fans' fervour, but not like Brookline where a game of golf seemed to be just a water cannon away from a riot. 'We're in complete agreement about everything,' said Strange. 'I expect nothing but wonderful behaviour from their fans, because they're great fans, with great golf knowledge. You see that at the British Open and at the Ryder Cup. Yes, they'll root more for their team, but there's nothing wrong with that; the Boston fans rooted hard for our team. So I expect nothing but to be treated with a lot of courtesy and respect over there.'

One of Torrance's first tasks as captain, other than to seek out world champion boxers to bolster his ranks, was to assemble his support staff. His first choice would be the Ryder Cup veteran and 1991 Masters champion, Ian Woosnam. 'Woosie' was cut from a similar cloth to his skipper. A gritty competitor on the course and one of the boys off it, he and Torrance had paired up for Woosnam's Ryder Cup debut in 1983 when they halved their fourball match against Ben Crenshaw and Calvin Peete. Since then, he had gone on to become a mainstay of the European side, playing on every side until age and form began to get the better of him for the contest at Brookline in 1999. But if Woosnam was an obvious choice – he had also been an assistant at Brookline – then Torrance's choice for his other right-hand man would cause consternation in European golf's corridors of power.

Having been the man in charge at Brookline, Mark James had come up short in his quest to win the Ryder Cup, but as he sat in the locker room after that painful defeat he had reassured his friend Sam Torrance that if the Scot ever got the job as European captain he would be on hand to help should he so require. Now, with Torrance leading the team, he had been asked to return to the fold once more.

It was a reversal of roles that would have made perfect sense if only James hadn't written his book about Brookline. Released in May 2000, *Into the Bear Pit* was named after the Royal and Ancient's secretary Sir Michael Bonallack's description of the scenes at the 1999 contest and was Mark James's detailed behind-the-scenes account of what really happened in that unseemly week in Massachusetts.

With an initial print-run of just 5,000, the book was picked up by the *Daily Mail* newspaper who bought the serialization rights and went to town on the revelations that James had thrown Nick Faldo's good-luck message in the wastepaper basket, rather than pin it to the wall, and also questioned the six-times Major winner's popularity among the European Tour's golfers. One month later, and with the central characters now engaged in an unseemly public spat, the book had been reprinted six times and sales had passed the 30,000 mark.

On the face of it, these were remarks that shouldn't have garnered the coverage or the controversy they did, not least because of everything else that happened at Brookline, but Nick Faldo believed that James's story contravened European Tour guidelines that maintained that all players were obliged to refrain from making comments that 'attack, disparage or criticize' fellow competitors.

The fall-out from the book would rumble on, threatening the very unity that Sam Torrance was so intent on establishing. In July at Loch Lomond, James had received the overwhelming backing of the tournament committee (which he chaired), much to the astonishment of Faldo and some high-profile supporters in the shape of Seve Ballesteros and Bernhard Langer, both of whom felt that James should never have gone public with the book.

Jean van de Velde, the Frenchman who had been left out by James for the first two days of the event at Brookline, meanwhile, also seemed determined to have his say. Ever since his 6&5 drubbing at the hands of Davis Love III in his one and only game in the Ryder Cup, van de Velde had held James personally responsible, claiming that his absence from the action until the final day was 'morally wrong'. Now, he was aghast at the support James was receiving. 'I was shocked by the committee decision,' he said. 'I thought my views would have been made clear to the committee and I fully expected some action to be taken... there was strong feeling around that the whole matter should be wrapped up and brought to an end. That obviously hasn't happened.'

It was a spat that threatened to overshadow what in 2000 was a spectacular summer for golf and, in particular, Tiger Woods. Now twenty-four, Woods had decimated the field in the US Open at Pebble Beach in June – he won by a record 15 shots – and then taken the Open Championship at St Andrews in July by eight strokes, setting a new record for the lowest 72-hole score in relation to par, –19, and becoming the youngest player in history to win all four of golf's major championships. A month later, he bagged the PGA Championship as well, pipping Bob May in a play-off at Kentucky's famous Valhalla Golf Club. To give an idea of just how far ahead he was of the rest of the professional golfing world in 2000, one need only look at his scoring in the four majors, where he boasted a total of 53 under par. His nearest challenger, the South African Ernie Els, was just 18-under. The following April, meanwhile, he would win his second Masters at Augusta to become the first man in history to simultaneously hold all four major titles. Some curmudgeons disputed whether it could be called a 'grand slam', given that one of the events was not in the same calendar year as the others. Others called it a 'Tiger Slam'. Whichever way you examined it, it was, indisputably, a phenomenal achievement.

As July melted into August, though, the Ryder Cup row showed no sign of abating. Despite Sam Torrance's desire to retain James as his vice-captain, the issue had remained the lead golf story of the summer and after the events at Brookline, it was the kind of controversy the European Tour could have done without. With pressure growing on Torrance from the media, from Nick Faldo and his cohorts and from the European Tour itself, the European skipper decided to put an end to the issue. He rang James on his mobile as the forty-six-year-old was holidaying in Spain. Asking him to step down, Torrance explained it was the only way for the team to move forward, stressing that while he wouldn't be an official vice-captain, he still wanted him as part of his support staff at The Belfry. To his credit, James accepted the decision without rancour.

The following day, at the International Tournament in Colorado, Nick Faldo welcomed the decision, although it was clear that the issue, in his mind at least, was far from over. 'I've now learned that Mark tore up my good-luck letter,' Faldo said. 'In his book he stated that he showed my letter to the whole team, but, in fact, that is incorrect. In fact, I don't think any of the team saw it except for two non-playing members.'

Not so, says James. 'We have all had our says,' he explains. 'It is old hat but all I will say is the book was a factual account and if there had been problems with it I think I would have been receiving a call from someone's solicitor... I knew there wasn't [any problems] because everything I wrote was the truth. I am not in the habit of not telling the truth anyway so I certainly wouldn't do it in a book.'

Following James's departure, Torrance turned to Joakim Haeggman, the first Swede to have played in the Ryder Cup (in 1993), as his replacement. It was a politic move, not least because the team was becoming increasingly European in its make-up, and Swedish golfers such as Niclas Fasth, Pierre Fulke and Jesper Parnevik were all likely to figure in Torrance's final team.

While Torrance had been the outstanding candidate for the job of captain, there was concern within the corridors of power at the PGA that while he would undoubtedly be able to create and unite his team, the unavoidable and innumerable presentations and appearances required of the captain could present problems. In short, Sam Torrance hated public speaking. It's a view reinforced by the veteran golf commentator Bruce Critchley. 'I remember thinking in the early days, God, this is going to be a nightmare,' he recalls, 'because [at] any gathering, he [Torrance] would get pissed, stand up and fall over because he was so nervous of public speaking,' he says.

Sit Sam Torrance in a smoke-filled snug, surrounded by his muckers, and the jokes, like the ale, would flow. Stand him in front of a room full of people, let alone the countless thousands of folk at The Belfry and the small matter of 500 million people around the world who would be watching the opening ceremony on television, and he was a nervous wreck.

It was hardly surprising. Here, after all, was a man who had left school at just thirteen and spent his working life treading the relative solitude of the fairways, with only his thoughts and a caddie for company. No private education. No university. No golf scholarship in the United States. Nothing. Now, though, he was charged with the task not simply of creating a team from twelve seemingly disparate individuals and sending them on their way, but of doing everything from press conferences to gala dinners to TV interviews, all of which, of course, would involve public speaking.

Faced with the very real prospect of embarrassing himself, the European team and the PGA in front of the watching world, Torrance decided to confront his problem head-on. In March 2000, just a few months into his captaincy, he had attended the centenary dinner of Sunningdale Golf Club at London's Claridge's Hotel where one of its members, a Scottish gynaecologist and acclaimed public speaker, Professor David Purdie, had entertained the guests with a speech that had them if not rolling in the aisles, then at least chuckling over the cheese and biscuits.

Torrance was impressed. Here, he thought, was a man, and a fellow Scot to boot, who could help him overcome his fear of public addresses. As the evening wore on, he sought out Purdie, as the Professor recalls. 'He said, "I'll get to the point. We're both from Ayrshire. You're from Prestwick. I'm from Largs. I want you for the Ryder Cup. "I knew what he meant at once but I thought I'd have some fun with him, so I said "Thank you Sam, but no".'

Torrance was crestfallen. 'But why not?' he asked.

'Because I'm an amateur,' replied Purdie, devilishly.

'No, no, no, I'm not asking you to play,' explained Torrance, taking the bait.

Purdie stopped him in his tracks. 'Sam,' he said. 'I know exactly what you mean and I'd be delighted to help you.'

With Purdie's help, Torrance set about conquering his fear. First, Purdie had Torrance write his four main speeches for the week of the Ryder Cup (including one in the event that his team lost), stressing the importance of structure, and between them they tweaked and tinkered with them, fine-tuning Torrance's words into speeches that were both functional and funny, respectful and to the point. In short, just like Torrance himself. Determined to be word-perfect come the competition, Torrance then learned all of his speeches by heart, considering the cadence, perfecting the pauses. He even commandeered the official lectern for the opening ceremony and set it up in his garage complete with nearby tape recorder so he could practise if not *in situ* then as close as he could get to it. It was like going to the driving range. Each day, every day, Torrance would stand at the lectern and practise for up to three hours. Sometimes he would have his wife Suzanne stand behind him and offer her opinion. 'It was a joint decision to use the lectern but I just wanted him to be completely at ease when he made his speech and to leave the stage one-up on Curtis Strange, which he did,' adds Purdie.

David Purdie would not be the only expert opinion Torrance would canvass. As manager of Manchester United Football Club, Sir Alex Ferguson had won virtually every honour the game of football had to offer. Like Torrance, Ferguson was also a working-class Scot made good, hailing from the shipbuilding centre of Govan, some thirty-five miles east of Largs, and the pair had met on several occasions when Torrance had taken his son, Daniel, to watch United play at Old Trafford. The pair spoke on several occasions about the task confronting the European team skipper. As a manager in the top flight of British football for more than a quarter of a century, Ferguson possessed unrivalled experience of handling players of vastly differing mentalities, from the most fragile personalities on the one hand to the most over-inflated egos on the other – and his record proved that he had done so outstandingly well. 'He said, whatever you do, you do not have a superstar in your team. Everyone is equal,' Torrance told the author in 2004. 'That was probably the best single piece of advice I received as captain.'

But while Ferguson was known for a management style that would see him confront any errant players with his so-called 'hairdryer' treatment, Torrance was the polar opposite, an avuncular, gregarious captain who believed that his role was to instil confidence through mutual respect and gentle persuasion, not fear or threats. 'I'm more like the naughty lieutenant who gets caught smuggling the booze in at midnight and then gets court-martialled,' he said.

Soon afterwards, Torrance found himself sitting next to the then manager of the England national football team, Sven-Göran Eriksson, on a flight to Spain. Ever the opportunist, he took the chance to get the Swede's take on the secret of successful team management.

As football coaches, Ferguson and Eriksson were both, obviously, skilled in team and squad selection, but for Torrance it was a new and potentially vexatious issue. While he had no say on the ten men who would qualify for his team automatically, he, like his predecessors, still had to make the difficult and delicate decision as to who his two wild-card selections would be. Invariably, when it comes to choosing, there is always one player whose mere presence and charisma, not to mention talent, are worth their place in the team. In 2001, it was the young Spaniard Sergio García, who, having divided his time between the PGA Tour in the States and the European Tour, was reliant on a wild-card pick if he was going to make his second Ryder Cup appearance.

Early in 2001, Torrance had assured García that he would be one of his two choices should he not qualify as of right, but the issue of the remaining place remained probelmatic. Indeed, Torrance had even requested a change to the selection system to give him three picks, but his appeal to the Ryder Cup committee fell on deaf ears.

At the final event that counted towards qualification, the BMW International in Germany in early September 2001, Torrance was still mulling over the second of his two picks and was torn between the Swede Jesper Parnevik and José María Olazábal, the Spaniard who, alongside Seve Ballesteros, had contributed so much to the Ryder Cup since his debut in 1987.

In Parnevik's favour was not just his form but his relationship with the other wild-card pick, Sergio García. At Brookline in 1999, the two had played four games together and had dropped just half a point against Davis Love III and David Duval. Against Olazábal was his poor form – he had failed to register a top-ten finish since winning the French Open in May – and ongoing problems with his driving and his putting. Yes, his reputation as a Ryder Cup stalwart preceded him, but faced with the option of a ready-made, not to mention tried and trusted, partnership, Torrance plumped for Parnevik. On hearing the news the double Masters winner Olazábal vowed to return while Torrance would later concede that informing 'Olly' of his decision was just 'awful'. Curtis Strange, meanwhile, urged the Spaniard to quickly take out US citizenship, saying, 'I'll have him.'

Today, though, Torrance believes that the Spaniard's commitment to the event remains unparalleled and that it is a matter of when and not if he becomes the European skipper. 'Olazábal,' he says, 'would be an outstanding future captain. He's put more heart into the event than anyone.'

Now, Torrance's team was complete. There was experience in Bernhard Langer and Colin Montgomerie, reliability in Lee Westwood and Darren Clarke and flair in García and Parnevik. There would also be four new faces to the European team, with Ireland's Paul McGinley, Wales's Phil Price, and the Swedes Niclas Fasth and Pierre Fulke entering the fray.

As ever, though, the US team, with its stellar cast list and proven winners throughout, looked the stronger side, with household names peppering their line-up, six of whom had also played at Brookline two years earlier. Like Torrance, Curtis Strange had also had to face the prospect of disappointing some of his friends and fellow professionals, with the likes of Brad Faxon, Chris DiMarco and Tom Lehman jettisoned in favour of Ryder Cup veteran Paul Azinger and, surprisingly, Scott Verplank.

Verplank received the news he had hoped for hours after the conclusion of the 2001 PGA Championship at the Atlanta Athletic Club in Duluth, Georgia. He had just landed at Oklahoma City airport and as his plane taxied on the runway, the Texan took the opportunity to furtively check his voicemail. There was a message from Strange. He was in. Verplank smiled to himself, saving a more effusive celebration for when he was in the terminal toilets where, he admitted, he let out a 'yelp'.

He was a controversial choice. Here, after all, was a player who had finished 14th on the qualification points list and, crucially, had never played in the Ryder Cup. That he had guts, though, was beyond doubt. A diabetic, he had also endured several operations on his troublesome elbow and suffered season after season of poor form and misfortune before winning the PGA Tour Comeback Player of the Year award in 1998 and, twelve years after his last win, winning the 2000 Reno-Tahoe Open. He was, as Curtis Strange explained, a 'fighter'.

The 1993 PGA Champion Paul Azinger had also had to fight his own battles. Soon after his successful appearance in the 1993 Ryder Cup at The Belfry, he had been diagnosed with Non-Hodgkin's lymphoma in his right shoulder and undergone six months of chemotherapy and five weeks of radiation treatment. The illness kept him out of golf for eight months and it would be another seven years before he would win again on Tour. Tenacious and unshakeable, Azinger had come to typify the spirit of the US team: in three Ryder Cups he had stared down the best European players of his generation and had never played on the losing side. That he was a fighter was unquestionable. That the US was a better team with him in it was obvious.

*

LIVING just fifteen minutes from his office at The Belfry had its benefits for Sandy Jones. Having popped home for a spot of lunch and to let his dog out, the PGA's Chief Executive had returned to work to find his PA Maureen Roberts running through the car park towards him. 'Hurry up,' she said, ushering him back into the building. 'Come and see the television. There's a plane flown into one of the Twin Towers!'

Jones quickened his step and made his way to his office, turning the set on and watching what he thought was footage of the aircraft hitting the World Trade Center. Only it wasn't. It was the second plane. 'That's not an accident,' said Jones, before he realized the implications of what had just happened in Manhattan. 'Christ, the Ryder Cup is in a fortnight... the Americans aren't going to travel.'

Across the Atlantic, Jones's US counterpart at the PGA of America, Jim Awtrey, was making a strategic presentation to the board of directors at Palm Beach Gardens, when he was interrupted and told to tune into the news. 'And that's when we saw it all together as a board,' he recalls.

On 11 September, just seventeen days before the 34th Ryder Cup was due to begin at The Belfry, two planes hijacked by terrorists and flown murderously into New York's World Trade Center had changed everything. Nearly 3,000 people would die, with another plane being flown into the Pentagon and another hijacked jet crash-landing in a field in rural Pennsylvania. Panic paralysed the planet and with the world facing a new terror and talk of war and retribution filling the corridors of power, something as flimsy and inconsequential as a golf contest suddenly became the last thing on anyone's mind.

For Jim Awtrey at the PGA of America and his counterpart in the UK, Sandy Jones, the horror of the attacks soon gave way to panic, followed by inevitable chaos. The Belfry, after all, was ready for the Ryder Cup; the contracts were signed, the TV towers and grandstands were up, the tickets were sold, the merchandise was waiting to be unpacked, and the caterers booked, as Sandy Jones recalls:

The attack was on the Tuesday and the next few days just flashed by me. We went through the week trying to figure out what was going to happen. On the Saturday night it was about 6.15 p.m. and I was sitting at home and my telephone rang. It was Jim Awtrey. The only words he said to me were, 'We can't get a team Sandy, we can't come over'. I remember I was sitting watching Celtic and Dundee on the telly and I thought 'Oh, right, that's interesting' and all I said to him was 'Thank you for letting me know Jim, that's fine'. I remember putting the phone down and thinking we better cancel dinner tonight, I think we've got a problem.

Over on the east coast of the United States, Jim Awtrey was also endeavouring to find a way through the myriad problems that now presented themselves:

When it happened everything was shut down in America. The airports were shut down and some of our board were from the west coast and [as] there was no way to get flights, people started driving. They drove right across the US to get home so it just created that turmoil where no one knew what was the next step, so it was really a tough time. But we [the PGAs] were talking regularly and we were trying to find a way and the players were committed to do it if that's what we wanted. Generally the discussion was that if we did, though, it was not likely that they would bring wives because many people had left their home, seen their children and seen their parents leave and some never came back and so a week later to take mother and dad and leave the country was just going to be a tremendous stress on the children of the families and ultimately we just didn't feel that it was the right thing to do.

Sam Torrance would learn of the attacks as he parked his car at Sunningdale Golf Club. Soon, his opposite number Curtis Strange would call and the two agreed that they could not now see the Ryder Cup taking place as planned. 'Curtis was on the west coast and he was driving back to get home,' recalls Jim Awtrey. 'We had talked on the phone about it. He was supportive whatever we decided.'

Discussions between the PGA of America and the European Ryder

Cup board, meanwhile, would also continue apace, but the truth was there wasn't anything to discuss. Certainly, the European Ryder Cup board were prepared to play and The Belfry was ready, willing and able to host it, but with the American team understandably reluctant to make the journey and the Europeans' appetite for the game dwindling, it was inevitable that something would have to give. 'They're human,' said Curtis Strange of his players. 'They want to be with their families, just like everyone else. They're talking to their children, trying to reassure them that we're not going to war. They were also very consistent in saying we really can't think much about golf right now. It's a tough situation all the way around.'

Four days after the attacks, it had become clear, painfully so, that there was no way that the 34th Ryder Cup could take place as scheduled. Even Sam Torrance, a man who had given his life to the game, conceded that 'Golf is nothing, nothing'. He was right, of course, but then he usually was. In the grand scheme of things, a little game like golf didn't mean a jot. Indeed, amid the horror and the wasted lives of September 11, everything else seemed insignificant, irrelevant, and if the events at Brookline two years earlier had seemed like the Ryder Cup was a matter of life or death, 9/11 was the brutal, sickening proof of the contrary.

On the evening of Saturday, 15 September, Sandy Jones began contacting the Ryder Cup board and a meeting was arranged at Wentworth for the following morning where the decision was taken to postpone, rather than cancel, the 2001 Ryder Cup. While Jones sent his financial director John Yapp to Wentworth, he stayed behind at The Belfry in a bid to close down the site, so as not to jeopardize the inevitable insurance claim. 'We had to shut down the site,' he explains. 'We had all the merchandising units set up, so we had to get security to quarantine the site otherwise we could lose our money. The insurance company was very insistent that we had to close down. Nobody could put another seat in place because they wouldn't pay the contractors for it. It had to be shut down at that moment.'

With the site secure, Sandy Jones informed Sam Torrance of the decision to postpone the match and later that evening, the European skipper began ringing round his team to tell them the news. Nobody was surprised. Relieved perhaps, but not surprised.

The following day, both of the competition's organizing bodies released statements. The European Ryder Cup board said that they had 'been placed in a position beyond our control, and therefore the matches, out of necessity, have been postponed'. Meanwhile, Jim Awtrey and the PGA of America said that 'the enormity of the tragedy in America' was such that they had also decided to seek a postponement 'of the matches until next year'.

That week at a ghostly Belfry, crews began dismantling the grandstands and the marquees, the signage and the pop-up shops, all without a ball having been struck. Some 15,000 seats had been installed for the event and not one had been touched by a single paying customer, while three cavernous two- and three-storey corporate hospitality centres would also have to come down, with case after case of champagne inside remaining unopened and uncorked. At the merchandising centre, meanwhile, the official Ryder Cup clothing supplier Glenmuir was also counting the cost of the postponement, as 40,000 'Ryder Cup 2001' monogrammed polo shirts sat unpacked, destined to become collector's items or lots on eBay. It seemed vulgar and inappropriate given the circumstances, but estimates suggested the final cost of the postponement would top £100 million. 'It was a major funding effort for the PGA, for the European Tour, for the British PGA and a significant commitment also to the American Tour, so from a business perspective it was a very big financial hit on everybody,' says Jim Awtrey.

Not surprisingly, there was still a mountain of off-site matters to attend to. In the UK, Sandy Jones cancelled his planned post-Ryder Cup holiday to Dubai and set about the mammoth job of reorganizing the event. 'It was just hell for three months,' he explains. 'I can remember having to go to a meeting with all the hotel operators. We had 5,000 rooms contracted in and around the area and we had to tell them

"We won't be using your rooms, but don't worry we are coming back next year". I made one of my Winston Churchill like speeches – "Don't worry guys, we'll be back, just hang on" and them going, "Well, what compensation do we get?"'

Jim Awtrey, meanwhile, had more lofty concerns. 'We were scheduled to be in the White House on the Sunday before the Ryder Cup,' he says. 'President Bush had invited us to have dinner... but when this happened we had to make contact and decide what to do.'

Ten years on, both Awtrey and Sandy Jones now feel that the attacks, horrific though they were, prompted the kind of communal response and cooperation that would not be possible ordinarily. Everybody, from merchandisers to hoteliers, TV companies to the various administrative bodies, seemed to understand the Ryder Cup's place in the wake of an event that had changed the face of the world. 'Everybody was working together to do the best thing,' says Awtrey. 'I remember talking to Dick Ebersol, President of NBC, because we had some significant revenue from rights fees from the Ryder Cup through our association, and when I talked to him about it he said ,"Jim, don't worry about us, you do the right thing and we are going to honour our commitment whatever you do". People – their whole attitude and their business relationships came together and really rallied in the face of a major terrorist threat... I am not sure that could happen again.'

Sandy Jones agrees. 'A lot of negotiation had to happen. We then had to have all sorts of debates with the PGA Tour, with the PGA in America and ourselves and the European Tour and the likes of hotels and venues and TV to find a date [for the rearranged match]. But people cleared the way for us and slowly but surely we got it in place, but it took a long time.'

Had it not been for 9/11 Sam Torrance and Curtis Strange would have had just three weeks from the time their teams were finalized to the event itself. Now Torrance had an extra twelve months, a year that he would use constructively. He held regular team dinners, encouraged the players to play the Brabazon course as and when their schedules allowed and caught up with his players as they made their way round the Tour. 'It was just a case of trying to get them to believe that they were part of the greatest team Europe's ever had,' he explains.

Torrance would also revisit the Brabazon course several times, to consider any further changes and ensure it gave his team the best possible chance of regaining the Ryder Cup.

He narrowed fairways, added some more bunkers, and thickened up the rough. In short, he made the course as un-American as he could. At the drivable par-4 10th hole, meanwhile, Torrance had the tee moved back, making the hole some 311 yards long and, with water guarding the front of the green, out of the reach of the USA's bigger hitters. 'We had a number of team meetings where we looked at each hole and decided how we wanted to change it to our advantage,' says Torrance. 'That was one of the reasons we took the tee back at the 10th, just so we could take the driver out of the hands of players like Woods and Duval.'

Even as late as the Monday afternoon of the Ryder Cup week itself, late into the afternoon and with the players practising, Torrance decided to shave the rough on the third hole by an additional half-inch after a rapidly convened on-course conference with his senior players, Colin Montgomerie and the man he called 'Fritz', Bernhard Langer. The German, meanwhile, also suggested trimming the rough near a bunker on the left of the 15th fairway, saying this could present problems for some of Europe's shorter hitters; so, once more, The Belfry's ground-staff were called into action.

Bevan Tattersall was The Belfry's course manager. He had become head greenkeeper at the Brabazon's sister course on The Belfry site, the PGA National, at the age of twenty-two. Now, aged twenty-nine, he was the youngest man in history ever to prepare a course for the Ryder Cup. Ordinarily, Tattersall had a staff of thirty-six to oversee The Belfry's three courses, but now, with the Ryder Cup in town (and despite the PGA National and the Derby courses being closed), reinforcements had been drafted in and his team totalled seventy.

GAME OFF... | 189

It would be a punishing few weeks for The Belfry's ground-staff, and not just because Sam Torrance continued to tweak the course. Every day from 5 a.m. until it became too dark to work, they would trim trees, cut grass, and top-dress.

For Sam Torrance and Curtis Strange there was little more they could do, save for prayers and finger-crossing. The speeches were written and rehearsed. The teams were picked and poised, and The Belfry pruned, preened and wearing its Sunday best. Everything, at long last, was set.

…Game On

THE long-awaited Ryder Cup week began with a bang. Shortly before 1 a.m. on Monday, 23 September, an earthquake measuring 4.8 on the Richter scale struck the nearby town of Dudley, shaking buildings and the locals alike. By the UK's standards it was a sizeable quake – the biggest in ten years – but not powerful enough to wake Sam Torrance from his sleep at The Belfry hotel some twenty miles away. According to West Midlands Police, there had been some 600 calls to emergency services in the hour after the quake, some 5,000 calls to police in total and even a dozen distressed locals who had walked into police stations dressed only in their nightclothes.

For Jesper Parnevik, however, it brought back some terrifying memories. The Swede had been in New York City on 11 September 2001 and witnessed at first hand the devastation of the attacks on the Twin Towers of the World Trade Center. When the tremor struck the West Midlands that Monday morning, he had awoken with a start and ran naked on to his balcony at The Belfry, believing the hotel had also been targeted by terrorists. 'I was very happy to find out it was an earthquake,' he said later. 'Being in Manhattan when September 11th happened, I still have very paranoid thoughts. So that was my very first thought, actually, because it was a big bang. My bedroom table just kept smacking into the window, and the bed was all over the place. I've never been in an earthquake before, but it was very scary.'

Whether it was the geological stirrings, scores of autograph hunters or the world's golf media, Sam Torrance would be a man in demand in the week of the 34th Ryder Cup. Before a shot had even been struck in anger, there was a raft of things to do and people to see. From players to presenters to Presidents – George H.W. Bush even gave Torrance's son, Daniel, a presidential golf ball – the Scot had to find time for everyone. He would also have to wade through reams of good-luck messages from well-wishers including the actor Sean Connery, the footballer Kenny Dalglish, Seve Ballesteros and the man he left out, José María Olazábal. None of these, however, would be filed in the bin.

A lot would be asked of the players too, especially as they weren't being paid for playing. As well as the opening ceremony, there would be a Gala Dinner to attend and a raft of functions, meetings and obligatory press conferences. When time allowed they squeezed some practice rounds in, too. At the Gala Dinner, for instance, held at Birmingham's NEC and hosted by the Irish Tourist Board to mark the announcement of Dublin's K Club as the venue for the 2006 event, the teams were treated/subjected to performances by Ronan Keating and the *Riverdance* cast and soon both teams were cutting the rug as well.

Ahead of the matches, there would also be plenty of advice for those players facing their first Ryder Cup. Paul McGinley, for example, learned to lean on the old hand that was David Feherty. Since playing in the Ryder Cup in 1991, David Feherty had transformed himself from promising pro into a TV analyst of rare insight and humour. Frank, plain-speaking and funny, he had become the wisecracker-in-chief on the PGA Tour, always there to offer a left-field perspective on the game or a quip to relieve the tension down the stretch on a Sunday. As the two Irishmen talked about the week ahead and what lay ahead for McGinley, and keen to help him out, Feherty presented him with a gold-plated four-leaf clover ball-marker. 'It was given to him by a member of his family and he'd used it in the Ryder Cup,' explains

McGinley. 'Now, he wanted me to use it in my first Ryder Cup. So I said thanks and used it all week.'

But not all players were enjoying the build-up and if Torrance's plan to create a star-free line-up was taking shape, there was little Curtis Strange could do to field anything but a star-studded team. In the world number one, Tiger Woods, of course, they had a player who had climbed rapidly to superstar status before then leaving it trailing in his wake to become one of sport's few megastars. Now in his sixth year as a professional and still only twenty-six years old, he had already won eight majors – more than Arnold Palmer, Sam Snead or Bobby Jones – and with a glut of commercial endorsements from the likes of Nike, GM Motors and American Express, was well on his way to becoming sport's first billionaire.

Since making his debut in the Ryder Cup at Valderrama in 1997, though, Woods's record in the event was in stark contrast to his ever-lengthening list of personal achievements. Having played ten matches in the event, he had won just three, halved one and lost six. Publicly, he had even begun to question the importance of the competition over the big pay days of Tour golf. The week before the Ryder Cup, for example, Woods had been playing at the American Express World Championship at Mount Juliet, near Kilkenny, Ireland, an event that carried a first prize of $1 million. After his first round – a course record 65 – Woods repaired to the press tent whereupon a reporter asked him whether he would rather win the tournament he was playing in or the Ryder Cup with the USA the following week. 'Here this week,' he shrugged, before adding, 'I can think of a million reasons why.' Three rounds later, Woods left Ireland, with another title on his resumé, a new record low score for the event (23-under) and his bank balance bolstered by another million dollars.

Yet in a week where Woods should have been using all his influence, all his renown, to help foster team spirit in the American camp, he had stated, publicly, that cash was more important than his country, even though he already had more than he could ever spend. In later years,

and with the benefit of experience, Woods would adopt a more diplomatic approach to the Ryder Cup, but for now it was patently clear that
this was one competition he could do without. 'I don't enjoy the lead-up
to the Ryder Cup because we're taken out of our normal routine,' he
continued. 'We're not able to practise and I am used to working out a lot
and we're not able to do that. We have to go to functions, getting home
late at night. If I'm at a big event I'm not spending all night hanging
out, I'm trying to get my rest.'

By the time the opening ceremony arrived, and with the brief
welcome dinner address already safely navigated, Sam Torrance now
faced his moment of truth – the opening ceremony in front of the
watching world and *that* speech. Before he left for the stage, Torrance
made his way via the hotel bar at The Belfry, downing a large Scotch
to help him on his way.

As the teams took to the stage, it was clear, however, that one lesson
had still not been learned from Brookline as, once again, fashion had
taken a back seat to functionality. The US team opted for checked
jackets, while their opponents went tieless with black shirts, cream
jackets and the kind of slacks that only golfers ever seem to wear.
Torrance's wife Suzanne, meanwhile, had suggested that the partners
of the European team members should be allowed to wear what they
liked, rather than an official outfit like the funereal black one worn
by the American wives. And while the European wives looked stylish
and relaxed, their American counterparts, as the Scottish *Daily Record*
remarked, looked like the 'Stepford Wives'.

With a moment's silence for the victims of 9/11 observed impecca-
bly, it was time for the captains to make their speeches. Confident and
assured, US skipper Curtis Strange rattled through his speech, empha-
sizing the importance of not merely restoring the image of the Ryder
Cup but also maintaining the competitive nature of the contest.

Then, it was Sam Torrance's turn to face the thousands of spectators at The Belfry and those hundreds of millions watching it live on
television, one of whom was his tutor, David Purdie. The Professor

had declined Torrance's offer of tickets to the event as he had a prior engagement giving a lecture at the University of Sydney, Australia. But there was no way he was going to miss his pupil's big day. Tuning in to the ceremony on television, Purdie sat on the edge of his seat, as Torrance walked to the lectern, which, fortunately, had been returned to its rightful place. 'I said to him, "Remember to smile at the audience," and when he did it he was immediately at ease and everyone relaxed,' recalls Purdie.

Slowly, deliberately and, to everyone's relief, faultlessly, Torrance made the speech he had fretted so much about, trying desperately not to catch the eye of his wife or his family in case his emotions got the better of him. Yes, it was short and funny, deferential and touching. It was, of course, also word-perfect. 'He was a star, and I was very proud of him,' adds Purdie.

Torrance's motto for the week, his mantra if you like, would be *carpe diem* or 'seize the day'. It was one of those all-too-common Latin phrases that non-speakers of the language use, primarily because they remember it sounding so stirring when Robin Williams used it in *Dead Poets Society*. Before the day's play, he would have a 'wee word' with each and every player to get them in the right frame of mind. No stirring speeches (he hadn't written any). No William Wallace-style addresses. Just some 'gentle mollycoddling'. It was, he says, 'just a case of trying to get them to believe that they were part of the greatest team Europe's ever had.'

For Torrance, the composition and order of his pairings for the first day would be key. With so many variables to consider, he wisely decided to disregard anything his opposite number Curtis Strange might or might not do, concerning himself only with those elements of captaincy that he had some semblance of control over. 'I never once looked at their pairings in practice,' he reveals. 'I didn't care who was playing with whom and didn't care about what order they were playing in. I was determined to do it my way, right or wrong – it took all that second-guessing out of the equation.'

When Torrance had arrived at The Belfry, he had what he thought would be his starting line-up for each of the days already mapped out, with everyone, including the four rookies in the team, scheduled to play before Sunday's singles matches. 'But,' adds Torrance, 'it just didn't work out that way.'

With form (or lack of it) and niggling injuries affecting some of his team, Torrance opted to split the usually dependable duo of Darren Clarke and Lee Westwood, largely because of the latter's inconsistency. Instead he paired Clarke with the Dane Thomas Bjørn and teamed Westwood with the irrepressible Sergio García, even though the pair hadn't even practised together. The old guard of Colin Montgomerie and Bernhard Langer and the new pairing of Ireland's Padraig Harrington and the Swedish rookie Niclas Fasth, meanwhile, would make up the remainder of the first morning's pairings.

A year on from the terror attacks in the United States, security at The Belfry was still tighter than ever. With 1,000 volunteer stewards drafted in, forty-five armed police officers and sniffer dogs patrolling the perimeter of the course and extra security checks for each and every one of the 35,000 spectators each day, nothing was being left to chance. Ticket-holders had been forewarned about precisely what they were permitted to take into the course and banned items would include mobile phones, cameras, spiked shoes, picnic boxes and bags larger than eight inches square. You couldn't take alcohol into The Belfry either. Yes, you could drink yourself dizzy in one of the many bars on course, so long as the booze was sanctioned, sponsored or both.

So, one year and eighteen days after the 34th Ryder Cup should have started, it finally began at 8 a.m. on Friday, 27 September, with the fourballs match between Paul Azinger and Tiger Woods and Darren Clarke and Thomas Bjørn. As was his prerogative, Sam Torrance had changed the order of the day's play, beginning with fourballs rather than the foursomes favoured by Ben Crenshaw at Brookline. Leading off, surprisingly, was Strange's wild-card pick Azinger who switched his clubs at the last moment, swapping a long-iron for a 3-wood and then proceeded to loop a huge slice over the galleries lining the fairway, to an accompanying chorus of 'fore' from what seemed like most of the population of the West Midlands. His playing partner, the world number one Woods, didn't fare much better either. He ditched his tee shot in a fairway bunker.

It would be an opening salvo that set the tone for the morning's matches, Clarke and Bjørn recording a one-hole win over Azinger and Woods, Lee Westwood and Sergio García dismantling David Duval and Davis Love III by 4&3, and the old guard of Colin Montgomerie and Bernhard Langer fighting off an array of aches and pains to beat Jim Furyk and Scott Hoch by the same margin. Only the new partnership of Phil Mickelson and David Toms, the man who had snuck into the team by winning the PGA Championship in August 2001, spared the Americans' blushes, their one-hole win over Padraig Harrington and the rookie Niclas Fasth preventing a clean sweep for Sam Torrance's team.

The Americans rallied in the afternoon, pegging the Europeans back and taking the session 2½ points to 1½, but for Woods it would prove to be a doubly disappointing day. A one-hole defeat in the game against Clarke and Bjørn would be followed by a 2&1 defeat against Sergio García and Lee Westwood in the afternoon foursomes where he partnered Mark Calcavecchia. For Europe, however, it had been a good day, not merely because the world number one had failed to register even half a point but because they had secured an invaluable lead going into the weekend.

After the loss to Mickelson and Toms, though, Ireland's Padraig Harrington was concerned by his lack of form and had asked to be rested for Saturday's morning session, leaving Torrance with some unforeseen pack-shuffling. And as Harrington headed for the range for some emergency repair work with his coach, Torrance's father Bob, the European skipper rearranged his pairings for Saturday. The net result was that a tiring Thomas Bjørn was taken out of the afternoon fourballs and Paul McGinley, who had originally been earmarked as Harrington's partner in the morning, was drafted in to partner Darren Clarke. 'I wasn't meant to be playing,' explains McGinley. 'My role for the week was going to be playing with Harrington in the foursomes, and then I was going to play singles. So I was dropped in to play with Darren in the afternoon.'

The points would be shared in Saturday morning's foursomes. Once again, the new partnership of Lee Westwood and Sergio García proved to be inspired, beating Jim Furyk and Stewart Cink 2&1. For Westwood, it was a long overdue return to something approaching his best form. At Brookline, the 2000 European Order of Merit winner had been the fifth best player in the world. When the week started at The Belfry he had plummeted to 148th in the rankings. Here, at last, was a player finally finding his way back and at a time when his touch and his talent were needed more than ever. 'I was apprehensive going into the 2002 Ryder Cup because I was playing awful,' he explains. 'But I had a great partner in Sergio García. There wasn't so much pressure on me when I was playing fourballs with him and I putted really well that week which can hide a lot of things. Holing a few 30- or 40-footers can mask quite a few faults elsewhere.'

With the ever-dependable Montgomerie and Langer beating the Scotts, Verplank and Hoch, at the last, it had seemed like Europe might extend its lead going into the afternoon. But it wasn't to be. The rookie partnership of Phil Price and Pierre Fulke went down 2&1 to the USA's strongest pairing of Phil Mickelson and David Toms, while Tiger Woods, partnering Davis Love III, finally registered a point, trouncing Darren Clarke and Thomas Bjørn 4&3.

That afternoon, three of the four games would go to the final hole. The rookie Niclas Fasth and his compatriot, the woefully out-of-form Jesper Parnevik, raced into a lead against Mark Calcavecchia and David Duval, but fell away, eventually losing at the 18th green. Padraig Harrington, meanwhile, returned to help Colin Montgomerie to another win, this time taking Mickelson and Toms out by 2&1. In the third game, meanwhile, Tiger Woods got his second point of the day, as he and Davis Love III snuck past Westwood and García in a tight finish.

In the final game, Clarke and McGinley had been 2-down with four to play against Scott Hoch and Jim Furyk, but had clawed their way back to all-square with two holes remaining. A birdie for Hoch at the 17th, though, had scuppered any chance of an unlikely victory for the Irish pair. Needing to win the last hole to salvage a half point, it would be McGinley who holed his par putt to grab a share of the points and take the teams into Sunday level at eight points apiece. 'I went out and played great,' adds McGinley. 'It was a huge mental boost for me to win that last hole. Yes, it was half a match but on the last green on the last match on a Saturday afternoon? It was crucial.'

Having secured a vital half point for Europe, Clarke and McGinley returned to the team room to high-fives and back-slaps. With the scores tied at eight points apiece and morale in the European side high, Torrance took McGinley to one side and crushed him with a bear hug. 'McGinley,' he whispered, 'you showed so much balls today that I'm going to put you out at number twelve tomorrow because I know I can count on you.'

Flushed with pride and relishing the opportunity of being the man tasked with possibly bringing the cup home, McGinley returned to his room to take a shower, returning forty-five minutes later for the team dinner. As he entered the room, though, Thomas Bjørn wandered over. 'Have you seen the team for tomorrow?' he asked. Picking up his meal, McGinley told the Dane he hadn't, even though he knew he had already been given the anchor role. As he sat down to eat, McGinley picked up the printed team sheet for the singles and scrolled down the list. Now, however, the Irishman found himself at number nine and not twelve. 'So now I am a bit pissed off with Sam,' explains McGinley. 'Only an hour ago he was going to put me at number twelve because he figured I was the guy who was going to come through and now I'm disappointed.'

McGinley carried on eating, waiting for Sam Torrance to finish a press conference so he could talk to him. Half an hour later, Torrance walked in and McGinley asked for five minutes of his time. 'I want to speak to you too,' said Torrance, dragging the Irishman into a corner. 'Before you say it, I know what you are going to say.'

Confused, McGinley asked for an explanation. 'Look,' said Torrance, 'I didn't have time to tell you but before I put in the team I had a think about it and in the history of the Ryder Cup it has never come down to the twelfth match. It's always been between number eight and eleven. I decided to put you in the middle of that at number nine.'

Suddenly, once more, McGinley felt like the most important golfer on the planet. 'For a Ryder Cup rookie like me,' adds McGinley, 'it was just brilliant man-management.'

The following morning Europe's four Ryder Cup rookies breakfasted together. The Swede Niclas Fasth, out eighth, the Irishman Paul McGinley ninth, Fasth's compatriot, Pierre Fulke, tenth, and Wales's Phillip Price eleventh. A distinct nervousness had descended over the dining table as the realization dawned that one of the four men sat buttering their toast could well be the man to bring the Ryder Cup home. McGinley broke the silence. 'Boys,' he said, 'it's going to come down to us. We are going to have to step up. We need to do something, guys.'

For Phillip Price, it would be a pivotal day in his career. The unassuming pro from the tiny coal-mining town of Pontypridd, a few miles north of Cardiff, was standing in the Players' Lounge with his teammates when the draw was announced. Like most of the players, Price's form had suffered in the twelve months that had passed since the postponement. 'Normally, you make the team just before September, then you play the Ryder Cup so it's very likely you will have been playing well,' he explains, 'but my form had deteriorated, which made it a little strange.'

In the week before the Ryder Cup, Price had taken some time off and played a couple of rounds with friends at Newport's Celtic Manor course. Away from the spotlight and those commentators who still questioned his place in the side, he suddenly found his touch returning. By the time the Cup started – having practised at The Belfry and felt the reassuring arm of Sam Torrance wrapped round his shoulder – Price was ready for the fight. 'He [Torrance] was brilliant,' recalls Price. 'He made everyone feel really important. There were a couple of us who weren't playing very well and I actually didn't feel particularly wanted beforehand. But when I got there [to The Belfry] everybody felt very important – and Sam made me feel like that, made me feel like I had to step up.'

Price wasn't the only player struggling to find form. Since making the teams for the original event in 2001, eighteen of the twenty-four players had fallen back in the world rankings, with just six boasting a tournament win in 2002. Just Tiger Woods, Phil Mickelson, Jim Furyk and David Duval from the American side, and Sergio García and Padraig Harrington from the European, had been able to maintain or improve their place in the rankings. And, in the case of Jesper Parnevik, his game had all but gone to pieces. The Swede's suggestion that he only be played in the singles on Sunday would fall on deaf ears, however, such was Torrance's belief that he would rise to the occasion.

Torrance would adopt a bold approach to his singles strategy, loading the top half of the draw with his form players, those big-game, big-name players he knew he could trust to deliver. 'It was a relatively simple plan. I just thought that whoever was playing better should go out first and whoever was playing the worst should go out last. I could never envisage a scenario when it wasn't right. If we were behind then we could get back into it. If we were ahead then we could go further ahead,' he explains.

In contrast, US skipper Curtis Strange had banked on the competition ending in another tight finish and, as such, had given his experienced and higher-ranking players the task of bringing the trophy home, with Paul Azinger, Jim Furyk, Davis Love III, Phil Mickelson and Tiger Woods filling the final five places in the singles line-up.

But not all of his players were relishing the opportunity. Scott Hoch,

'I lost the Ryder Cup – it said so on the front page of the *Daily Telegraph*.' Europe's Costantino Rocca collapses at the final hole at The Belfry in 1993.

Nobody expected the USA to win at The Belfry in 1993, but under the guidance of captain Tom Watson they triumphed again, winning 15–13.

Ireland's Philip Walton becomes the unlikeliest of heroes, holing the putt that won the Ryder Cup for Europe at Oak Hill in 1995.

European celebrations at Valderrama in 1997. Somewhere under the champagne spray is the victorious captain, Seve Ballesteros.

For two days at Brookline in 1999, Mark James was the one of the most successful European Ryder Cup captains ever...

...then came the greatest comeback in the history of golf, culminating in Justin Leonard's monster putt against José-María Olazábal.

With his unexpected win over Phil Mickelson, Philip Price was one of the stars of Sam Torrance's team in the victory at The Belfry in 2002. Sergio García hugs the exultant Welshman.

The luck of the Irish – Darren Clarke, Paul McGinley and Padraig Harrington celebrate another memorable European victory, 2002.

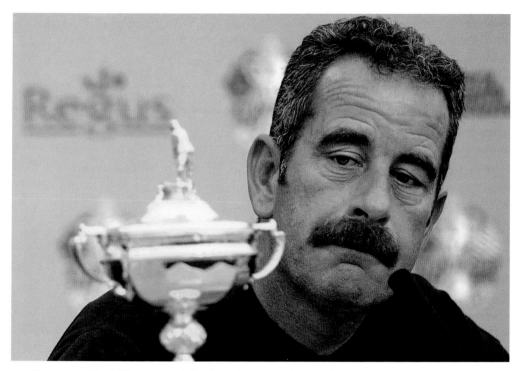

Sam Torrance at The Belfry, 2002: a Ryder Cup winner as a player and a captain.

At Oakland Hills in 2004, Tiger Woods and Phil Mickelson should have been one of the strongest pairings in Ryder Cup history. They weren't – and Mickelson's expression suggests he knows it.

While Colin Montgomerie never won a major, his record in the Ryder Cup, especially in the singles, was among the very best. Here he celebrates holing the putt that won the Ryder Cup in 2004.

At the end of an emotional week at the K Club in 2006, Europe's Darren Clarke wins against Zach Johnson in the singles and the floodgates open.

As players, Nick Faldo and Paul Azinger enjoyed some hard-fought and often antagonistic matches but it was Azinger's America that took the spoils at Valhalla in 2008.

Sunshine after the rain – it was left to Northern Ireland's Graeme McDowell to take Europe over the winning line at Celtic Manor in October 2010.

for instance. Straight-talking and never prone to enthusiasm, Hoch, forty-six, was the oldest player in the event, and if his pre-match confessions were anything to go by, not exactly looking forward to the challenge of a weekend in the West Midlands. 'If the weather is bad, I'll tell Curtis [Strange] to sit me down because the weather is not going to help me any,' he said. 'He can sit me out until singles, like the European team does. And if the weather is bad then, he can put me in the envelope. I'll come up lame.'

Slowly, the draw unfolded and Torrance's strategy of loading the top half of the draw with his strongest players seemed to have paid dividends. 'We looked at the singles draw and we just knew when we saw it this could not have come out any better for us,' recalls Mark James. Montgomerie drew Scott Hoch once more, García would play David Toms and Darren Clarke would take on the 2001 Open champion David Duval. Bernhard Langer, meanwhile, would face Hal Sutton while Padraig Harrington would battle it out against the veteran Mark Calcavecchia.

At the foot of the draw, meanwhile, sat Tiger Woods, drawn in a game against his Florida neighbour, the Swede Jesper Parnevik, while above him was the world number two, Phil Mickelson. His opponent? The world number 119, Phil Price. 'I thought, "Oh dear",' says Price. 'I did expect to go out in the middle, a little bit under cover.'

Mickelson, like Woods, was one of Curtis Strange's bankers. A right-hander who played left-handed, he made the game look easy and effortless. Brutally long off the tee but blessed with a short game that was among the best in the world, he had won twenty-one times on the PGA Tour. 'I didn't really mind who I was playing,' admits Price, 'But I was more concerned that I was going out in eleventh spot and I'm thinking, "Hang on, the Ryder Cup is coming down to me".'

Predictably, Colin Montgomerie, had once again proved that he was a different, altogether more resolute figure in the Ryder Cup than he was in major championships. Having played all four games over Friday and Saturday and conceded only half a point (and that thanks to a gutsy salvage operation by Phil Mickelson and David Toms in the Friday foursomes), he had led the charge yet again for Europe.

Relaxed, cheerful and thriving on the challenge, Montgomerie seemed a world away from the man who seemed to labour in the majors. On the range before his lead-off singles match against Scott Hoch, the Scot was loosening up, hitting balls towards the 100-yard marker. As he played, a voice piped up from the watching gallery. 'Why don't you hit the target?' said the man.

Ordinarily, such an interjection would have provoked a scowl at best and a full-on fit at worst, but here in the Ryder Cup, where everybody was on his side, Montgomerie simply invited the spectator down, handed him his wedge, and looked on, laughing, as the divots flew and passers-by ran for cover.

From that moment on Montgomerie was imperious. On the 1st tee, his opening drive flew fully 50 yards past that of his opponent and, in the flash of that 3-wood, the game was as good as over. Fourteen holes and a little over two and a half hours later, Montgomerie had triumphed 5&4 and given Europe the perfect start to the vital singles games. The massacre over, Scott Hoch congratulated his opponent on what was a masterful showing. He even smiled.

Buoyed by Montgomerie's example, the other European team members also rose to the occasion. The Irishman Padraig Harrington crushed the 1989 Open champion Mark Calcavecchia by 5&4, Bernhard Langer defeated Hal Sutton 4&3 to remain undefeated all week, and Thomas Bjørn accounted for Stewart Cink 2&1. With Darren Clarke gaining a half point against David Duval, only Sergio García from Torrance's bankers came up short, falling to David Toms at the last hole.

At the Price–Mickelson rubber, meanwhile, the game had turned in the space of three crucial holes. All-square, Price had taken the 5th hole, while at the 6th, the Welshman had, improbably, doubled his lead. Off the tee, Mickelson had found the safety of the fairway while Price tugged his tee shot left, perilously close to the water, leaving him with an awkward, ungainly stance for his second shot. Sensing an opportunity, Mickelson compounded Price's misery, firing a short iron in to three feet, maybe even less, and setting up what seemed a nailed-on birdie.

The shot that followed from Price, though, was scarcely believable. With the ball over the hazard line, not only was Price unable to ground his club at address, but his ball was well above the level of his feet, forcing him to grip well down the club in a bid to get any kind of shot away. But with his head down and a swish of an 8-iron, his ball sailed high over the water, landing softly on the green and rolling to within a foot of his opponent's. And while Price rolled in his putt for an unlikely three, Mickelson missed his, pushing it three feet past. Clearly rattled, the San Diegan then lost the 7th to a par from Price and the Welshman knew the match was his to lose. 'I was like a dog with a bone,' he recalls. 'I had gone 3-up and all of a sudden I had something to cling on to.'

At the 16th, Price was still two holes to the good and closing in on an entirely unexpected victory. When both men found the green, Price was confronted with a snaking 25-foot downhiller from near the edge of the green. It was a vicious putt from a position that the Welshman could easily find himself three-putting from. With Mickelson maybe five feet closer to the pin and unlikely to make anything worse than a four, Price knew it was imperative to put it close. He gathered himself and set the ball on its way, meandering down the hill. Moments later it dropped, and the roar could have been heard back in Ponty. Price, meanwhile, was violently pumping his fist, his slender face contorted by a combination of surprise and unbridled joy. 'I was rolling it down there and in it went,' he says. 'All of a sudden I started to get a little carried away I think. Looking back I should probably have kept my composure a little more… I lost control, I suppose.'

He has a point. Mickelson, after all, still had a putt to halve the hole and take it to the 17th. Eventually, the bedlam subsided long enough for the San Diegan to make his shot but his putt fell away on the low side of the hole. Now, Pontypridd's Man of the Year 1994 had something else, something much more significant, to shout about. 'It was a fantastic day,' he reflects. 'The momentum was with us from the first game. I think that made it a lot easier for us four rookies at the end, because the atmosphere we were going out in was a good one. I think that really made a difference.'

With Europe closing in on victory, Torrance received word on his walkie-talkie of Price's improbable triumph. Now, as his team moved ever closer to regaining the Ryder Cup, the tears were once more welling in his eyes. On the 18th green, the Swedish rookie Niclas Fasth was 1-up on the veteran Paul Azinger and with his opponent in the greenside bunker, it appeared as though the Swedish rookie was destined to win the cup for Europe. But with The Belfry galleries poised to erupt, Azinger, remarkably, flipped his ball out of the sand, rolling it straight into the hole for a three, prompting a series of adrenaline-fuelled but largely unsuccessful high-fives with his caddie and a rare moment of joy for the American contingent in the crowd.

Moments earlier, Fasth had stood over his putt expecting to have two putts to win the Ryder Cup for Europe. Now he faced a 30-footer to win it, or, as it would transpire, a two-putt to halve the match and take his team to the brink of victory. It was as Sam Torrance concedes, a 'welcome back to reality'.

In the game behind, Paul McGinley was oblivious to Azinger's miraculous recovery. Indeed, he would find out only at 11 o'clock that evening, when the topic cropped up over a few beers in the team room. His opponent, Jim Furyk, found the same bit of sand with his approach as Azinger, while McGinley found the rough, chipping his third shot on to the green and leaving himself with an unappetizing ten-footer for his four. Like his teammate ten minutes earlier, Furyk produced another exquisite bunker shot, only failing to replicate Azinger's masterstroke by a matter of inches and causing respiratory problems amongst the watching European players.

Now, exactly three hours after Colin Montgomerie had secured Europe's first point of the day, McGinley had a putt to halve his match and win the Ryder Cup. 'When you are so involved you get so caught up in what you're doing… but you don't go there – you don't go into that dark place of thinking about the huge amount of pressure on you,' explains the Irishman. 'Of course I was nervous but I was also very excited too – it was a real rush of adrenalin.'

If McGinley was nervous he certainly didn't look it. After a consultation with his caddie J. P. Fitzgerald, during which the bagman reminded him of a similar putt he had faced on the green some two years before at the Benson and Hedges International, McGinley settled over his ball, aiming for the left lip.

Silence. Deathly, uncomfortable silence. McGinley pulled back his putter and started the ball rolling. The closer it got to its target, the louder the volume became. When it finally dropped into the hole, it was as though another earthquake had shaken the West Midlands. As McGinley star-jumped his way across the green, on came the rest of the European team, not to mention their wives, the support staff, the caddies and some people who patently shouldn't have been there. Lee Westwood kissed Sam Torrance, the captain cried (again) and Sergio García leapt around like a kid with a sugar rush. Meanwhile, a couple of hundred yards down the 18th fairway sat Curtis Strange, resting on the steering wheel of his golf cart, with just a walkie-talkie and his thoughts for company.

Back at greenside at the final hole, and with the remaining two games halved, the hero of the hour, Paul McGinley, had been commandeered by the BBC for an interview. As McGinley struggled to make himself heard above the din, he saw his close friend and teammate Padraig Harrington coming towards him, backed up by several European team reinforcements, all intent on mischief. Moments later, the Irishman had been hoisted into the air and was heading for a celebratory dip in the lake by the 18th green. 'I knew exactly where I was going,' he recalls. '[But] all I could think of was Feherty's ball-marker… I was trying to get my hand in my pocket to make sure this ball-marker was going to be secure.' Powerless to prevent the inevitable, McGinley took the safer option and dived in himself, emerging from the water with an Irish tricolour draped over his shoulders and still with that seemingly immovable grin on his face.

For Torrance, it would be another memory to cherish. Seventeen years after his putt had won the Ryder Cup for Europe, he had returned to the same course and watched as Paul McGinley, on the very same hole, had completed his own personal Ryder Cup story. Yes, he was wider around the waist and greyer round the temples but the moustache was just as magnificent and his heart was as proud and as passionate as ever. Typically, Torrance would downplay his role in the victory, saying, 'I just led them to water and they drank copiously.'

After a quick change and several tots of whisky, Torrance made his way to the closing ceremony and, with David Purdie's advice reverberating in his dizzy head, delivered another word-perfect speech, praising Curtis Strange and his team for the way in which they played the match and thanking his family, friends and his 13th man, The Belfry crowd. The losers' speech he had written and rehearsed so many, many times would, to his eternal delight, remain unread. 'I thought Curtis Strange and Sam Torrance were fantastic because they weren't only leaders on the course they were leaders off the course,' reflects the PGA's Sandy Jones. 'They kind of laid out how the matches were to be played in the true spirit of the game, both very feisty competitors themselves but equally they understood how important the integrity of the game was. We had lost Payne Stewart not months after, weeks after [Brookline] and then with 9/11 too. I think all those things conspired together. It was almost as though all these things happened and it was as if someone was saying that that is not how it is meant to be, so maybe you should get your act together.'

At the party that night in the main bar at The Belfry, the celebrations continued apace with Lee Westwood acting as the MC for the evening, announcing each and every member of the European team, all to a rousing reception. When he reached Phillip Price, the Welshman was already at his side, prodding him in the side and reminding him to

'Tell 'em who I beat, tell 'em who I beat.' And, as the night wore on, the booze flowed and the speeches became ever more slurred, David Feherty approached Paul McGinley. 'I suppose my ball-marker's at the bottom of the lake, is it?' he asked.

Smiling, Paul McGinley reached into his pocket and handed it back.

A Ten-Gallon Trouncing

OAKLAND HILLS, BLOOMFIELD, MICHIGAN

17–19 September 2004

IT had been a taxing time for the Ryder Cup. Since its heady trans-formation from anachronistic, two-bit tournament to global sports phenomenon, everything had grown – and not just the size of the driver heads or the players' egos. The galleries, the viewing figures, the ticket prices – everything was bigger, everything was, for the most part, better. Of course, the net result of such staggering, seemingly unhindered growth was that the competition itself was now more lucrative than anyone could ever have envisaged back in the life-support-machine days of the 1970s. Inevitably, as the revenues had risen, so too had the murmuring about who was getting what and, more pertinently, why.

The Ryder Cup, of course, was central to the plans of Sandy Jones and the British PGA but also to the European Tour, which felt that as it was its players who were the (unpaid) stars of the show, they should be better recognized and/or remunerated for their services. 'The rela-tionship between the two [the PGA and the European Tour] was a bit fraught because we had kind of lost our way,' explains Sandy Jones. 'But our role within the match was a differing one. We weren't really managing the players any longer and I had a view that the players belonged to the Tour, and we were borrowing them for the week.

I thought the Tour needed to have a better position within the Ryder Cup and I set about thinking that through at the time and eventually talked to Ken Schofield about the need to change the structure of the Ryder Cup, not to the disadvantage of the PGA but to the advantage of the Tour.'

With four months to go to the 35th Ryder Cup matches at Oakland Hills, the PGA, the European Tour and the PGAs of Europe convened for a meeting in Milan to discuss the way forward for the Ryder Cup. On the face of it, the deal that came out of the summit looked as though the PGA of Britain had surrendered a lot, perhaps too much, of the control they had. Previously, the European Tour and the British PGA had split the profits down the middle but now the European Tour would receive 60 per cent of all profits, with 20 per cent going to the PGA of Britain and the remaining 20 per cent to the PGAs of Europe. The British PGA, however, would retain the ownership of the Ryder Cup trophy, receiving a licence fee against it, thereby providing the organization with a guaranteed base financial figure every two years, before any profits had been made and distributed.

The agreement, which saw the formation of Ryder Cup Europe LLC, also saw the creation of a new charity, the Ryder Cup Development Trust, meaning that from now on a portion of all net profits would be given over to developing the game at grassroots level across the continent, and putting money back into the member clubs, many of which had helped the Ryder Cup players as they started out in golf. 'My own personal view was that the PGA had been given the trophy by Sam Ryder – and we still own the trophy,' says Jones. 'A lot of our members will always accuse me of selling our crown jewels but that's why financially we do better out of the event today, because I believed we could draw a line where we were and grow the match so that we were still benefiting. That is how we have been able to invest in our educational programme and subsequently the Tour has benefited from better players across Europe.'

While it appeared as though the British PGA had made some fairly drastic concessions, it was a politic move by Sandy Jones, not least because his organization had retained the ownership of the trophy. Moreover, the fact that he now had a guaranteed income, dedicated solely to grassroots golf, meant he and the PGA were now fulfilling their very *raison d'être* in developing and promoting golf in the wider community. 'My belief was that the players needed to be recognized more for what they gave back to the game for playing that match and that is where the Ryder Cup Trust came up,' adds Jones. 'Our job is to make sure that the success of the Ryder Cup is then taken back into the game – that's not for the Tour to do.'

As the vexatious issue of money occupied the minds of the administrators, the thoughts of the new captain, Bernhard Langer, turned towards how he might erase the sole blot on his Ryder Cup record – that missed six-foot putt, courtesy of a spike mark, at the last hole at Kiawah Island in 1991. Only the second captain from continental Europe, Langer couldn't have been more different from the first, Seve Ballesteros. While the Spaniard had led his team with passion, flair and an inherent, unshakeable belief that he was always right, Langer was quiet, considered and extremely thorough: a man for whom attention to detail was just as vital as the rousing speech delivered as he sent his troops off into battle. Of course, he also had the kind of track record in the game that nobody could argue with. You want medals? Try forty-two European Tour titles, ten Ryder Cups, two Green Jackets and a place in the World Golf Hall of Fame for size. 'Every player had such enormous respect for Bernhard Langer and everybody still does,' explains Bernard Gallacher. 'He is such a strong figure, a dominant figure. That's why he's enjoyed such longevity in the game.'

Hal Sutton, meanwhile, was already tiring of fielding questions about the last time the Ryder Cup had been held in the USA, at Brookline in 1999, when the behaviour of some tired and emotional fans had been exacerbated by an extraordinary circumstance in which the participants, players and spectators, had all been engulfed, Sutton included. 'You've all been kind of like a bad marriage partner,' said Sutton, a man who had been through three divorces. 'We've apologized for five years for what happened in 1999. So y'all need to forget about it. I've told our players to be gentlemen and to be themselves. I can't be concerned or try to control everybody in the world.'

Five years earlier, captain Ben Crenshaw had sought help in his hour of need, calling in George W. Bush to talk to his team. Enlisting the help of the future President was undeniably impressive, but Sutton trumped his predecessor by getting the greatest basketball player of all time, Michael Jordan, to come and talk to the team at their team dinner on the Monday night before the start of the competition. Now 41 and having finally retired from the NBA just a year earlier, Jordan had long been a golf obsessive, playing off a handicap irritatingly close to scratch and making a lot of new friends in the sport, Tiger Woods included, along the way. For Sutton, Jordan's cameo appearance was the perfect fillip for his star player, whose Ryder Cup record was now being called into question. 'I feel strongly that Tiger Woods is ready,' said Sutton. 'I think y'all might see some of Tiger's greatest golf this week, so buckle your chinstraps.'

For the first time since 1981, Europe would field a side without a single major winner in it and where once a Faldo or a Ballesteros, a Lyle or an Olazábal, would have carried the team, now the responsibility fell to the likes of Westwood, García, Clarke, Harrington and the captain's pick, Colin Montgomerie. Getting the call-up from Langer had been a fillip for Colin Montgomerie. While he had qualified with ease for the previous six Ryder Cups, the Scot's form had nosedived in 2004, leaving him at just 19th in the world points list and 16th in the European list in qualification. That said, he had his excuses, not least a separation from his wife that would end in a divorce costing him a reported £8 million. When the author interviewed him that year, though, he seemed relaxed and content, despite his dip in form, and having lost a lot of weight he was also happy with the way he was looking. 'Nothing,' he told me, 'tastes as good as slim feels.'

For all his achievements in the game it was still a mystery why

Montgomerie had never won a major title. Sure, he had come close, losing in two US Open play-offs to Ernie Els in 1994 and 1997, and in another to Steve Elkington at the PGA Championship in 1995, but for whatever reason – fate, (mis)fortune, nerve – he had failed to finish the job. But in a game where, rightly or wrongly, the four major championships were deemed more worthy than any other, the fact that Montgomerie, winner of seven consecutive Order of Merit titles and the leading money-winner in the history of the European Tour, hadn't won one was a constant source of irritation, primarily because at every press conference he ever gave the issue invariably came up. That he was a stronger player in the Ryder Cup, however, was undeniable. That it had become his own major was obvious.

Situated in the suburbs of the motor city, Detroit, Oakland Hills had been awarded the 2003 Ryder Cup in October 1998, and boasted a long, illustrious record of hosting major championships, dating back to 1924 when Bobby Jones was surprisingly beaten by Cyril Walker in the US Open. Later, in 1951, Ben Hogan had inadvertently presented the course with its nickname when he took his third US Open Championship, saying, 'I'm glad I brought this course – this monster – to its knees.'

Bernhard Langer would take time and trouble acquainting himself with the 'monster'. Having played under four captains, each of them winners, the forty-seven-year-old had seen how each man had brought something new, something different to the captaincy. Langer, though, would go way beyond anything that had been done before. Meticulous and methodical, there was no facet of the job he didn't explore. He spent time researching the psychological impact of the colours the team should wear, noting which ones made players feel comfortable and confident. He would make a point of speaking to each of his players on a one-to-one basis every day, particularly the ones who found themselves sidelined for a session or two. He even selected the wine for the team meals and the cigars for after it too. 'Langer was probably the best of our captains in every aspect,' says the PGA's Sandy

Jones. 'He was totally professional, there was nothing left to chance. Everything was perfect in that Germanic sort of way.'

Bruce Critchley, the Sky Sports commentator, agrees. 'Bernhard Langer had this tremendous attention to detail [and] the realization that captaincy is a tremendous exercise in organization,' he explains. 'It is this business of creating a team, of taking yourself out of it and making them, this unit, this nebulous unit, the most important thing. It is very difficult.'

During practice, Langer would be a constant source of advice for his players, not in the same manic manner that Seve Ballesteros was at Valderrama, but more considered, more convivial. At each of the par-3 holes, he would tell them which club to play and where to hit it, before then justifying why he had made the suggestion. 'He's gone through the whole thing, explaining the shape and everything about it on every par-3 I've played this week in the foursomes and the fourball,' said Padraig Harrington. 'He's been right there, describing exactly what was needed.' It was testament to the respect his players had for him that Langer, like Ballesteros, could tell a player in the top ten of the world rankings how to hit a golf shot, without finding an 8-iron wrapped around his neck.

That week, the word in the media centre was that one of Hal Sutton's plans was to pair the two players that pretty much everyone in the game assumed were incompatible. Between them, Tiger Woods and Phil Mickelson had won sixty-three PGA Tour titles and, having won the Green Jacket at Augusta in April, Mickelson had also finally shed the tag of the best player to never win a major, taking one of the big four titles after forty-two attempts as a professional. But it wasn't all going swimmingly for the left-hander. In a much-publicized change of equipment supplier, triggered by his early release from his contract with Titleist, he had signed for rivals Callaway Golf and when he reached the Ryder Cup he was still adjusting to his new clubs. Hal Sutton would then compound Mickelson's problems by insisting he play with Woods's Nike ball, rather than his own, the net result being that the left-hander would now be hitting an unfamiliar ball with unfamiliar clubs, alongside a partner for whom he cared little.

It didn't help that Woods, too, had had an indifferent season, at least by his own cosmic standards. Without a major win, he had failed to win any strokeplay event and had fallen to fourth in the PGA Tour money list as he tinkered with his swing and switched coaches from Butch Harmon to Hank Haney. He had even been overtaken at the top of the world rankings by the Fijian Vijay Singh, who, having won the PGA Championship, followed it up with a win at the Deutsche Bank Championship in Norton, Massachusetts, and in doing so ended Woods's run of 264 consecutive weeks as the world number one.

Though Phil Mickelson had never held the number one position in the world rankings, he had long been seen as the only real challenger to the hegemony of Woods, and this despite the rise of Singh. The rivalry between Mickelson and Woods had been built up largely by the media, and while there was undoubtedly a certain antipathy between the pair, it was hardly the simmering hatred that the press clearly longed it to be. Hal Sutton, though, was determined to make the biggest, quickest impact he could, and threw the duo together, putting them out first in the opening morning's fourballs. 'I felt like history needed it. I felt like the fans needed it,' Sutton said at the opening ceremonies. 'And most of all, I felt like Phil Mickelson and Tiger Woods needed it.' When he was then asked if it was a risky strategy, Sutton was adamant that the pair would put aside whatever differences they had for the benefit of their team and their country. 'There's a risk every day in life,' Sutton said, losing patience with anyone who didn't see his side. 'You cross the street and it's a risk; someone may run over you. This is a risk Hal Sutton is taking. I'm not afraid of this risk. And I challenged them not to be afraid of this risk.'

Langer's strategy, however, was one based less on risk and hunches and more on deliberation and inclusion. One of his many innovations that week would be to send each of his players a card asking them to write down the names of one or two teammates whom they would like to play with, as well as the names of those teammates whom they would rather not pair up with, all in the strictest confidence. With the replies all in, Langer could then assemble his partnerships without having to waste any time on more speculative pairings that might or might not gel.

Instead, Europe, for the most part, would field four pairings that seemed to be composed of natural bedfellows, and not to have been thrown together in hope or for the sake of headlines. There was the Celtic duo of Montgomerie and Harrington, Darren Clarke and his fellow cigar aficionado and *bon viveur* Miguel Ángel Jiménez, the successful 2002 pairing of Westwood and García and the new but dependable partnership of Paul McGinley and the debutant Luke Donald. 'There's no stars, and there are no rookies as such,' he said, echoing Sam Torrance's philosophy of 2002. 'There are twelve fantastic players and I'm here to serve them and lead them and guide them in any way possible.'

Rarely has such a strategy paid such huge dividends for the captain. That morning, Europe went ahead in all four games within the first hour and never looked back. Indeed, the US team would never lead during any of the opening session's games and it was only a seven-foot putt from Chris Riley at the last hole that salvaged something for the home side, as he and Stewart Cink halved with Paul McGinley and the captain's pick Luke Donald.

Matters got worse for the US team in the afternoon foursomes. In a session where Colin Montgomerie set a new European Ryder Cup record for consecutive games played – twenty-nine – that dated back to the distant second-day fourballs at Kiawah Island in 1991, Hal Sutton's decision to pair Woods and Mickelson reached its nadir in their game against Darren Clarke and Lee Westwood. By the 18th tee, the game was all-square, the Americans having won the par-3 17th with a par. Opting for the safety of a 3-wood, Mickelson then hit a tee shot so errant, so scandalously wild, that it veered 80 yards off line and ended up deep in the trees, hitting the perimeter fence and giving Woods no shot whatsoever. What started out as the Dream Team was fast turning into Laurel and Hardy, with Mickelson leaving Woods to deal with another fine mess.

While the shot was indisputably poor, the look on Woods's face was priceless. As he stared into the distance he resembled a tired housewife who, having arrived at the airport at the start of the annual vacation, discovered that her husband had gone and left the passports at home. Part-resignation, part-fury, it would be the final conclusive proof that Hal Sutton's hunch to pair the world's best two players was as wide of the mark as Mickelson's tee shot.

Forced to take a penalty drop, the best Woods and Mickelson could muster on the hole would be a double bogey, leaving Clarke and Westwood to take the hole and the match 1-up. There is a story, doubtless apocryphal, that as Woods watched their ball disappear into the woods and dance with the out of bounds, he sighed, prompting Mickelson to tell him, 'If you're the number one player in the world, you can just get it fucking out of there.' The truth was, of course, that Vijay Singh was now the number one player in the world, and being Fijian, was not eligible for the Ryder Cup. Besides, even Singh couldn't have extricated the ball from the dark place where Mickelson had left it.

Standing in the background with a Stetson on his head and an ever more perplexed expression spreading across his face, Sutton looked like an extra from *The High Chaparral* whose horse had just bolted leaving him stranded at the pass. Others said he looked more like Fred Flintstone's little friend, Barney Rubble. 'Hal Sutton just didn't grasp it as a captain,' suggests the PGA's Sandy Jones. 'He had that Texan bit, firing, let's go and shoot these guys, shock and awe… but he just didn't grasp it.'

The only bright spot on an otherwise gloomy horizon for Sutton was the point gleaned by Chris DiMarco and one of his captain's picks, Jay Haas, over Miguel Ángel Jiménez and Thomas Levet. The choice of Haas as a captain's pick had been another of Sutton's more curious decisions.

It had been nine years since Haas had handed Philip Walton the point that had given Europe the victory at Oak Hill and, as he told the press in August, that game had played on his mind ever since. 'I still see the replays of that moment when I'm sitting at home flicking through the sports channels. And every time I just turn it off because I don't want to see it,' he said. 'It's not just one guy who loses the Ryder Cup but you can't help thinking it's your fault, especially if it turns out to be your match that decides it.'

Haas was, at fifty years of age, the second oldest Ryder Cup competitor in history (after Raymond Floyd). But he was still seen, improbably, as a better, safer bet for the team than the new Open champion and PGA Tour rookie of the year Todd Hamilton and the revitalized John Daly. Despite a catalogue of incidents and accidents on and off the course and with the revolving door that was his marriage spinning off its hinges, Daly had returned to the PGA Tour winners' circle at the Buick Invitational in February.

Haas and DiMarco's point, however, would do little to halt the unstoppable tide of European success. Ahead by 6½ points to 1½, the spectacular failure not just of Woods and Mickelson but pretty much every other pairing had left Hal Sutton with no choice but to juggle his line-up for Saturday. It seemed laughable, but with two full days and four sessions of golf still to play, it already seemed like a last throw of the dice. Conversely, and with an unprecedented advantage, Bernhard Langer could have been forgiven for following Mark James's line of thinking at Brookline in 1999 and keeping things the way they were in a bid to snuff out any chance of the opposition mounting a comeback. But as he had said all along, the players who had missed out on day one – Paul Casey, David Howell and Ian Poulter – all came in on day two.

Hal Sutton awoke on Saturday to the kind of headlines he didn't want to see. 'Euro Thrash' and 'Woe is US' yelled the papers. The previous evening, sensing the media onslaught to come, Sutton had conceded that his much-vaunted Woods–Mickelson experiment had failed. He opted to change his pairings for the Saturday session, swapping Mickelson for Chris Riley, the young Californian. Riley had known Tiger Woods from their time in junior golf where they had often teamed up to play together. On Friday evening, when Sutton had informed the thirty-year-old former Walker Cup player that he was now going to play with Woods, Riley had, by his own admission, 'free-wheeled' out of the team room, so excited was he to be playing with the world's best golfer.

Initially, the new duo seemed to make a difference, an impressive 4&3 win over Darren Clarke and Ian Poulter helping to set up a 2½–1½ morning fourballs session win for the US, and priming the galleries for what appeared to be the beginning of another US comeback. And yet it could have been even better for the US. By sending out two rookies together, Paul Casey and David Howell, Langer had, by common consent, made his first real gamble of the match. With two holes to go of Casey's and Howell's game against Jim Furyk and Chad Campbell, it looked as though it was destined to backfire. Remarkably, at the 203-yard 17th, Howell hit his tee shot to six feet and holed the birdie putt to square the match going down the last, whereupon Casey returned the favour and, as the only player to par the 494-yard par-4 hole, gave Europe another priceless point.

Casey's and Howell's point had not only pricked the bubble of a possible US comeback but left one player, Chris Riley, feeling flatter and more fatigued than most. Despite his win with Woods, the San Diegan had decided to sit out the afternoon session, citing tiredness and an unfamiliarity with the alternate shot format for his decision. 'To tell you the truth, I'm really tired,' he said. 'This is my first time at the Ryder Cup and I'm pretty drained right now. So I told him [Sutton] I wasn't ready to go and, you know, look at our US team, we have tons of guys that will step up and play. I just told him that if I could, could I sit down this afternoon?'

Given that he was still only thirty years old, had played just two rounds of golf in two days, and was already the US team's most

successful player, remaining undefeated to this point, it was a perplexing decision by Riley. This was a rare opportunity for any professional
golfer and, besides, men much older than Riley, like Davis Love and
Colin Montgomerie, were playing two rounds a day despite being well
into their forties, eager to do whatever was asked of them. A stronger
captain might simply have thrown Riley under a cold shower, given
him a cup of coffee and kicked his backside back out on to the golf
course. Instead, Sutton acceded to Riley's request, teaming Tiger Woods
with Davis Love for the afternoon foursomes, and watching as Woods
and his third partner in two days went down 4&3 to the Irish pairing
of Paul McGinley and Padraig Harrington.

Riley's reluctance seemed to personify a wider unease in the
American team, and a sense that they had already lost was inescap-
able. It looked for all the world as if the hideous failure of their two
best players had been a hammer blow to their collective solar plexus,
a sure sign that if the might of Woods and Mickelson couldn't see them
through, what chance – and point – was there in the rest of the tie.
That afternoon, they floundered again as Europe twisted the knife still
further, winning the session at a canter, 3–1, to leave Langer's team
needing just 3½ points from the 12 on offer on Sunday to take the
Ryder Cup back across the Atlantic. That the US team had failed to
click was clear to even the most casual observer. It was also clear – and
far more telling – that neither the US team nor its captain had any kind
of answer to their malaise.

At Brookline in 1999, Ben Crenshaw's team had faced a four-point
deficit on the final day, and through some inspirational – and presidential – team talks and, though nobody tends to mention it, some
frankly astonishingly amazing golf, clawed their way back into the
game before going on to win. Five years on and Hal Sutton's team were
a further point in arrears and with no Commander-in-Chief on hand
to help out.

All Sutton could do was summon the spirit of Brookline and
hope, perhaps pray, that his team could respond. With no room for

manoeuvre, he had little choice but to send his strongest players out first. As Woods, Mickelson, Love and Furyk all surged into leads, there was a brief surge of enthusiasm from the Detroit crowd.

Come the singles, Woods was a markedly different player from the one who had skulked and scowled his way through the fourballs and foursomes. With only himself to worry about, he did what he always did week in week out on the PGA Tour: he set about grinding his opponent, Paul Casey, down, culminating in a 3&2 victory. Yet Woods's point would prove to be a false dawn for the US. As the initial momentum faded, the scoreboard soon turned blue as Phil Mickelson surrendered an early 2-hole lead to lose 3&2 to Sergio García, while Davis Love III was pegged back by Darren Clarke, the Ulsterman over-turning a two-hole deficit with three to play to snatch a half point. Only the 2003 US Open champion Jim Furyk, recently returned from wrist surgery, kept the European charge at bay, battering the debutant David Howell 6&4. When Lee Westwood defeated Kenny Perry at the last, taking Europe to the brink of victory, all eyes turned to the remaining matches out on the golf course, eager to see which European would become the hero of the hour.

For once, Colin Montgomerie hadn't been thrust forward in the singles or been asked to shoulder the responsibility of seeing his team home at the business end of the list. No, this time he had been secreted in the middle order, where the makeweights and minor players were often to be found. It was as though Bernhard Langer, after all his planning, preparation and attention to detail, knew that it would come down to one of the middle-order games and knowing what it meant to him, put Montgomerie, his old Ryder Cup playing partner, in precisely the position where he thought the match would be decided.

Requiring a par at the last to secure a one-hole win over David Toms, Montgomerie left himself with a four-foot putt to win his game – and the Ryder Cup. When the putt dropped – it had no choice – Montgomerie simply dropped his belly putter on the green and turned to his teammates to begin the celebrations. It may not have been a major but Montgomerie's face radiated sheer elation. This was his arena, his event, and nobody could deny him another precious Ryder Cup memory, even if there was still some debate as to whether he had actually holed the winning putt. Back at the 15th hole, Ian Poulter had just holed a bride putt moments earlier to go three up – and dormie – against Chris Riley, thereby securing a half point at the very least and taking Europe, theoretically, to 14½ points. 'Did I hole the winning putt in the 2004 Ryder Cup and not Monty? Well, yes and no,' says Ian Poulter. 'I'd holed a putt to secure a half point but my game wasn't actually finished so there's two ways of looking at it. But you know, it doesn't really matter who holes the winning putt. It's a team event. It's not about individuals.'

With the win assured, Europe's players could have been forgiven for easing up. Instead, those players, like Ian Poulter and Thomas Levet, who had yet to contribute any points all week, helped turn another European triumph into a record-breaking victory, both recording wins, against Chris Riley and Fred Funk respectively. The final scoreline – 18½–9½ – equalled the biggest-ever win in the competition achieved twenty-three years earlier, when Nicklaus, Watson, Trevino, Floyd *et al.* had dissected the European team amid the quagmire of Walton Heath.

The scenes around the final green resembled an end-of-season pitch invasion at a football match, as the European players found themselves engulfed by the fans: they even sang 'You'll Never Walk Alone'. As Langer got sucked into the throng, his normally implacable exterior gave way to something approaching emotion. 'I always thought we'd win it but I wanted to win big. I'm so proud of all the guys. I've enjoyed every single minute of it,' he said. 'It's been awesome.'

Tears in Heaven

IF you've ever visited Straffan you'll know that there's very little there. You may well have even passed through it, oblivious to its charms. While it's a picturesque, well-heeled, blink-and-you'll-miss-it village with a shop, a petrol station, a church and a pub (obviously), it's not exactly a tourist mecca. That said, it has got a rather nice five-star hotel with a couple of tidy golf courses tagged on, both designed by no less a legend than Arnold Palmer.

The Kildare Hotel and Golf Club – the K Club – was just half an hour west of Dublin if you put your foot down and the Garda weren't looking. Built in the 1830s, it was a majestic, magnificent house set in a 550-acre estate and, with the River Liffey meandering through the woods, boasted the kind of sumptuous elegance rarely seen outside of Merchant Ivory films. As a young boy, Michael Smurfit used to climb over the perimeter wall of Straffan House and help himself to apples from the orchard. Decades later, as the head of the paper and packaging company Jefferson Smurfit and one of the richest men in the Republic of Ireland, Smurfit would return to Straffan and buy the house, transforming it from stately home to luxury hotel and resort and in 1991, the new K Club opened for business.

Michael Smurfit, or Dr Michael Smurfit, as he preferred to be known, not because he'd studied long and hard for his doctorate but because he had been given an honorary one and liked the sound of it, was, like Jimmy Patiño at Valderrama, a millionaire on a mission. Central to his plans for the K Club was the creation of two golf courses, and he retained Arnold Palmer to help turn his dreams into reality. Smurfit was determined to make the venue capable of hosting not just a European Tour event but, more importantly, the Ryder Cup itself.

Within four years of the new resort opening, Smurfit had fulfilled the first stage of his golfing masterplan, as the European Open relocated to the K Club, becoming the Smurfit European Open. The Ryder Cup, however, would prove problematic. While the European Open had grown into one of the most lucrative and best-attended pit-stops on the Tour, now the K Club had to go up against some of the most renowned golf courses in Ireland to win the right to stage the 2006 Ryder Cup. There was the Irish Open venue at Druids Glen, the Jack Nicklaus-designed Mount Juliet in Kilkenny and the fabled links at Portmarnock just north of Dublin.

Smurfit's undoubted passion, however, not to mention the estimated £40 million investment he had made in the resort, would tip the balance in favour of the K Club. In mid-January 1999, a little over a decade since his pet project began in earnest, the Kildare Hotel and Golf Club was awarded the 36th Ryder Cup matches. Finally, Smurfit's dream was realized. Finally, the high-flier's paradise on the banks of the Liffey was going to take centre-stage in the biggest golfing event in the world.

Fast forward seven and a half years and the Irish singer Van Morrison is standing on the stage at Dublin's Citywest Hotel singing 'Brown-Eyed Girl' to 1400 people all done up to the nines for the Ryder Cup Gala Dinner. Amid the VIPs and the great and the good of Irish life, though, somebody had forgotten to reserve a table for Michael Smurfit, which, given he'd spent £40 million on the Ryder Cup, was the very least he may have expected.

For the European captain Ian Woosnam, the extracurricular events couldn't have ended soon enough, not least because he didn't look too good in a tux. Like Sam Torrance four years earlier, the Welshman wasn't one for public speaking or the small talk of formal functions. It was simply a case of grinning and bearing it until the real business of the week got underway.

Woosnam had been appointed on his 47th birthday when, for the first time, the Ryder Cup committee had also announced Nick Faldo as captain for the 2008 event at Valhalla, Louisville, Kentucky. Like Faldo, Woosnam had always been one player high on the Ryder Cup committee's list of potential captains. Short in stature – he is just 5 feet 4 inches tall – but blessed with a compact, powerful swing, he had been the best ball-striker in the game when he had risen to world number one in 1991, the same year he had also won his sole major title at the Masters at Augusta. His Ryder Cup record was remarkable too. Over eight consecutive matches from Palm Beach in 1983 to Valderrama 1997, he had won 16½ points from his thirty-one games, a record that would have been immeasurably better if he had won any of his eight singles games.

Seated nearby, in a white dinner jacket and red bow-tie and looking just as uncomfortable as the rest of his teammates, was Darren Clarke. 'All I needed to look like a proper magician,' he said later, 'was a top hat and three rabbits tucked up my sleeve.' With his parents, Godfrey and Hetty, his sister Andrea, his aunt and uncle and some of his closest friends in attendance, Clarke was well supported at the Gala Dinner, but there was one person missing.

On 13 August, the day before her husband's thirty-eighth birthday, Clarke's wife of six years and mother to his two young boys, Tyrone and Conor, had lost her battle with breast cancer, passing away at London's Royal Marsden Hospital. She was thirty-nine. A week or so later, Ian Woosnam had called Clarke, not as his captain but as a friend, offering his condolences. It was Clarke, though, who chose to broach the subject of the Ryder Cup, telling Woosnam that if he wanted him in his team, he would make himself available, even though he hadn't wielded a club in anger in months.

A fortnight later, as the final qualification tournament for the European Ryder Cup team took place at the BMW International in Munich, Woosnam called Clarke again and told him that his place in the European team, if he still wanted it, was assured.

For Woosnam, selecting Clarke was straightforward and a decision which, once he had gained the Ulsterman's consent, was an easy call. Yes, he lacked form and the edge of competition, but he had worked hard with his coach Ewen Murray since making himself available and, more importantly, if there was anywhere on earth and any competition that could inspire Clarke, then it had to be a Ryder Cup in Ireland at the K Club. 'I think Heather would have wanted him to play in the Ryder Cup,' said Woosnam, 'and I think that's why he put his name forward.'

Darren Clarke had always found the K Club to his liking. In 1999, he had shot a round of 60 at the Smurfit European Open, which, given that he had missed putts from 15 feet at the penultimate hole and from 25 feet at the last, could have been the lowest round in European Tour history. Two years later, meanwhile, he returned to the Palmer Course and took the title, winning by three strokes from the local favourite Padraig Harrington, the Dane Thomas Bjørn and his Ryder Cup captain Ian Woosnam, and pocketing £436,000.

But if the choice of Darren Clarke had been clear-cut, Woosnam's second wild-card spot would be less so. Narrowing the candidates down to the Dane Thomas Bjørn and Clarke's close friend and stablemate at Chubby Chandler's ISM group, Lee Westwood, Woosnam was faced with a dilemma. Did he go with Bjørn, higher in the rankings, with a good record in the event and having enjoyed a much better season than his rival, or did he go with Westwood, a man with proven Ryder Cup credentials and two wins at the K Club to boot?

When Woosnam finally opted for Westwood, he did so knowing that what he needed – and what Darren Clarke needed, in the light of his devastating loss – was someone who could walk alongside the Irishman that week and offer him strong personal support. Westwood was understandably delighted in claiming his fifth appearance in the Ryder Cup, but Bjørn, a player not exactly known for biting his lip when the red mist descended, declared himself to be 'gutted,' before launching into a tirade against the European captain.

'I think he [Woosnam] has been very poor. A friend of mine he isn't – and I don't have a problem saying that. He's not taken charge of the captaincy in the way I see a captain should take charge and it's disappointing.

'He's put a lot of guys through misery by not talking to them… he never called me. He came into the bar at the hotel and gave me 20 seconds about Lee having won twice at the K Club, in a bar – that kind of sums it up.'

Woosnam himself conceded that Bjørn 'wasn't a happy chappy' when he had informed him of his decision. But if he thought the matter was closed he was wrong. As the British media seized on the row, Woosnam began to doubt himself. He considered legal action against Bjørn but held back, appeased by a reported fine of £10,000 from the European Tour and a public apology from the Dane. He even considered quitting.

With just two weeks until the Ryder Cup began, Woosnam decided to gather together at the K Club clubhouse those members of his team who weren't playing in that week's European Masters in a bid to establish once and for all whether he had the full support of his players. With Darren Clarke, Luke Donald, David Howell, Padraig Harrington, Paul Casey and José María Olazábal in attendance, Woosnam laid his captaincy on the line, asking if any of them agreed with Bjørn's opinion.

Silence.

With the rest of the team also pledging their support, Woosnam's fears, it seemed, had finally been allayed and the serious business of plotting and planning his Ryder Cup strategy could continue apace.

But it had, undeniably, been an unnecessary and troubling distraction on the eve of the competition. While Woosnam had never been the greatest of communicators, he could certainly never be accused of prevarication. That a senior player on the Tour such as Bjørn could harbour such negative opinions about him and his style of captaincy – even if they had been fuelled by rejection and dejection – had rocked the Welshman.

For the American team, with the calming influence of captain Tom Lehman at the helm, the K Club represented an opportunity to restore some pride to their performance after the horror show that was Oakland Hills. In the summer of 2006, when I interviewed Tom Lehman for the magazine *Golf Punk* ahead of the Ryder Cup, he was considerate and affable, charming and witty. He even chose a lob wedge as the club he would most likely use against a burglar in his home, adding that he'd open up his stance to 'get him up and out quicker' as well as 'get more spin too'.

Gone was the man who had been caught up in the madness of Brookline. Now, as the US team skipper, it was clear that he understood not just what the job entailed but what was expected of him and his players. 'The Ryder Cup is everything golf should be. It's pride, it's passion, it's emotion, it's nationalism. It's competition in its purest form,' he said, adding, 'I've been on winning Ryder Cup sides and I've been on losing Ryder Cup sides. Let me tell you, it's much more fun when you win. Much more fun.'

His captain's picks aside, Lehman's team had been finalized, as ever, after the PGA Championship at Medinah Country Club. Having shot four rounds in the 60s and eased to a five-stroke victory and his twelfth major title, Tiger Woods led the qualification table, with almost twice as many points as the second-placed player, Phil Mickelson. With the exception of Jim Furyk and David Toms, though, there was precious little Ryder Cup pedigree elsewhere in his line-up, with Chad Campbell and Chris DiMarco both having played just one Ryder Cup (in 2004) and the remaining four, Zach Johnson, J. J. Henry,

Vaughn Taylor and Brett Wetterich all poised to make their debuts in the contest.

The sudden influx of younger, less experienced players into Lehman's side had been the result of a change in the US qualification system in which the points were still collated over a two-year period but extra weight was now given to the tournaments in the year of the Ryder Cup itself. The thinking behind the change was that the final team would, at least, feature some players who were in some kind of form, and not those who had won a Tour event nearly two years ago and had since slipped off the rankings radar.

If Lehman was worried by the lack of experience, though, it didn't really show. 'I'm not afraid of having so many Ryder Cup rookies in my team,' he told me. 'Nick Faldo was a rookie in the Ryder Cup once upon a time. So was Seve Ballesteros. So was Jack Nicklaus. You have to start somewhere.'

That said, Lehman was under no illusion about the size of the task confronting him and his team. 'I think we'll be underdogs going into the Ryder Cup,' he shrugged. 'After what happened at Oakland Hills in 2004, I don't see how we can be favourites really. Everything came together for the European side [in 2004] and our team had nothing in return.'

Whatever he said publicly, Lehman, clearly, was concerned by the make-up of his side. That Sunday night, just a few hours after the culmination of the PGA Championship, Lehman set about selecting his wild-card picks, eliminating those men who were surplus to requirements and calling those players who stood between 11th and 25th in the qualification table to tell them the bad news. He also spoke to Tiger Woods and had a thirty-five-minute midnight phone conversation with Phil Mickelson to see how he felt about the make-up of the US team. Feeling tired and only marginally clearer in his mind about the make-up of his side, Lehman retired for the night. His two picks would be selected from a shortlist of six players, featuring Lucas Glover, Davis Love III, Scott Verplank, Stewart Cink, Steve Stricker and his assistant captain Corey Pavin, who had returned to winning ways for the first time in a decade with a victory at the US Bank Championship in Milwaukee in July.

That night, a nervous Scott Verplank went to bed, slipping his mobile phone under his pillow just in case Lehman too couldn't sleep and decided to give him a call. The following morning, as the sun rose, Verplank was already awake, pacing around his room waiting for Lehman to call. When he did, it was good news. 'When I woke up at 5:30, I was so pumped,' he said. 'I've been dreaming about this for two years.'

As it had been in 2002, when Curtis Strange selected the Dallas native for his one and only other Ryder Cup appearance, Verplank's selection seemed curious. Though he had a reputation for the kind of grit and steel that was always useful in the daze of a Ryder Cup contest, he had finished 20th in qualification, had suffered a shoulder injury in May and hadn't won a tournament since taking the 2001 Canadian Open.

Lehman's other pick, Stewart Cink, was an easier call to make – he had finished 12th in the qualification standings and had a couple of Ryder Cups under his belt. Verplank, however – described by some papers as an 'injury-prone diabetic' – had edged out the likes of Davis Love, a member of every US team since 1993, and a proven winner like Corey Pavin. It was a testament to his determination and his indomitable spirit that Lehman had seen fit to include Verplank once more.

While Cink and Verplank were both versatile, reliable players, capable of playing with anyone, they were hardly the kind of box-office names that could provide a much-needed fillip for US golf fans tiring of defeat after sapping defeat. Indeed, with four American reverses in the last five outings, the idea that the Ryder Cup was now suffering from the same kind of apathy in the States that, conversely, had afflicted the competition when the Americans were dominant in the 1960s and 1970s, began to take root. Now that they weren't winning, or to put it more accurately, now that they were losing and losing badly, it seemed as though the importance of the competition was once more in danger of dwindling.

Crucially, it was, as former captain Curtis Strange revealed to *Golf Digest*, a feeling that was fast filtering through to the players themselves. 'Our guys just aren't as excited about the Ryder Cup as they used to be, certainly not as excited as the Europeans, who always are motivated by beating the big, bad USA. For an American who plays in one of these things every year — there's the Presidents Cup, too — it's only a matter of time before you blow a big match and get fried by the media. For guys like Tiger and Mickelson it's not just about playing for their country, it's about getting scrutinized and hammered if they don't play well.'

For Lehman, it was imperative that the unity and spirit displayed by the European team, Thomas Bjørn notwithstanding, should be replicated within his own team. With his team finalized, he arranged a team trip to Ireland (minus Woods and Mickelson, absent because of prior commitments) to go fishing, play some golf, 'sign a bunch of autographs' and, of course, 'drink some Guinness'.

'Team morale is key,' he told me. 'In 1999 at Brookline we were losing badly, really badly, but we all felt to a man that we could still do it. Ben [Crenshaw] did a great job of keeping us up and maintaining that belief. That's what I want from my team. I want that spirit. I want each player to look around the locker room at the other eleven players and have absolute confidence in their ability.'

And, as ever, behind every good Ryder Cup captain, there was a good woman. 'Being captain isn't just about picking the pairings,' he added. 'I even have to find the right company to make our uniforms and have some input into the design. My wife's been helping me out there.'

While fashion wasn't exactly high on Ian Woosnam's list of priorities, getting the right team behind him certainly was as he roped in Des Smyth, D. J. Russell, Sandy Lyle and his partner from 1993, Peter

Baker. 'My role throughout the year was to watch the players and see who was coming through or hitting top form,' Baker explains. 'But you do what the captain wants you to do really.'

A wet Wednesday had made practice difficult for the teams and disappointing for the spectators while the weather on Thursday was just as overcast, reflecting, perhaps, the mood of those Europeans who had just been told that they would not be playing on the first day, namely Luke Donald, David Howell, Paul McGinley and Henrik Stenson. 'The hard bit was dropping the guys the first day,' recalls Peter Baker. 'Some of them were in the top twenty on the Order of Merit, maybe even higher. Everyone was playing so well and people were on top of their game. It was a tough one.'

It was here that Woosnam produced the moment of leadership he is plainly most proud of. 'It was the last practice round on the Thursday and Peter Baker [my assistant] was out with the boys who were not picked for the fourballs. He buzzed me on the walkie-talkie saying, "Woosie, get over here, we've got a problem". I arrived at their hole, only to find four of the worst cases of bad body language you'll ever see. They were just so miserable at being left out. That's when I made my mind up – everyone's going to have a game on the first day, nobody's going to feel excluded. I walked across the fairway and told them they were all playing in the afternoon foursomes. The effect was immediate; suddenly they all had a spring in their step.'

Too often, captains, like, say, Hal Sutton go with their gut instincts, persevering with pairings that simply won't work, but here Woosnam could see the bigger picture beyond the first day's games. Many perceived his change of heart as a weakness, an uncertainty born out of trying to keep all of his team happy, but, if anything, that readiness to change his mind, contrary though it may seem, was a sign of decisiveness, of real strength. With the mood swinging back the way he wanted and smiles returning to everyone's faces, Woosnam and his team went into the 36th Ryder Cup.

The opening match saw Tom Lehman, predictably perhaps, send out two of his strongest players. Rather than repeat the dismal experiment of Hal Sutton two years earlier, instead he paired Tiger Woods with Jim Furyk, a two-time winner on the PGA Tour in 2006. Ian Woosnam, meanwhile, would return fire, choosing Colin Montgomerie and the home favourite Padraig Harrington to lead the European charge, just as Langer had two years earlier. 'In terms of pairings, we both felt that it was something Bernhard Langer had done so well in America that if it wasn't broken why try and fix it,' says Woosnam's assistant Peter Baker.

Octopus swing or not, Furyk did what he always seemed to do, finding the fairway at the 418-yard par-4 1st hole. His partner, meanwhile, wasn't so precise, carving his tee shot some 40 yards off target and into the lake that lined the left side of the hole. For once, it seemed like nerves had got the better of the world number one.

Everybody suffers 1st tee nerves in the Ryder Cup and whatever the coaches say, it's not something you can control with deep breaths or stretches. From wide-eyed rookies to weathered veterans to multiple major winners, it is an event that has a unique ability to render all the preparation and practice that players devote hour after hour to entirely futile. Even the very best sometimes struggle to get the tee in the ground on the 1st tee, as the PGA's Sandy Jones confirms. 'I have seen Monty's hand shaking on the tee and Monty will be the first to admit that it happens. And Paul Lawrie, who I have known really well since I signed his forms when he turned pro – I can remember standing on the tee with him when he played with Monty in his first Ryder Cup, and he was just shaking.'

It's the captain's job, then, to prepare his players for the onslaught to the senses that the 1st tee will inevitably bring. 'Woosie was such a great captain because he engaged with the players and lifted the players, because they wanted to play for him,' adds Jones. 'He didn't tell them how to play. He just told them what to expect, particularly the young players, you know, when you go out there, the hairs are going to stand up on the back of your neck, you might feel like you want to cry and you might cry, but it is not a sign of weakness, it doesn't make you a bad player overnight.'

Furyk and Woods would eventually prevail at the last hole, the world number one's progress around the K Club course being followed, as ever, by huge galleries. These were dwarfed, however, by those waiting to see Darren Clarke. Since the death of his wife Heather and his subsequent decision to play in the event, Clarke had spent eight hours a day for two weeks working on his game with his coach Ewen Murray at his home club of Queenwood in Ottershaw, Surrey, in a bid to be competitive for the K Club.

As Murray explained later in the *Daily Telegraph*:

They were hard days with emotions running high and I would say little progress was being made. I stopped the car one night on my way home trying to figure out why. It struck me that Darren was nervous. Sometimes we think great players don't suffer from nerves, but they are just like the rest of us. I tackled him about it next morning and the reply was music to my ears. 'Of course I'm bloody nervous, now let's get down the range and hit a couple of hundred balls,' he said. That was the moment I knew he was going to be OK.

Paired his with friend Lee Westwood, Clarke practised his putting, as a tangible sense of anticipation swept over the Palmer Course. When the pair got the signal to make their way to the 1st tee, Westwood accompanied Clarke, but backed off as they got nearer to the start to allow his partner the welcome he deserved and, indeed, needed.

Announcing the teams, as ever, was the official starter of the European Tour, Ivor Robson. 'When Darren Clarke came on to the 1st tee with Lee Westwood it was unbelievable. Totally awesome,' he says. 'I'd never experienced anything like that in my life and I doubt I will again. Even Lee Westwood had tears in his eyes... You couldn't help but get caught up in it all. My throat was tightening up as well – I could barely speak.'

Fortunately, Robson finally managed to get his words out. 'On the tee, from Ireland – Darren Clarke.' What followed, though, was a roar that would have the world's seismologists scurrying for safety. 'It was down to me, as the player who knew him best, to partner Darren,' explains Clarke's playing partner Lee Westwood. 'What he had been through was tragic and it was always going to be an emotional time for him. That 1st tee was horrible. Me, Phil Mickelson, Chris DiMarco, the caddies, Ivor Robson – we were all in tears. Then Darren steps up, hits a driver down the middle, knocks the approach to 15 feet and holes it for birdie. Amazing.'

Other, lesser men might have struggled to contain their emotions or could have been forgiven for topping it short of the ladies' tee, but for Clarke not only to get the ball away, but to play the hole in exemplary, faultless fashion, spoke volumes for the man. 'I've no idea how he got the ball off the tee. He can't be a normal human being,' adds Robson. 'But it was an incredibly courageous decision of his to play.'

That morning, damp and overcast, saw Clarke and Westwood motor to a 1-up victory, carried along on a tsunami of goodwill around the K Club. Clarke was rested for the afternoon ('it was emotionally draining and tiring for him,' says Peter Baker), but the fact that he had made it to the match and then played so capably, helped to propel his teammates to a 5–3 lead by the end of the first day.

When Europe maintained their solid start with a 2½–1½ session win in the Saturday morning fourballs, it seemed as though the expectant crowd were getting ahead of themselves. During the first game out, for instance, the Swede Robert Karlsson was lining up a short three-foot putt at the 8th green when he became distracted by a spectator getting a little too close for comfort. With a scowl and a lecture, Karlsson asked the fan to move away, not realizing that it was Dr Michael Smurfit himself, eager to get as close to the action as possible.

Inspired by the courage of Clarke, Woosnam's men seemed relaxed and in control, despite some stubborn resistance from Lehman's team. Confidence surged through the European ranks. During the foursome game between Paul Casey and David Howell and Stewart Cink and Zach

Johnson, for example, Casey ended the match in the most emphatic manner, dumping his ball in the hole at the par-3 14th for an ace and a 5&4 win.

The US's chief tormentor, however, was the Spaniard Sergio García. Seven years on from wowing the world at the PGA Championship at Medinah, García was now, at just twenty-six, a Ryder Cup veteran. Like his idols Ballesteros and Olazábal before him, the young Spaniard seemed to thrive on the intensity of the Ryder Cup. All high-fives and fist-pumps, he may have been older and marginally wiser, but he still retained a youthful vigour and impetuosity around the golf course. Moreover, his performance at the K Club over the first two days, where he had played in all four sessions and won every game, had, Clarke aside, set him apart as the outstanding player in the Ryder Cup.

Come Sunday, the outlook for Europe was bright, even if the Kildare climate wasn't. Ian Woosnam's team had won each and every session and were now heading into the singles with a commanding 10–6 lead, the same lead they had held in 1999 at Brookline – and then surrendered.

Not everyone was relishing the day ahead though, especially Lee Westwood who had been felled by the flu. The Palmer Course was also under the weather: endless Irish rain had given the ground-staff the kind of overtime they could have done without, especially as there was golf to watch. At the sodden 15th tee, for instance, the squeegees were abandoned in favour of stamping scores of the hotel's embroidered towels into the ground just to try to soak up the puddles, before taking them to the rough, wringing them out and then going back to do it all over again.

If there was any concern that Europe would once more fall victim to the sort of shattering comeback that the US had launched at Brookline, it would be allayed almost immediately by Colin Montgomerie leading the way, as ever, at the top of the European singles order. Faced with the sturdiest of opponents in David Toms, the 2001 PGA champion, the Scot put in another peerless performance, taking the lead on the

3rd hole and staying ahead before winning with a birdie at the last and maintaining his unbeaten record in the singles.

American points would be few and far between. As the afternoon progressed, the scoreboard became a sea of blue with only Stewart Cink – who ruined Sergio García's 100 per cent record – and Tiger Woods, a 3&2 winner over Robert Karlsson, sparing US blushes in the top half of the draw.

Once more, Tiger Woods seemed to be a different player in the solitude of the singles. He was focused, diligent, and free, even if his caddie Steve Williams was doing his level best to scupper his chances. At the 7th hole, Woods's 9-iron approach had spun just off the green towards the lake on the right. As he arrived at the putting surface, Woods had marked his ball and handed it to Williams, who was busy trying to wash Tiger's muddy 9-iron. As he struggled, though, the Kiwi caddie slipped on the rocks on the banks of the water, before dropping the club into the water. 'It was either going to be him or the 9-iron,' shrugged Woods, 'so he chose the 9-iron.'

Sheepishly, Williams tried to retrieve the sunken club but short of getting in the water himself there was no way he could reach it. Instead, a frogman would be sent for and the club would be returned to its owner at the 15th hole.

A hole later, Woods, having played half the round with just 13 clubs, had wrapped up his victory over Robert Karlsson, 3&2. Though people had questioned Woods's record in the Ryder Cup, his record in the singles remained extremely strong. But for a defeat in his debut in 1997 to the Italian Costantino Rocca and a half point against Jesper Parnevik, agreed when the result at The Belfry in 2002 was already over, Woods had won all of his other games and a week that had started with a 5-wood splashing down in Michael Smurfit's lake had finished with another win, for him, if not for his country.

The 16th green would also prove to be the scene of perhaps the most emotional scenes ever witnessed in the Ryder Cup. After his heroics on the opening two days, Darren Clarke was out seventh in the singles, listed to play the American debutant Zach Johnson, the man who would go on to win the following year's Masters at Augusta.

Poor Johnson could have been forgiven for shaking hands and conceding the game on the 1st tee. After all, it was hard enough being a rookie in the Ryder Cup but playing Darren Clarke on his return to golf, in front of an Irish crowd and with everybody – probably even some of your teammates – wanting the home favourite to win, made it almost impossible. 'I expected it to be loud, but it was like an 80,000-people stadium amassed around one tee box,' explained Zach Johnson. 'It was pretty remarkable. Frankly it was like that on every tee box for him.'

Of course, it didn't help that Clarke had played the kind of round that would have been a match for almost any opponent, the highlight of which was an implausible 100-foot birdie putt at the par-3 12th hole, which suggested that it wasn't just his wife who was looking down on him from above.

By the time the pair reached the par-5 16th, Clarke was dormie-three. As he played his approach into the green, Henrik Stenson, in the match behind, had holed a 7-foot putt that had given him a comfortable 4&3 victory over Vaughn Taylor and Europe the point they needed to carry them over the 14½-point threshold. As the news filtered through the course and the sonic boom of another K Club eruption subsided, marginally at least, Clarke lagged his birdie putt up to the hole, leaving Zach Johnson to pick up his opponent's ball and concede the match.

Three days. Three games. Three points. Clarke's perfect Ryder Cup had defied belief and all the odds. Even the American team ringing the green stood and applauded his effort, with Tiger Woods and Tom Lehman leading the way. Now, at the end of an emotionally draining week, a week which he could have quite easily and understandably dodged, Clarke could let go and the dam broke. With tears streaming down his ruddy face, he was embraced by his captain Ian Woosnam, who held his arm aloft like a prizefighter at the end of a long, brutal bout. Even Bill Clinton was filling up.

When he gathered himself, Clarke finally managed to speak. 'This is as good as it gets,' he said. 'My team have been unbelievable all week, so have the American guys, their wives and the crowd – their support has been incredible. Being part of this team has done a lot for me and for people who have shown how much they care about me and Heather.'

It had been so close to being the dream conclusion to the 36th Ryder Cup but even though Henrik Stenson had dealt the crucial blow, it wasn't as though the Swede had stolen Darren Clarke's thunder. This, after all, had been Clarke's Cup, from the thunderous drive off the 1st tee on Friday to the tearful climax come Sunday afternoon. Besides, perhaps it would have been just too much to take if Clarke had been the man to hole the winning putt as well. Maybe someone, somewhere, was saving us from the trauma of it all.

For the European vice-captain Peter Baker, though, Clarke's efforts were justification of Ian Woosnam's decision not merely to pick him but to gauge just how he was faring and play him accordingly. 'Our big concern with Darren, and why we rested him, was because it was emotionally draining, obviously, and very tiring. It was tough for him [but] he did a great job,' he says.

Today, the US assistant captain Loren Roberts believes there was an air of inevitability about the result. 'Obviously they [the Europeans] had passion and emotion on their side that week [but] Darren is so close to so many of the players over here, that play on the US team, that it was always going to be an emotionally tough situation. Let's just say the odds were stacked against us.'

A record third consecutive win secured, the players still out on the course persevered amid a party atmosphere; Scott Verplank even notched a hole-in-one at the 14th in his 4&3 win over Padraig Harrington in the last game out. It has long been protocol for the players still out on the course to continue playing their games to a conclusion. That said, it has also long been protocol for the players still out on the course to ignore that protocol, shake hands and, if the scores are tied, agree on a half and head for the clubhouse. The only remaining singles match that would reach the 18th would be Paul McGinley's match with

J. J. Henry. McGinley was 2-up at the turn, but he had then been pegged back by the thirty-one-year-old New Englander.

Going down the last, the pair were all-square but it was advantage to the Irishman. With the American lining up a 20-footer to salvage a half point from his game, though, his attention was distracted by the sight of a naked man careering across the green. 'It wasn't even a woman,' huffs McGinley.

Forty-one-year-old Liverpudlian Mark Roberts was a serial streaker who had begun his 'career' in 1993 when he streaked at the Hong Kong Sevens rugby tournament and then proceeded to display his 'talent' at innumerable major sporting events, including the Wimbledon men's final in 2002, the 2004 Superbowl and on the final green at the Old Course, St Andrews, when John Daly took the Open Championship in 1995 (with the words '19th hole' scrawled on his back and an arrow pointing to his posterior).

As the police and stewards surrounded the green, Roberts, with a golf ball wedged between his buttocks, headed for the only available escape route, belly-flopping into the greenside lake, before being dragged out and taken away, his body, if not his dignity, intact.

The distraction over, McGinley decided that it wasn't right or proper for Henry to try and make his putt given the circumstances and conceded his putt to share the spoils. In the grand scheme of things, it had no effect on the outcome of the match, but if Henry had missed his putt, which was more likely than not, McGinley would have taken the point and the US team would have suffered a record 19–9 defeat and not merely the record-equalling margin of 18½–9½.

In McGinley's defence, he had already asked one of the vice-captains, Des Smyth, if he should concede the putt but, having been met with a shrug and no definitive answer, had been left to decide for himself. Greenside was the US vice-captain Loren Roberts. 'It was out of reach for us, but I think he [McGinley] may have caught a little heat for giving that putt and not setting a blow-out record,' he reflects. 'But I think it was a wonderful display of sportsmanship, you know.'

Save for a few ruined betting slips and a few people still bitter about Colin Montgomerie's similar concession to Scott Hoch at Valderrama in 1997, it didn't really matter that McGinley had given Henry the putt, not least as a naked man had stolen the moment. McGinley had merely done what he thought was fair and appropriate in the circumstances. It was a gesture of goodwill and a nod to Ryder Cups past. It was, perhaps, the right thing to do, even if Ian Woosnam felt a little peeved. 'I'll have a talk with Paul McGinley later,' joked the skipper.

With the mauling over, though, Woosnam and his team took to the roof terrace of the K Club's clubhouse. The champagne corks popped all around and the European team sprayed the crowd and each other like podium finishers at a Grand Prix. Woosnam grabbed a bottle of his own, but, as he drank, the bubbles got the better of him and he was forced to jettison a mouthful of cuvée on those below.

Undeterred, Woosie simply wiped his face and turned his attention to a pint of Guinness he had been presented with. Following Darren Clarke's lead, he downed it with all the gusto of a student in rag week. Somehow, you couldn't quite have imagined Tom Lehman doing the same thing. But it didn't matter. This was Woosie's moment, arguably Europe's greatest moment, and the captain could drink what he bloody well liked.

As the celebrations continued, and the beer and the bubbly flowed, it was left to Woosnam's vice-captain, Peter Baker, to remind his captain, that the job wasn't quite done yet. 'I remember saying to Woosie, you've still got to make a speech and he was like, "Oh Christ, yeah!"'

A quick (and necessary) change of clothes ensued and, with booze-soaked hair slicked back, the teams mounted the stage for the presentation and closing ceremony. After the criticism he received in 1999, Tom Lehman had been the perfect ambassador for American golf. Courteous, eloquent and generous with his time, he had done everything asked of him. Sadly, his team had not. His speech was gracious, his congratulations genuine.

Dressed in a kind of salmon-pink blazer that looked like it had been through the same wash as one of Tiger Woods's Sunday shirts, Ian Woosnam, meanwhile, was typically to the point. Receiving the Ryder Cup from the Irish Taoiseach Bertie Ahern, he thanked Lehman and his team, dedicated the victory to the late Heather Clarke and then wished everyone a 'safe journey home' as though he were packing an elderly aunt off after Sunday lunch.

The European team would continue where they had left off, only this time it was in the team room, not on the roof of the clubhouse. And following the rowdy scenes moments earlier, a team of K Club staff had been hastily dispatched to remove some of the more valuable pieces from the room. 'There were hundreds of thousands of pounds of antiques knocking about,' recalls Peter Baker. 'And just before it really kicked off, I remember some of the staff taking the antique tables out and putting them away safely, just in case.' Then, with the master-pieces on the wall encased and safely secured and U2's 'Beautiful Day' shaking the ceiling, the inevitable happened. 'We just got absolutely hammered, really,' shrugs Baker.

Over in the American team room, Darren Clarke had popped by, opening the door to find another party in full flow. No long faces or finger-pointing. No grudges or gripes. No protracted post-mortem. Just a few laughs, more than a few drinks and the surreal sight of Jim Furyk rapping along to a 50 Cent soundtrack. A swift beer later, Clarke would be summoned back to the European team room whereupon he was presented with the flag from the 16th green, which had been furtively removed by Lee Westwood's caddie and then signed by all the players.

The following day, Darren Clarke slipped out of the K Club bright and early to fly home, making it back in time to do the school run with Tyrone and Conor. It would be fifteen months before he fully resumed his playing career again.

Stars and Gripes

VALHALLA GOLF CLUB, LOUISVILLE, KENTUCKY

19–21 September 2008

LOUISVILLE, Kentucky, 6 November 2006. As the world's sports media file dutifully into the conference room at Valhalla Golf Club, Paul Azinger waits in the wings, ready to take to the stage and be introduced as the new captain of the US Ryder Cup team. With moments to go, though, his phone buzzes into life. It's a text message from his opposite number, Nick Faldo, wishing him well for the task ahead of him.

It was perfect – and quite fortuitous – timing by Faldo, who unwittingly and inadvertently came close to stealing Azinger's thunder on his big day. Not that Azinger seemed to care. 'It'll be a good rivalry,' he shrugged. 'It adds a lot of intrigue, but it will still be America versus Europe, not Nick versus Paul.'

That, of course, was baloney. This, more than any other Ryder Cup contest, was all about the two captains. It was a deliciously enticing clash. Azinger, the vocal, vibrant heart on the US team's sleeve versus Faldo, the Ryder Cup record-breaker known for his perfectionism and an insularity often perceived as aloofness or even arrogance.

Theirs was a rivalry that went back decades, to the final day of the 1987 Open Championship at Muirfield. Having led the whole week, Azinger had bogeyed the last two holes of the final round and then watched on as a monotonously steady Faldo overtook him with a

run of 18 pars to claim his first Claret Jug. Later, at the trophy presentation, all Faldo could say to his opponent was 'Sorry about that,
old bean', prompting Azinger to say, 'I confess that it hurt a little that
he wasn't more consoling... I don't think he knew I existed.' A year
later, Faldo had poked fun at Azinger's swing in a magazine piece,
suggesting that it would never hold up under the pressure of a major
tournament and that it was, on the face of it, 'a homemade grip and a
hatchet swing'.

From then on, their clashes simply seemed to be scheduled around
the Ryder Cup, as if they had booked them in, years in advance. From
1989, when Azinger pulled Faldo up for paying a little too much
attention to his playing partner Chip Beck's line, to Faldo's refusal to
concede a meaningless putt to Azinger at The Belfry in 1993, and on to
1995 and the American's dig in the ribs about Faldo's slow play, there
was an element of needle between them. Even when they became colleagues as co-summarizers on ABC's network coverage of the PGA Tour
in 2004, they still didn't see eye to eye. 'I've felt my accomplishments
have been minimized in comparison with Nick's,' Azinger suggested.
'I try to brush it off, brush it off, but that's a real feeling. There's always
a little something there.'

Few players in Ryder Cup history had gone out in more style than
'Zinger'. In 2002, with Europe on the brink of victory, the US team's
scrapper-in-chief was standing in a greenside bunker at the 18th hole
at The Belfry with his opponent, Niclas Fasth, set fair to take his team
over the 14½-point line. But the Swede could only watch, incredulous,
as his moment in the Sutton Coldfield sun was stolen by the kind of
preposterous holed bunker shot only a player of Azinger's calibre could
have conjured up.

Azinger typified the kind of doughty attitude that the American side
had lacked so conspicuously over recent years. He possessed what the
American military are wont to call 'intestinal fortitude' – or what the
rest of the world calls guts. Had the PGA of America invested some of
the vast revenues from the Ryder Cup in cloning technology and made

three or four Azingers it's unlikely that Europe would ever have got within sniffing distance of the Ryder Cup, let alone come to dominate it in such magnificent fashion.

Given his exploits in the event (four matches, fifteen games, just three defeats and undefeated in the singles), and the way he had gone toe-to-toe with Seve Ballesteros when most players would have turned and headed for the hills, Azinger was always going to be a US Ryder Cup captain. It wasn't so much a matter of if but when. Indeed, the 1993 PGA champion had been asked to lead the US team at the 2006 matches at the K Club but had declined, leaving Tom Lehman to fill the vacancy. When the PGA came calling again in November 2006, though, Azinger willingly stepped into the fold, declaring himself to be 'awestruck' by the appointment. Veteran Ryder Cupper Jim Furyk typified the reaction to Azinger's appointment. 'I think he's a great choice,' he said. 'He's feisty. He brings a little bit of an attitude to a team that I think needs it right now.' Furyk was wrong, though. Azinger didn't bring 'a little bit of an attitude' to the contest. He brought a bunker full of the stuff.

Though commentators had long since stopped using provocative military metaphors to describe the Ryder Cup contests, Azinger's backroom staff appointments suggested the new US captain was assembling something more akin to a war cabinet than a support team. In calling up two of the competition's most combative former captains, Raymond Floyd and Dave Stockton, as his assistants, alongside Olin Browne, Azinger was not merely surrounding himself with experi-ence (not that he really needed it) but issuing a clear signal of intent that, after the humiliations of 2004 and 2008, the Americans would be showing some cojones the next time Europe's golfers rode into town. 'I'm really counting on them [Floyd and Stockton] to help shape and mould the personality of the team,' said Azinger.

For 'shape and mould the personality of the team' read 'whip them into shape'. As captains, both Floyd and Stockton's teams had shared that same dogged resolve, that same passion and inherent belief so conspicuous by its absence in recent US Ryder Cup teams. For Floyd, who had already played in eight Ryder Cups and captained one, it was another Ryder Cup call he was only too happy to accept. 'Coming back and being asked to be an assistant captain was tremendously rewarding,' he says. 'You know some of the guys who were on that team I had never met until we got to Louisville. I mean I knew most of the players but there were two or three players that I had never had the opportunity to shake their hands, I knew who they were. Very special.'

Yet Paul Azinger's captain's strategy would go way beyond a reliance on veteran lieutenants or barking sergeant majors. On his appointment, Azinger had demanded an immediate rethink of the selection process for the US team, something that, given the recent results, was desperately needed. Now, rather than having the standard two picks, Azinger was given four wild-card spots by the PGA of America and also introduced changes to the points qualification system. Now, one point would be awarded for every $1,000 earned at the four majors in 2007 and PGA Tour events in 2008, with double points for the 2008 majors, the idea being that the team the US ended up with would be one with the requisite balance of talent, form and, with the two extra picks, experience, if it was needed.

What Azinger had little control over, however, was the fate of his star player, Tiger Woods. Since his first appearance in the Ryder Cup in 1997, Tiger Woods's career had been propelled into realms hitherto unseen in the modern game as he collected major after major and closed in on Jack Nicklaus's record of eighteen majors, a record previously thought unbeatable. In the process, Woods had become not just the richest golfer in history, but sport's first billionaire, bagging titles and endorsements by the truckload and a Swedish swimsuit model for a wife as well.

But it was his last major victory at the US Open at Torrey Pines, near San Diego, in June 2008 that had suggested that maybe Tiger Woods wasn't human after all. Just two months after surgery, and with his knee still causing him severe discomfort, Woods had returned to competitive golf and, after a play-off with his compatriot Rocco Mediate, won his 14th major title, despite clearly being in pain throughout the tournament. Not everybody had been sympathetic though. The South African Retief Goosen, for example, had questioned just how injured Woods was, noting that he only ever seemed to grimace whenever he hit a bad shot. 'Nobody really knows if he was just showing off or if he was really injured,' said the two-times major winner. 'I believe if he was really injured, he would not have played.'

Two days after his third US Open victory, however, Woods revealed that he had played the tournament not just with a torn ligament in his left knee but with a double stress fracture of his left tibia also. He promptly booked himself in for further surgery, ruling himself out for the rest of the season, the Ryder Cup included, and making Retief Goosen look, well, a bit silly.

Ordinarily, the absence of a player as gifted and as influential as Woods would have had most captains reaching for the bourbon, or even the revolver, but not Azinger. If anything, Woods's injury, it could be argued, was a blessing in disguise for the US. Without the media circus that surrounded the world number one's every move and waited on his every word (even though most of them were vague and largely inconsequential), the American team benefited from a new-found freedom, forging a bond unlike any US team in recent memory. It helped, of course, that there was now a healthy new crop of players coming through the American ranks: some young, some not so, but all approaching the form of their lives. Yes, some of the old guard, like Phil Mickelson, Jim Furyk and Stewart Cink, were still in there, steady as ever, but in much the same way that Europe had prospered in the early and mid-1980s, now the USA found themselves blessed with a new breed of confident, cocksure golfers, most notably Anthony Kim, the University of Oklahoma graduate who had already won twice on the PGA Tour in his fledgling pro career and the flamboyant 'young lion' Hunter Mahan.

While broadcasters and sponsors alike bemoaned the absence of the biggest box-office draw in the game, so too did Azinger, who would later invite Woods to join the US team as an unofficial 13th member. 'I'm going to have an open phone line to Tiger during the event,' he said. 'I am curious to see how he feels as things unfold. He's really intelligent and has a great golf mind, so I'm looking forward to talking to Tiger. It's one of my great regrets of this Ryder Cup that he's not going to be participating in these matches.'

Unfazed by Tiger's absence, Azinger's Ryder Cup revolution continued apace. Not only did he allow those players who had qualified automatically to assist in choosing the wild-card picks for him – the first time such a radical move had been implemented – but he also split his twelve-man team into three sub-groups of four, after an evening spent watching a television documentary on the training programme of the US Navy SEALS. 'Military experts knew that in the heat of battle you couldn't get a battalion or a company to jell as a single fighting unit. The numbers were too big,' Azinger wrote in his book *Cracking the Code*. 'But you could get three, four, five, or maybe as many as six guys to lay everything on the line for the men beside them. Small groups – men who ate, slept, trained, hung out and sometimes fought together – were a key to military success. At that moment, I thought it could be the answer to America's Ryder Cup woes as well.'

Taking a leaf out of Seve Ballesteros's book, he would also tinker with the format of the event, switching the opening games back to alternate shots for the first time since 1999. 'I felt like the Americans had an edge in alternate shot,' Azinger said. 'And I think playing foursomes first is partly responsible for why Europe has gotten off to a pretty hot start.'

If it appeared that Paul Azinger was the captain with all the ideas, all the energy, it was because he simply had no option but to try to make things happen, as Bernard Gallacher explains. 'They are all such great players in the Ryder Cup [but] we shouldn't be winning in America by nine points, no matter how good a captain Bernhard Langer is, no matter how good a captain Ian Woosnam is,' says the three-times captain. 'The winning margin just shouldn't be so wide, because the teams are much closer than this and there is something wrong in the other camp when you are winning by nine points.'

After three crushing defeats, in which the one-sided nature of the contests had turned Europe from perennial underdogs to overwhelming favourites, it was clear that emergency surgery was needed and only Paul Azinger could perform it. Even Seve Ballesteros, Azinger's other arch-enemy in the event, wanted the Americans to win, just to preserve the future of the competition. 'I see the Ryder Cup getting very boring because we are beating them so badly,' he mused. 'Everybody is losing interest. I think it will be good if they win the next one. It would give the Ryder Cup a lift.' Conversely, Nick Faldo seemed settled, confident and happy that the system that had served the European team so effectively in recent years would see them right at Valhalla as well. The US captain, however, viewed the challenges ahead in a positive light. 'I have more of an everything-to-gain situation,' reflected Azinger. 'There will be a little more heat on Nick to get it right. A little more of the microscope on him if he loses.'

The line-up for Nick Faldo's team was announced after the final qualifying event at the end of August, the Johnnie Walker Championship at Gleneagles. Like Azinger's team, Faldo's side also included some established stars in the form of Lee Westwood, Sergio García, and, fresh from his third major title victory at the 2008 PGA Championship at Oakland Hills, Padraig Harrington. While Luke Donald was absent with a wrist injury, there were some extremely able deputies ready to step in, not to mention four rookies in the shape of England's Justin Rose and Oliver Wilson, Denmark's Søren Hansen and Northern Ireland's Graeme McDowell.

It would be one of Faldo's choices for his two captains' picks, however, that would cause consternation. While the selection of Paul Casey was hard to argue with, it was the decision to pick Ian Poulter that garnered the most column inches, not because he wasn't equipped to do a job for Europe, but because he had a) decided not to play at the Johnnie Walker Championship at Gleneagles, preferring to play in the

States, and b) it was at the expense of Darren Clarke, the man who had reduced the watching world to tears two years earlier at the K Club. Although he was behind Poulter in the world rankings, Clarke was in fine form, having won at the KLM Open in Holland the week before the team announcement. Moreover, the fact that Poulter had skipped Gleneagles led some of the press to conclude that he had already been assured of his place on Faldo's team and that the claims of players like Clarke and, to a lesser extent, Colin Montgomerie, were never going to he heard anyway.

As Poulter bore the brunt of the criticism – unfairly so – Darren Clarke was keen to point out that the fault, if any, lay with the captain and not the player. 'I think Poults has been dragged into a situation which was caused not by his own doing, but because Nick has changed his mind and gone back on it,' Clarke told Sky News. 'Earlier in the year, Nick had stated he wanted his players to be on form, he wasn't going to pay particular attention to the rankings. I thought I was on good form, my record this year has been a couple of good wins and lots of top tens, but unfortunately he changed his mind.'

A fortnight before the start of the Cup, Azinger invited Nick Faldo and his European team to make exclusive use of Valhalla for two days' practice. It looked like a generous gesture on Azinger's part, but there was an ulterior motive. 'I said to Mark [Wilson, the Valhalla superin-tendent], "Hey, Mark, wouldn't it be something if it was so hot that you couldn't mow the greens the Monday and Tuesday that Europe is here playing practice rounds?"... Mark could read between the lines. The greens rolled about a six [very, very slow] on the Stimpmeter on those days.' Whether Faldo and his charges realized the trap that was being laid for them or whether they simply had prior commitments, not one of the European team would take Azinger up on his kind offer. Thanks, they said, but no thanks.

But if Azinger was constantly thinking of new ways to wrongfoot Faldo, so the European captain was finding new ways to irritate his opposite number. Whether they were intentional was by the by.

As the European team disembarked from their plane at Louisville International Airport, Faldo stood at the top of the stairs jubilantly holding the Ryder Cup aloft before shielding it from Azinger as the two posed for photographs on the tarmac. If it was Faldo's idea of a joke, it fell flat, as it did when he thanked the press from 'the heart of my bottom' and then sang a toe-curling rendition of 'My Way' in his winner's speech after the 1992 Open Championship at Muirfield.

That said, the incident had illustrated just how the two men were approaching the task in hand. While Faldo had fallen into his default 'comic' mode, Azinger was, despite his experience, canvassing opinion and advice, empowering his players and, well, getting ideas from the US military. For Azinger, inclusion was key, the team was every-thing. 'Azinger is an old warrior, he is shrewd,' says Sandy Jones. 'The Americans came unfancied, unfavoured, but through Azinger they formed a very strong, bonded team and got on with one another. We lacked leadership in the team. While I would never criticize Nick Faldo, because he has done things in the game that I could only dream of, I don't know what it was with him, he just didn't grasp the captaincy role properly. He is such a strong-minded individual, he never figured out that he had to tell the guys how to play, because he thought once you have made the Ryder Cup team – and this is me putting in my thoughts here, not what he has said – you must know how to play so who am I to tell you?'

In an interview with the *Guardian* newspaper in July 2007, Faldo had admitted that he had been surprised by the lack of contact he had with those players in the reckoning for Ryder Cup places. 'They don't pick up the phone and ask for advice but maybe they're learning from a distance,' he said. 'They usually want to pick my brains for Augusta – "Can I play a practice round with you? What shot should I play on this hole?" But it's not as many as you would think given that I've made it clear I am here for them.'

Azinger had his own version of why Faldo seemed to be struggling to impose himself on the job and his team.

Nick Faldo is trying to redefine himself… He is at the fork in the road. He is who he is, and he was who he was. Some people buy it, and some people don't buy it… If you are going to be a prick and everyone hates you, why do you think because you're trying to be cute and funny on the air, they're all suddenly going to start to like you?… The players from his generation really don't want to have anything to do with him. He did it the way he did and there are relational consequences from that.

With egos bruised and apologies duly issued, attention finally turned to the match. Typically, Valhalla looked sublime. Named after the 'Hall of the Slain' in Norse mythology, Valhalla was a permanent fixture in the top 100 golf courses in the US listing. Designed by Jack Nicklaus on a 486-acre plot twenty miles east of downtown Louisville, it had opened in 1986 to almost universal acclaim. With its contoured fairways, large undulating greens and spectacular backdrops, populated with dense collars of Kentucky bluegrass, it was, undoubtedly, an American-style course but with more than a little nod to some of Nicklaus's favourite Scottish links courses. The PGA of America certainly liked it too. In the early '90s, the organization had bought a 25 per cent share in Valhalla. Shortly after, it had hosted its first major, the PGA Championship won by the American Mark Brooks. Three years later, they upped their stake to 54 per cent, before eventually assuming total control in the early 2000s. Valhalla was a great venue for the Ryder Cup, undoubtedly, but also one that would save the PGA of America a lot of money. By hosting the event at their own club, it was estimated that the PGA would avoid around $6 million in course rental fees. The PGA would also get to keep all the profits, as it wouldn't have to share the revenues with the host course.

Over the preceding eighteen months, Paul Azinger had worked with the course's managing superintendent Mark Wilson to create a course that would give his team the best possible chance of winning back the Ryder Cup. Virtually every hole had been tweaked or, in some cases, reworked. There were also four new putting greens, many new bunkers and, to allow the US team to make the most of their length advantage off the tee, he cut back the rough and added an extra 329 yards in total, taking the track to a topped tee shot short of 7,500 yards long.

Other significant changes had been made to the Valhalla club. Some 5,000 trees had been removed to help improve viewing and a small town had been created to accommodate the 1,500 media personnel needed to relay the event to 600 million people in 177 countries. And, in the event of a confrontation between the two captains, there would be 650 police and security staff on hand if things turned ugly.

What nobody had allowed for, though, was the weather. On the Sunday before the Cup, as the European team headed across the Atlantic from Heathrow to Louisville, the tail end of Hurricane Ike paid Valhalla a visit on its way across the US South. When the storm, with its 60 m.p.h. winds, had blown over, the damage was widespread. A TV camera tower had crashed on to the 12th green, scoreboards had collapsed, trees were brought down and many of the marquees had been damaged, leaving the tournament director Kerry Haigh and his 150-strong team an unexpected overnight clean-up operation. By the time Faldo and seven members of his team arrived, much of Louisville was still without power; even the first press conference had to be held in the nearby Kentucky Exhibition Center, with generators being fired up to help power the television lights. Regrettably for those who don't enjoy country music sung by reality TV stars, power was restored in time for the Gala Dinner, at which Carrie Underwood, winner of the fourth series of *American Idol*, regaled the guests.

After all his years playing, working and winning in the States, Nick Faldo seemed relaxed. It was as if that air of superiority, so long the preserve of the US team, had, in the wake of three European wins in succession, drifted into the visitors' team room. Indeed, so at ease was Faldo that he walked round the course with his potential pairings scribbled down on a piece of paper there for all the long lenses of the press photographers to see. Asked if these were his pairings for Friday, the European captain maintained that it was 'the lunch list.

It had sandwich requests for the guys, just making sure who wants the tuna, who wants the beef, who wants the ham. So that's all it was – a sandwich list.'

The match started well for Faldo and Europe. Within an hour, the holders were ahead in all four of the matches but once the Americans had reeled them in, thanks largely to an inspirational effort from Justin Leonard and Hunter Mahan against Paul Casey and Henrik Stenson, they held on to emerge from the session with a 3–1 advantage. When they followed it up with a 2½–1½ win in the afternoon fourballs, the USA found themselves in that rarest of positions with not just a first-day lead, but the largest they had enjoyed since the match at The Greenbrier in 1979.

But if day one had given the home support reasons to be cheerful, day two would prove to be one of those spellbinding days that every Ryder Cup invariably features and that left Paul Azinger's stomach 'churning'. A spirited comeback from Europe in the morning foursomes, ignited by Oliver Wilson and Henrik Stenson's comeback from 4-down to win 2&1 against Phil Mickelson and Anthony Kim, saw them reduce their deficit by a point. The US's only win came in the final match out, in which the local favourite Kenny Perry teamed up with Jim Furyk to eclipse Padraig Harrington and Robert Karlsson 3&1.

That afternoon, the US continued to keep the Europeans at arm's reach, a 2–2 scoreline failing to do justice to what was an extraordinary session of golf, in which three of the fourball games would be decided on the 18th green. The only game that failed to go the distance was the first match, involving Søren Hansen and Lee Westwood, in which Westwood's twelve-match unbeaten streak in the Ryder Cup – a record he shared with Arnold Palmer – was ended by the big-hitting, meat-eating, all-American pairing of J. B. Holmes and Boo Weekley, a player who had called time on a promising career cleaning ammonia tanks at petrochemical plants to turn professional in 1995 and '97 respectively.

It would be an afternoon where the players were holing putts for fun. The last match out between Phil Mickelson and Hunter Mahan and Robert Karlsson and Henrik Stenson was a case in point. Back and forth went the lead, and despite six birdies for Karlsson on the back nine, the European duo still couldn't pull clear. Finally, at the last, both Karlsson and Mahan had putts for eagles but both missed and instead shook hands on a terrifically hard-fought half.

Yet the key moment would come in the third game, where Ben Curtis and Steve Stricker seemed all set to lose against Sergio García and Paul Casey. Having been in the greenside rough at the last hole, Stricker had holed a clutch 15-foot putt, giving the US a half point they may have thought would elude them. Indeed, Stricker's stroke would prove to be one of those precious, pivotal moments that almost every Ryder Cup contest inevitably hinges on. 'How close it would have been had Stricker not made the putt at the 18th on the second day?' wonders US assistant Raymond Floyd. 'People don't realize that there are little movements during the play that can change everything. A half point loss or win. Maybe a half that turns into a win. It is huge.'

Europe's star, unquestionably, had been the captain's pick, Ian Poulter. Having played in all four sessions and with only the singles to come, Poulter had returned three points already and would go on to be the highest points scorer in the match from either side, wrapping up a singles win over Steve Stricker on Sunday. His form and dedication to the cause had been the most public vindication of Faldo's decision and had finally silenced those critics who maintained he should not have been there. 'The 2008 Ryder Cup was great for me,' he says. 'To get picked by Nick Faldo in the first place was huge but then to back it up by being the only player to play all five sessions and emerge as the highest points scorer was just fantastic. It's given me a lot of confidence and I like to think it kick-started my rise up the world rankings.'

Graeme McDowell, too, had risen to the occasion, his captain describing his performance as 'absolutely amazing'. Propelled into the team on the back of a season in which he had won two titles on the European

Tour, the man from Portrush, Northern Ireland, had clearly found the heat of the Ryder Cup battle to his liking, winning 2½ points from his four games.

Buoyed by another thrilling session where they had refused to yield the momentum, Paul Azinger's US team headed into the singles with their first final-day lead since Oak Hill some thirteen years earlier. Key to Europe's chances was their start. If they could get a quick lead and steal some early points the match would be there for the taking. But if Faldo had been criticized for his leadership style, now it was his tactics that would be called into question. While sending senior players such as García and Casey out first and second made sense, the fact that the other experienced players were left at the tail end of the order meant Faldo was banking on the earlier exchanges going his way. It was a gamble, but then the singles list always was. By leaving his player of the week, Ian Poulter, to play in the tenth game against Steve Stricker, followed by Lee Westwood versus Ben Curtis and his three-time major winner, Padraig Harrington, out last, there was a real possibility that they could still be playing when the game was already over and the destination of the Ryder Cup decided.

Initially, though, Europe appeared to have the upper hand, taking 2½ points from the first four games, and with the debutant Justin Rose defeating the world number two Phil Mickelson 3&2. But the American team seemed beyond determined, beyond focused. Anthony Kim, for example, was a man on a mission. The twenty-three-year-old rookie was so wrapped up in his game with Sergio García that when he holed his putt at the 14th green he stormed off to the 15th tee, failing to realize that he'd just won the match 5&4. When somebody stopped him to tell him he had won, Kim headed back to the green to take a bow. Boo Weekley, meanwhile, was 8-under through 16 holes in his 4&2 win over Oliver Wilson and virtually unstoppable. 'I don't really pay much attention to golfing history but this is really unreal,' explained Weekley, who was roared home by cheers of 'BOO-S-A!'. 'I honestly didn't know what the Ryder Cup was like but the feeling you get when they shout your name... It ain't nothing like shooting a deer, it's a whole lot more.'

As each European point was trumped by an American one, it became clear that there was only going to be one winner. Inside the ropes on Sunday was the former Ryder Cup captain Bernard Gallacher who was working for BBC Radio 5 Live. As the home side edged ever closer to the finishing line, he could see a distinct difference between the two sides.

It is a very lonely place for the players in the Ryder Cup and although you may have huge support behind the ropes, players like to see faces inside the ropes; they like to see their wives, they like to see their friends, they like to see their colleagues inside supporting them. That's why it is important that a captain has quite a strong support. You have got players round about you that the players like and then the captain can send a couple of players out to see each match so when the players look about they can see these players rooting for them. I felt at Valhalla that was what was missing. I could see all the support they [the USA] were getting inside the ropes from Paul Azinger, from Raymond Floyd, from Dave Stockton and from other players and I didn't see that same level of support for our players. I just thought it makes a difference.

Support or no support, this was simply one match that was beyond the European team. Their challenge would finally be unpicked by an American middle order carried along by an expectant home crowd. The Kentuckian Kenny Perry, for instance, was mesmerizing in his win over Henrik Stenson, draining putt after putt and suggesting he had found 'the putting touch of Tiger Woods and Jack Nicklaus' combined. J.B. Holmes, a player with forearms as thick as most men's thighs and who was playing on the satellite Hooters Tour the last time the USA won the Ryder Cup, grabbed three birdies in the last four holes to beat Søren Hansen and take the US team to within a point of the winning line, while Boo Weekley romped to a 4&2 win over Oliver Wilson, cheered on by a delirious home gallery.

As the scoreboard turned red and an expectant crowd waited and wondered, the game between Jim Furyk and the pony-tailed forty-eight-year-old Miguel Ángel Jiménez seemed destined to be the deciding rubber. For Furyk, a player often ridiculed for his idiosyncratic swing but who, whatever you thought of his bizarre action, was among the most consistent players in the game, it would be a moment to savour. Having led from the opening hole, Furyk had been in complete command and he reached the 17th hole 2-up. Though Furyk missed his birdie putt, it left Jiménez, whose hairstyle suggested he was slap bang in the depths of a mid-life crisis, needing to hole his birdie putt to take the game down the last. After an eternity spent reading the line, the crowd fell silent as the Spaniard slid his putt wide and to the right, before offering his hand to Furyk and conceding their match.

After three failed attempts and for the first time in the twenty-first century, the USA had won the Ryder Cup. It had been a victory engineered by the tireless, inspirational and imaginative captaincy of Paul Azinger. It was, moreover, a victory in which twelve Americans had played as a team. 'I took the players in and came in with a plan,' said Azinger. 'These guys came together as a group and stuck to a message. In the end it comes down to putting and heart and our guys had a lot of heart.'

This is a view shared by Europe's Ian Poulter. 'People say the US were a better team in 2008 without Tiger Woods but what happened was that their rookies really stepped up to the plate and they all delivered points. That's why they won,' he says.

Nick Faldo's singles strategy had been a counter-intuitive gamble that had backfired spectacularly. Still out on the course, after all, were some of Europe's strongest and most experienced players from the week – Poulter, McDowell, Harrington and Westwood – their games now rendered meaningless by Furyk's decisive victory. Faldo's team had been outplayed all week, while he himself had been out-thought and out-fought by his rival Paul Azinger.

'There were twenty-four guys giving their all and we came up short,' said Faldo. 'The shot-making and putting were unbelievable – we are talking fractions. In this particular week they have done us and congratulations to them. The difference between a win, a loss or a half... you are talking maybe a chip or a putt. You can't point fingers. I've no regrets. One of my goals was to leave knowing I did my best and I'm more than happy. I've got to be proud of everyone.'

Faldo's talk of 'fractions' was wide of the mark. The European team had been comprehensively outplayed at Valhalla, so much so that the *Guardian* newspaper suggested that Faldo had forgotten 'that the details don't matter, the outcome does; that a beaten Ryder Cup captain is a bad Ryder Cup captain'.

Despite suggestions from Lee Westwood that he had once more suffered some 'shameful' abuse during the games, the matches had been played in a good spirit, not that it made losing any easier. 'Obviously, I'd have rather won the Ryder Cup,' says Ian Poulter, 'but I guess you could say it was good for the future of the Ryder Cup for America to win as they'd taken two big defeats in 2004 and 2006. I don't see that as being a problem – as long as we take it back this year [2010].'

Sandy Jones puts it more succinctly. 'In any two-horse race,' he says, 'you've got to let the other horse win sometimes.'

It was a thoroughly well-deserved victory for the US team – their biggest since Walton Heath in 1981 – and, thankfully, Paul Azinger and Nick Faldo had made it through the week without any major diplomatic incidents occurring. The pride, passion and, yes, patriotism had returned to the American Ryder Cup experience and, for once, it wasn't misplaced or uncomfortable.

A couple of months later, Paul Azinger assembled his team once more and took them to the White House to meet the man Stewart Cink would later call 'a normal dude', President George Bush. Posing for pictures, Azinger presented the President with a personalized Ryder Cup golf bag, the same Sunday red golf shirt and sweater vest worn by the team and, for some reason, a Ryder Cup money clip which, presumably, was left over in the Valhalla merchandising store. 'This was the icing on the cake for me and the players,' said Azinger afterwards.

Nick Faldo, meanwhile, would have to content himself with a visit to Buckingham Palace to receive a knighthood, the first living British golfer to be granted the honour. And so what if Valhalla hadn't panned out the way he had hoped? After six majors, 30 wins on the European Tour, 11 Ryder Cups and a record 23 points, it was all Britain's greatest-ever golfer deserved.

A River Runs Through It

IT's the closing ceremony at the 2008 Ryder Cup at Valhalla Golf Club. After a comprehensive victory for the American hosts, the defeated European captain Nick Faldo is concluding his speech to the thousands of fans who have stayed behind. After congratulating his opposite number, Paul Azinger, and his triumphant team, Faldo turns back to the crowd for one final word. 'See you in Wales,' he says, referring to the next Ryder Cup at Newport's Celtic Manor resort, adding, 'Bring your waterproofs!'

Stand-up comedy never was Faldo's forté. Nor, it seemed, was marketing. In the wake of that defeat, his latest ill-judged wisecrack had maybe tickled a few fans at Valhalla – OK, not that many – but it had left the 2010 Ryder Cup delegation biting their lips and scrunching their official programmes in their hands.

The central member of the delegation was Sir Terry Matthews, Wales's first billionaire and, more importantly, owner of the Celtic Manor Resort. Newport born and bred – he was born in a hospital on the site of Celtic Manor – Matthews was the local lad made good, or rather, the local lad made very good. Since making his fortune in tele-communications, the former BT engineer had made it his life's work to bring the Ryder Cup to his homeland, spending £125 million on developing the resort, creating three hotels and three championship golf courses, including the track that would host the 38th Ryder Cup, the Twenty Ten course.

But much had changed since Celtic Manor had been awarded the Ryder Cup back in September 2001, and not just the spectacular countryside in the Vale of Usk where the resort had taken shape. Buoyed by the record-breaking antics of Tiger Woods, professional golf, especially in the US, had become more lucrative than ever. Every event on the PGA Tour now boasted one million dollar-plus winner's cheques as a matter of course, and of the 258 players that competed on the PGA Tour in 2009, the first ninety-one players all earned over a million dollars in prize money.

But that, it seemed, still wasn't enough. In 2007, the PGA Tour commissioner Tim Finchem had announced a new competition, the FedEx Cup, a protracted and slightly convoluted new season finale of play-offs to the PGA Tour, played from late August and through September. If the timing wasn't great for the Ryder Cup, then the prize money – a frankly obscene $10 million to the eventual winner – was certainly a way to focus the American players' minds on their paymasters' competition, rather than that quaint team event they had nothing to do with. Of course, the PGA Tour was perfectly within its rights to play the event whenever it wanted. After all, they had no financial interest in the Ryder Cup so if it meant that the Ryder Cup got booted down the pecking order and the players decided to chase the pot of gold at the end of Tim Finchem's rainbow then hey, that wasn't their fault.

So it was that the 38th Ryder Cup would come to be played in October, the latest it had been played since Ben Hogan's US team demolished Dai Rees's men in Houston in 1967. After Nick Faldo's failure in Kentucky, Colin Montgomerie had emerged as the only serious contender to take over as captain. Certainly, he ticked all the boxes for a European Ryder Cup skipper; mid-forties, slightly past his best, still familiar with the guys on Tour and, crucially, with a natural affinity with, not to mention an outstanding record in, the Ryder Cup. He called his appointment 'the greatest honour of my career' and you knew he meant it. Montgomerie would surround himself with a backroom staff that could, in all likelihood, have played on the European team as well that week. There was Darren Clarke, Paul McGinley, Thomas Bjørn and, having ruled himself out of playing on account of some poor recent form, Sergio García. Though they were vice-captains, the truth is they were all captains-in-waiting, all men you could one day envisage stepping into Montgomerie's shoes. They, like Montgomerie, lived and breathed the Ryder Cup.

Though he had been afforded three captain's picks for Celtic Manor, Montgomerie would also find himself stymied by the lure of the FedEx Cup. With Justin Rose, Paul Casey, Luke Donald and Padraig Harrington all committed to playing in the States, rather than teeing it up in the final qualifying event at Gleneagles in Scotland, the Johnnie Walker Championship, the European captain found himself in the position of having to disappoint one or more of a group the press were now calling the 'FedEx Four'.

Yet any plans Montgomerie may have made would be thrown into disarray by the result at Gleneagles, where the Italian Edoardo Molinari had birdied the last three holes to win the event and force himself into Montgomerie's shortlist for a wildcard. It wasn't just his victory at the Johnnie Walker that gave him a real chance. Molinari's younger brother, Francesco, had already qualified for the team as of right and together the pair had won the 2009 World Cup. They were, in short, a natural, ready-made Ryder Cup pairing, primed and ready to go and one that Montgomerie, ultimately, couldn't resist. 'In my time as a player on the European Tour, and I've been a member for twenty-four years, I don't think I've seen a finish of that quality under pressure by anyone anywhere,' said Montgomerie, who also selected the ever-reliable Luke Donald and the three-time major champion Padraig Harrington. 'He is the type of player we need to regain the Ryder Cup from America.'

If Colin Montgomerie had cured his selection headache (and it was an extremely brave call leaving Justin Rose, who had won two PGA Tour titles in 2010, and the world-ranked number 7 Paul Casey on the sidelines), Corey Pavin was still dealing with the fallout from the mother of all sports scandals. As a Ryder Cup captain, Pavin seemed an entirely different beast to Pavin the Ryder Cup player. Older and wiser, he was a much more considered and affable opponent than the one who had stomped and snarled his way around Kiawah Island in 1991, with his violent fist-pumping and his Desert Storm cap. But his captaincy – indeed, virtually everything else in the game of professional golf in the preceding year – had been overshadowed by the one story that had dominated the front and the back pages and most of the ones in between.

On Friday 27 November, the world number one Tiger Woods had left his house in Isleworth near Orlando at 02.25 hours, but crashed his Cadillac Escalade into a fire hydrant at the end of his driveway. Initially, the news reports suggested Woods had been seriously injured in the crash, although it was later revealed he had only suffered some facial lacerations. While the accident itself was big news, what then unfolded was unlike any other sports – or celebrity – scandal in living memory and in the days and weeks that followed, the career and the personal life of arguably the greatest golfer in the history of the game, imploded in a whirlwind of sleazy tabloid revelations about the many women with whom he had had affairs.

Every day, it seemed as though another woman came forward, claiming to have been one of Woods's mistresses. Cocktail waitresses, porn stars, models and mums, there seemed to be no shortage of ex-lovers only too eager to tell tales of their torrid times with the Tiger. Day by day, the life and career of the world number one suffered hammer blow after self-inflicted hammer blow. Within days, his wife Elin would move out, taking their kids, Sam and Charlie, with her.

As the allegations mounted and the coverage intensified, Woods headed to Mississippi and to the Pine Grove sex addiction centre in Hattiesburg in a bid to save his marriage, his career and, no doubt, his sanity. His sponsors got spooked too. Soon, Gatorade, AT&T, Accenture and GM Motors would all announce they were parting ways with the fallen star and Woods would be forced into an extraordinary media statement broadcast live across the world's TV networks in which he apologised for what he had done, saying: 'I felt that I had worked hard my entire life and deserved to enjoy all the temptations around me. I felt I was entitled. Thanks to money and fame, I didn't have to go far to find them.' Woods also announced an indefinite break from the professional game before heading off back to Pine Grove for further treatment.

Woods's demise was as spectacular and shocking as it had been rapid. Here was a player, a man, who had built his career not just on a God-given golf game but on an image that was cleaner than clean. The family man. The doting dad. The good guy. And here he was, the greatest sportsman of his generation imploding in a blizzard of sleaze.

Woods would finally return to action in the relative security of the 2010 Masters, and while he would challenge for the Green Jacket once more, eventually finishing in a creditable tie for fourth place, his game, as later events would prove, had largely deserted him, leaving him well adrift of qualification for the US Ryder Cup team. Not that Corey Pavin cared. Despite everything that had happened in the months since that November night, Woods had managed to retain his number one world ranking and there was no way that Pavin was going to leave the highest ranked player in the game out of his team.

While Woods's selection as a pick, despite everything, was a given, the call-up for twenty-one-year-old rookie pro Rickie Fowler was a surprise. At twenty-one, Fowler was the third youngest US Ryder Cup player in history (after Horton Smith and Tiger Woods) and the first player to play the Walker Cup and Ryder Cup in successive years. With his boyish looks, ice white teeth and a hairstyle pulled fresh from a Playmobil set, Fowler didn't look a day over fourteen but certainly, the kid could play. He had a track record in team golf too. In the 2007 Walker Cup at Royal

County Down in Newcastle, Northern Ireland, he had lost just once in four games as the USA pipped Great Britain and Ireland. Two years later, in the same event at Pennsylvania's Merion Golf Club, he had won all four of his games as his team cantered to a comfortable seven-point victory.

Back in Europe, Colin Montgomerie was leaving nothing to chance in his attempts to prise the Ryder Cup from Corey Pavin's grasp. Meticulous to the point of obsession, he was the kind of captain who had his entire week organized with all the precision of a military operation. Though there's no evidence to prove it, you kind of know that he had all his clothes laid out in his hotel room, day by day. In the build-up to the play, he had enlisted a string of motivational speakers to drop by and speak to his team. But on the Tuesday evening, as the players relaxed, playing table tennis and watching television, Montgomerie summoned them into the European team room and sat them down around a telephone. He flicked it on to the speakerphone. On the other end of the line was Seve Ballesteros, still recovering at home in Santander, Spain, after several operations on a brain tumour. For ten minutes, the Spaniard spoke to the team, regaling them with anecdotes from his time in the event and leaving them with the perfect rallying cry. 'Go get them so hard that they'll all be caddies in the future,' he said. After the chat, Northern Ireland's Graeme McDowell jumped straight on his Twitter site, declaring Ballesteros to be, quite accurately, 'A legend!' and adding that the team were 'trying to win it for him this weekend'.

Meanwhile, Sweden's Peter Hanson, in typically Scandinavian fashion, said the conversation was 'cool'.

The blue skies and good times of the opening ceremony soon gave way to more typical Welsh weather. Overnight on Thursday, the Usk valley was soaked by the kind of rainstorm not seen since Noah set sail, leaving the Twenty Ten course, even with its £1 million drainage system, virtually waterlogged.

When the opening fourball match between Dustin Johnson and Phil

Mickelson and Lee Westwood and Martin Kaymer reached the first tee at 7.45 am on Friday it was still raining, still soggy. Despite some heavy going, the players ploughed on but progress was painfully slow. Even with preferred lies in play it was almost impossible to find a place on the fairway to place the ball. Gradually, the matches ground to a halt. The first hole of Graeme McDowell's and Rory McIlroy's match against Stewart Cink and Matt Kuchar, for example, took twenty-six minutes to complete, while Luke Donald's and Padraig Harrington's game versus the rookie duo of Bubba Watson and Jeff Overton saw their first two holes completed in a little over an hour.

The slow play was the least of the American team's problems. Having taken to the course in their new Sun Mountain Sports waterproofs, they soon found that after a proper working over from the Welsh weather, the waterproofs were anything but. Selected by Corey Pavin's wife Lisa – the self-styled 'captainess' of the US team – the outfits were a heavily-embroidered design in blue and white, described by the golf coach and commentator Butch Harmon as 'the ugliest things I have ever seen'.

Even the golf bags weren't holding up. Steve Williams, the caddie of Tiger Woods, had placed a towel in one of the pockets of his official bag but by the third hole it was sopping wet. It was like the 'Carry On' days of the British team in the 1970s, and when the former European captain Ian Woosnam learned of the American's wardrobe malfunction, the 2006 skipper maintained that Corey Pavin 'should have been shot' for not employing more rigorous testing procedures.

Mercifully, he wasn't. Instead, Pavin dispatched a search party to Celtic Manor's merchandising tent, and £4,000 and twenty-four sets of new waterproofs later, they returned to the team room with new armour for the troops, provided by the same company, ProQuip, who had also supplied the European team with their wets.

It was a bumper day for the ProQuip stall, with over £100,000 of business done. As the official supplier to the home team and now the unofficial supplier to the away team, they were also faced with a queue of ill-prepared golf fans, eager to get their hands on the same kit that Rory, Westy, Tiger and Phil were now wearing. 'The American officials came over with the European team officials and said could I help them out with some waterproofs. They didn't say much and nothing negative about their waterproofs,' said ProQuip's Managing Director Richard Head. 'I was delighted to help them out.'

The president of Sun Mountain Sports, Rick Reimers, meanwhile, was sheltering inside from the rain when he heard of the problems with his waterproofs, admitting that he 'may have underestimated the kind of rain they would get over there'.

Later, as his company achieved the kind of publicity they didn't quite anticipate from their Ryder Cup involvement, Reimers announced that Sun Mountain would apologise to the US captain and his wife at its 'earliest opportunity and hope they will accept our heartfelt apology for the stress this must have caused'.

Less than two hours into play, though, the persistent rain had turned the Twenty Ten course into a new tributary of the River Usk, causing the first stoppage in the Ryder Cup since the storm that swept over Valderrama in 1997. Play would resume, over seven hours later, at 5.00 p.m. It was a testament not just to Terry Matthews much-vaunted drainage system but to the Director of Golf Jim McKenzie and his 110-strong team of groundstaff who managed to turn the course round in a little over an hour so that they could get at least some play in before dusk.

But the downpour would very nearly do for the 38th Ryder Cup and while the course would recover, miraculously so, the sodden walkways and spectator areas around the Celtic Manor soon became a quagmire. It was like the worst Glastonbury Festival imaginable, only with less fashionable clothes, slightly better toilet facilities and, for the most part, nicer manners.

Though the Twenty Ten course had been built with a major tournament like the Ryder Cup in mind, with its huge banks creating natural amphitheatres around the greens, the deluge had seen the same banks become virtually impossible to climb without the aid of crampons. Over the course of the weekend, the black runs of the banks would claim more victims than just the day's play. The *Independent* newspaper, for instance, reported that nine people had fallen and broken their legs in the treacherous conditions, which was another record Celtic Manor would rather not hold.

As the players headed off the course to the comfort of the clubhouse, 45,000 spectators headed for cover in the tented village, availing themselves of beer at £5 a pint (in special commemorative plastic cups) and a mere £9.50 for a slender serving of fish and rather disappointing chips. It was more expense on a day that would prove to be very expensive. With no games completed on the opening day and no refunds on offer to ticket holders, the costs had mounted up. There was £130 for a day ticket, travel to and from the venue, maybe some hotel accommodation and doubtless some dry cleaning bills too. And all for a handful of holes.

With more bad weather forecast over the weekend, a plan was hatched with the agreement of the two captains, and a new schedule of play was agreed. At 6.30 p.m. on Friday evening, it was announced that in order to try and ensure a Sunday finish, rather than the traditional session of foursomes followed by an afternoon session of fourballs on Saturday, there would now be six foursome games played immediately after the conclusion of the opening fourballs, and then two more foursomes and four fourball games after that. Confused? So were most of Celtic Manor.

While it now meant that some players would be playing constantly on Saturday, it also meant that every player would now be playing in every remaining session of the Ryder Cup. It also meant that Montgomerie would need some more assistance to keep track of his players, given that they were all out on the course. As luck would have it, the Spaniard José María Olazábal was at Celtic Manor as an ambassador for Nestle Nespresso. Montgomerie thought he could be better employed and hardly needed to ask. He lobbed him a walkie-talkie, pointed him in the direction of a golf buggy and off he went, splashing through the Vale of Usk.

Amid all the very British talk of the weather, the Americans would make the better start in the match, taking a 2½–1½ lead from the fourballs, with Europe's only win coming from Westwood and Kaymer in the first game out. But if Friday had been frustrating, Saturday would prove to be a day unlike any other in Ryder Cup history – fast, frenetic and at times frantic. Every team member would be called into action and with nobody sat skulking on the sidelines, there seemed to be a constant conveyor belt of players arriving at the first tee. Provisional tee times would be arranged and then re-arranged as players who were due on the first tee were still out on the course. Then, as soon as they had finished their games, there would be a quick turnaround before they headed back out again. For those fans who had been starved of golf on Friday, it must have been galling to see such a feast of golf on the Saturday – especially if they were back home, grumbling as they watched it all on television.

Sunday morning brought further bad news. Heavy overnight rain had once more soaked Celtic Manor and the start would be delayed until midday. As the groundstaff did what they could to clear the course of this latest deluge, the day's spectators were kept in the car parks for their own safety as much as anything, and sat waiting for hours until the gates were finally opened and they could make their way to the overpriced fish and chips. This, though, would be one suspension too many. With no possibility of the singles being concluded before the sun went down, it was decided that for the first time in Ryder Cup history, a fourth day would be added. The singles would have to wait.

Sunday would be Europe's day. And how. Despite a 6–4 deficit after the expanded foursomes session, they mounted a comeback that not only pulled the rug from under the feet of the visitors but gave them a lead they could not have imagined earlier in the day. It was stirring stuff. Now the only thing raining was European points. Charged with showing more passion on the golf course, Montgomerie's men won all but one of the day's games. Just when it seemed that Stewart Cink and Matt Kuchar would take the point against the Molinaris in their fourball game, it was left to Francesco to hole a short putt at the last, to win the hole and steal a half point they had no right to snaffle.

Westwood's and Donald's brutal 6&5 foursomes battering of Tiger Woods and Steve Stricker – a pairing that was unbeaten in the Presidents Cup – was not only the stand-out result, but also the world number one's heaviest ever defeat in the Ryder Cup. Westwood was simply imperious. Cast as the on-course captain of the Europe team, he had led from the front and in winning he had extended an unbeaten foursomes record that stretched back to the previous century and the matches at Brookline, Massachusetts. It was also six victories in seven games against Woods in the Ryder Cup.

So three days became four. The organizers had harboured concerns that concluding the Ryder Cup on a business day would have an adverse effect on the attendance. They needn't have worried. Whether sickies were thrown or not, some 35,000 poured into Celtic Manor on Monday and, as it had been all week, the atmosphere around the first tee was buzzing, the energy palpable. Some of the songs and comments too were inspired. When Stewart Cink and Rory McIlroy waited to go, a group piped up with 'He's got more hair than you', at which point Cink removed his cap and patted his bald pate. When either of the Molinari brothers appeared, back came the chant: 'Two Molinaris, there's only two Molinaris.' And then there was the inevitable 'Where's your water-proofs, where's your waterproofs... gone, gone, gone...'

Celtic Manor looked like a different venue on Monday. In many ways, it was. Though it was still treacherously muddy on the walkways, the sun now baked the valley. From waterproofs and wetsuits, now it was t-shirts and if not flip-flops, then at least it was golf shoes and not wellies. In the press conference on Sunday evening, Pavin had pledged that his team would not shirk the responsibility ahead of them. Besides, there were only three points to make up. 'We have got twelve of the best players in the world, [and it's] match play, anything can happen,' he shrugged. 'And the one thing I can guarantee you, is that Team USA is going to come out tomorrow and play hard and try to win the Ryder Cup.' While it wasn't quite on a par with Ben Crenshaw's premonition at Brookline in 1999, there had been too many impossibly strong singles showings by the USA over the years to doubt that Pavin's side would be giving the home team a proper contest.

He was right. Save for Ian Poulter's 5&4 demolition of Matt Kuchar, early European success would be scant. Lee Westwood, surprisingly given his exploits all week, lost out to Steve Stricker while his partner from the first day, the new PGA champion Martin Kaymer, had nothing to offer in a thumping 6&4 defeat to Dustin Johnson. Later, Jeff Overton, the effervescent rookie from Bloomington, Indiana, accounted for another fellow rookie, Ross Fisher, while Tiger Woods silenced the boisterous galleries following his game with Francesco Molinari. Despite losing the first two holes, Woods had moved through the gears, dismantling the course in a way even the old Tiger would have struggled to match, going on a 9 under par run through 11 holes in his 4&3 win. At times he was even seen to be smiling.

Guarded and uncommunicative he may have been in his press con-ferences – and who can blame him, really? – but the notion that Woods didn't care about the Ryder Cup should have been finally laid to rest in Wales. Three points from four made him the joint-highest points scorer in the US team (alongside Steve Stricker) and took his record to thirteen wins, fourteen defeats and two halves from his six Ryder Cup appearances. Contrast that with Phil Mickelson, a man whose Ryder Cup record is rarely questioned as much as that of Woods. In his thirty-four games, he has won just eleven, lost seventeen and tied six. Indeed, his defeat in the Sunday foursomes, when he partnered Rickie Fowler to a 2&1 reverse against Ian Poulter and Martin Kaymer, would set a new record for the highest number of losses in US Ryder Cup history.

At the tail end of the order stood Graeme McDowell. Since winning the US Open at Pebble Beach in June 2010 – the first British player to do so since Tony Jacklin in 1970 – McDowell had grown in stature and at Celtic Manor he never looked anything other than in total control. Exuding purpose, swagger and confidence, he had seized the mantle of becoming a major winner and used it to propel his golf game to even greater heights. Some players, too many to mention, win their first major and struggle to live up to the expectations that go with being one of golf's elite band. Not McDowell. Now, the thirty-year-old Ulsterman looked as though operating on a higher plane was something he was always destined to do.

All of which made Colin Montgomerie's decision to send him out in the number 12 spot in the singles, a match which, in all likelihood, was going to be concluded when the result was done and dusted, all the more perplexing, as McDowell explained.

I remember sitting there on Sunday night when the singles draw came out. We were sitting as a team and Monty was reading through the line-up. We got to number seven, eight, nine my name still hadn't come and I was like, 'OK'. And then he [Montgomerie] said Harrington 11 and myself 12. I remember feeling a mixture of emotions; disappointment because I felt like I wasn't going to have a chance to be part of a winning euphoria. I thought maybe sixth, seventh, eighth spot might be the man. I was on the verge of saying something. I think I had a blank look on my face. I remember Thomas Bjørn saying to me, 'G-Mac, you OK?' I was like, 'yeah, I think I'm OK'. I did put the question to Olly [José María Olazábal] and to Monty, 'how do I do this, how do I play number 12?'

If McDowell had felt his match at the tail end of the singles line-up would be largely irrelevant, he – and Europe – had not anticipated another typically gutsy American comeback. His game with Hunter Mahan had been largely ignored by the galleries for the first twelve or thirteen holes, but now, as the afternoon wore on, it began to look like the decisive tie, not least because Rickie Fowler ahead of him had, miraculously, birdied the final four holes to turn around a three-hole deficit against Edoardo Molinari and eke out a half point when everyone had already chalked up another blue point on the scoreboard. Fowler's reaction after his comeback did little to suggest that he hadn't just stepped off the set of *High School Musical*. 'It's awesome!' he beamed.

Though Montgomerie's European team had started the final day with a healthy three-point lead, they had been pegged back by a US team shaken into action by the appalling session they had suffered on Sunday. The difference in the team when they played as individuals was as marked as ever. Phil Mickelson had finally realized what he was there for, breezing past Peter Hanson 4&2, while Zach Johnson completed a miserable Ryder Cup for the captain's pick Padraig Harrington, winning comfortably 3&2. Prior to the Ryder Cup, Colin Montgomerie had bitten back against those in the media who had criticized his selection of Harrington, asking to be judged when the event was over. It was, perhaps, the one bad call of his captaincy.

When Fowler had stolen a half point in his match, it had tied the scores at 13½ apiece. Behind them, meanwhile, was Graeme McDowell and his opponent Hunter Mahan. Though Mahan, a stalwart of the US team at Valhalla two years earlier, had got within a hole of McDowell, winning the driveable 15th when the Ulsterman had carved his drive into the rough on the right of the green, McDowell had responded magnificently, draining a deadweight birdie putt at the 16th to leave him dormie two.

Though it had restored McDowell's two-hole advantage, Mahan was still in a position to deprive Montgomerie's side of the victory. If he could win the remaining two holes, he would secure a half, levelling the scores up at 14 points each, meaning the USA, as holders, would retain the Ryder Cup. Which, as anyone knows, is as good as winning the thing.

Their approaches to the 17th both revealed how they were coping with the pressure. McDowell pushed his right, narrowly avoiding the deep bunker at the front right of the green and landing in the fringe. Mahan's, meanwhile, came up one or even two clubs short of the green. Mahan's next shot, though, would prove pivotal. It was the kind of shot played by every weekend wannabe the world over, the kind of shot you've hit too many times to remember. Striking the ground first, he advanced it forward just a few feet, leaving his ball still short of the putting surface. When McDowell trickled his putt to within five feet, it left Mahan having to hole his next shot to have any realistic chance of taking the game down the last. When he missed – and it was an admirable effort given what had just gone before – Mahan strode forward and, rather than make McDowell putt, simply took off his cap and offered an outstretched hand to his opponent. It was Europe's Ryder Cup once more. Just.

It had been a day that had started with Europe as overwhelming favourites but had seen the Americans, for so long the stronger side in the singles, claw their way back into the match. As the crowd engulfed the 17th green, the sense of relief around Celtic Manor was tangible, the joy unbridled. Battling his way through the crowds to congratulate McDowell, Colin Montgomerie was showered with champagne on his way to embrace the Ulsterman. How any of the players extricated themselves from the mêlée around the green remains a mystery.

In the press conference later, as a dejected American team sat in front of the media, Mahan, now without his trademark shades, fell to pieces, breaking into tears and leaving Phil Mickelson to answer his questions for him. It was tough on Mahan. It wasn't his chip that cost the US team the Ryder Cup, not really. Stewart Cink may have been the only unbeaten player all week but he had missed a short birdie putt at the 18th to take the point against Rory McIlroy. Jim Furyk, meanwhile, pushed his approach into the greenside bunker at the same hole to hand Luke Donald the win. And as for Bubba Watson, well, he may as well have stayed in the clubhouse than venture out against an ebullient Miguel Ángel Jiménez.

It would be the forty-six-year-old Spaniard who led the European celebrations. With his dark shades, his glistening jewellery and looking every inch like a ganglord from *Miami Vice*, he had appeared on the clubhouse balcony with a huge cigar and swigging straight from a bottle of Rioja. Ian Poulter, meanwhile, was draped in the cross of

St George while a beaming Rory McIlroy was backtracking at indecent speed. 'I would not have said this a year ago,' he said, 'but this is the best event in golf by far.'

For Montgomerie, it was mission accomplished, albeit a day later than anyone had planned. Though he would make noises about returning as a player to the Ryder Cup fold, it was clear that this was the culmination of a journey that had begun nearly twenty years earlier in the heat of South Carolina's Kiawah Island and that epic comeback against Mark Calcavecchia. As he accepted the trophy, Montgomerie addressed the crowd. 'This is one of the greatest moments of my golf career,' he said, before adding a transparent and clearly scripted correction. 'No wait, this is *the* greatest moment of my golf career.'

The 38th Ryder Cup had – eventually – got the finish it deserved. It had survived torrential weather, a last-ditch format change and an unprecedented extra day of play, but it had got there, producing another typically tight, nerve-shredding climax. Certainly it was a fitting finale for the man whose vision – and money – had brought the Ryder Cup to Wales, Terry Matthews. The only damp spot, literally, was the weather and there's nobody in the world with sufficient wherewithal to control that. But what did anyone expect? It's not as if the UK can guarantee sunshine, even in the fleeting, momentary joy that passes for the British summer. Besides, there's a reason the valleys in Wales are so green.

But Celtic Manor may not be a one-off. The next time the Ryder Cup will be played in Europe will be in 2014, when the fabled Scottish course Gleneagles will host the event. It goes without saying that the weather north of the border may also become an issue, which is why in the wake of what happened at Celtic Manor, the calendars are already being examined to see if it can be pushed forward into the middle of September when the weather may, theoretically at least, be marginally better.

But what chance do they have? It's unlikely the PGA Tour is ever going to budge. It's their FedEx Cup, after all, and they can stage it whenever they want. But for the players it may prove to be the ultimate test of patriotism. While the days of the team members demanding payment for playing may have gone, the fact that the Ryder Cup is played when it doesn't clash with a tournament makes it an easy event to sign up to. Schedule it head-on against a tournament that pays $10 million to the winner and faced with the choice of a huge payday at home or a wet, wild and unpaid week in Scotland, they may find their appetite for another Ryder Cup contest severely tested.

There is, of course, the distinct possibility that after Gleneagles in 2014, it may be some time before the Ryder Cup actually returns to British shores. With the team's increasingly cosmopolitan make-up and a flourishing European Tour, there are several countries, like Germany, Holland, France, Portugal and Spain that all have a valid claim to host the event. And as for Wales? Well, it's safe to say that it probably won't host another Ryder Cup, at least not in our lifetimes.

Inevitably, history will remember the woeful weather in that wet weekend in Wales, but it will remember that magical Monday even more, a Monday when the sun finally shone on the valleys and the Ryder Cup returned in all of its wondrous, maddening, unpredictable glory.

Appendices

Ryder Cup Results: 1983–2010

14–16 October 1983, PGA National Golf Club, Palm Beach Gardens, Florida
Captains: Tony Jacklin (Europe), Jack Nicklaus (US)
EUROPE 13½ – USA 14½

Foursomes: Friday morning

B. Gallacher & A. Lyle	0	T. Watson & B. Crenshaw (5&4)	1
N. Faldo & B. Langer (4&2)	1	L. Wadkins & C. Stadler	0
J. M. Cañizares & S. Torrance (4&3)	1	R. Floyd & B. Gilder	0
S. Ballesteros & P. Way	0	T. Kite & C. Peete (2&1)	1

Fourballs: Friday afternoon

B. Waites & K. Brown (2&1)	1	G. Morgan & F. Zoeller	0
N. Faldo & B. Langer	0	T. Watson & J. Haas (2&1)	1
S. Ballesteros & P. Way (1 hole)	1	R. Floyd & C. Strange	0
S. Torrance & I. Woosnam (halved)	½	B. Crenshaw & C. Peete (halved)	½

Fourballs: Saturday morning

B. Waites & K. Brown	0	L. Wadkins & C. Stadler (1 hole)	1
N. Faldo & B. Langer (4&2)	1	B. Crenshaw & C. Peete	0
S. Ballesteros & P. Way (halved)	½	G. Morgan & J. Haas (halved)	½
S. Torrance & I. Woosnam	0	T. Watson & B. Gilder (5&4)	1

Foursomes: Saturday afternoon

N. Faldo & B. Langer (3&2)	1	T. Kite & R. Floyd	0
S. Torrance & J. M. Cañizares	0	G. Morgan & L. Wadkins (7&5)	1
S. Ballesteros & P. Way (2&1)	1	T. Watson & B. Gilder	0
B. Waites & K. Brown	0	J. Haas & C. Strange (3&2)	1

Singles: Sunday

Severiano Ballesteros (halved)	½	Fuzzy Zoeller (halved)	½
Nick Faldo (2&1)	1	Jay Haas	0
Bernhard Langer (2 holes)	1	Gil Morgan	0
Gordon Brand	0	Bob Gilder (2 holes)	1
Sandy Lyle	0	Ben Crenshaw (3&1)	1
Brian Waites	0	Calvin Peete (1 hole)	1
Paul Way (2&1)	1	Curtis Strange	0
Sam Torrance (halved)	½	Tom Kite (halved)	½
Ian Woosnam	0	Craig Stadler (3&2)	1
José María Cañizares (halved)	½	Lanny Wadkins (halved)	½
Ken Brown (4&3)	1	Raymond Floyd	0
Bernard Gallacher	0	Tom Watson (2&1)	1

13–15 September 1985, The Belfry, Sutton Coldfield, England

Captains: Tony Jacklin (Europe), Lee Trevino (US)

EUROPE 16½ – USA 11½

Foursomes: Friday morning

S. Ballesteros & M. Piñero (2&1)	1	C. Strange & M. O'Meara	0
B. Langer & N. Faldo	0	C. Peete & T. Kite (3&2)	1
A. Lyle & K. Brown	0	L. Wadkins & R. Floyd (4&3)	1
H. Clark & S. Torrance	0	C. Stadler & H. Sutton (3&2)	1

Fourballs: Friday afternoon

P. Way & I. Woosnam (1 hole)	1	F. Zoeller & H. Green	0
S. Ballesteros & M. Piñero (2&1)	1	A. North & P. Jacobsen	0
B. Langer & J.M. Cañizares (halved)	½	C. Stadler & H. Sutton (halved)	½
S. Torrance & H. Clark	0	R. Floyd & L. Wadkins (1 hole)	1

Fourballs: Saturday morning

S. Torrance & H. Clark (2&1)	1	T. Kite & A. North	0
P. Way & I. Woosnam (4&3)	1	H. Green & F. Zoeller	0
S. Ballesteros & M. Piñero	0	M. O'Meara & L. Wadkins (3&2)	1
B. Langer & A. Lyle (halved)	½	C. Stadler & C. Strange (halved)	½

Foursomes: Saturday afternoon

J.M. Cañizares & J. Rivero (4&3)	1	T. Kite & C. Peete	0
S. Ballesteros & M. Piñero (5&4)	1	C. Stadler & H. Sutton	0
P. Way & I. Woosnam	0	C. Strange & P. Jacobsen (4&2)	1
B. Langer & K. Brown (3&2)	1	R. Floyd & L. Wadkins	0

Singles: Sunday

Manuel Piñero (3&1)	1	Lanny Wadkins	0
Ian Woosnam	0	Craig Stadler (2&1)	1
Paul Way (2 holes)	1	Raymond Floyd	0
Severiano Ballesteros (halved)	½	Tom Kite (halved)	½
Sandy Lyle (3&2)	1	Peter Jacobsen	0
Bernhard Langer (5&4)	1	Hal Sutton	0
Sam Torrance (1 hole)	1	Andy North	0
Howard Clark (1 hole)	1	Mark O'Meara	0
José Rivero	0	Calvin Peete (1 hole)	1
Nick Faldo	0	Hubert Green (3&1)	1
José María Cañizares (2 holes)	1	Fuzzy Zoeller	0
Ken Brown	0	Curtis Strange (4&2)	1

25–27 September 1987, Muirfield Village, Columbus, Ohio

Captains: Jack Nicklaus (US), Tony Jacklin (Europe)
EUROPE 15 – USA 13

Foursomes: Friday morning

S. Torrance & H. Clark	0	C. Strange & T. Kite (4&2)	1
K. Brown & B. Langer	0	H. Sutton & D. Pohl (2&1)	1
N. Faldo & I. Woosnam (2 holes)	1	L. Wadkins & L. Mize	0
S. Ballesteros & J.M. Olazábal (1 hole)	1	L. Nelson & P. Stewart	0

Fourballs: Friday afternoon

G. Brand Jr & J. Rivero (3&2)	1	B. Crenshaw & S. Simpson	0
A. Lyle & B. Langer (1 hole)	1	A. Bean & M. Calcavecchia	0
N. Faldo & I. Woosnam (2&1)	1	H. Sutton & D. Pohl	0
S. Ballesteros & J.M. Olazábal (2&1)	1	C. Strange & T. Kite	0

Foursomes: Saturday morning

J. Rivero & G. Brand Jr	0	C. Strange & T. Kite (3&1)	1
N. Faldo & I. Woosnam (halved)	½	H. Sutton & L. Mize (halved)	½
A. Lyle & B. Langer (2&1)	1	L. Wadkins & L. Nelson	0
S. Ballesteros & J. M. Olazábal (1 hole)	1	B. Crenshaw & P. Stewart	0

Fourballs: Saturday afternoon

N. Faldo & I. Woosnam (5&4)	1	C. Strange & T. Kite	0
E. Darcy & G. Brand Jr	0	A. Bean & P. Stewart (3&2)	1
S. Ballesteros & J. M. Olazábal	0	H. Sutton & L. Mize (2&1)	1
S. Lyle & B. Langer (1 hole)	1	L. Wadkins & L. Nelson	0

Singles: Sunday

Ian Woosnam	0	Andy Bean (1 hole)	1
Howard Clark (1 hole)	1	Dan Pohl	0
Sam Torrance (halved)	½	Larry Mize (halved)	½
Nick Faldo	0	Mark Calcavecchia (1 hole)	1
José María Olazábal	0	Payne Stewart (2 holes)	1
José Rivero	0	Scott Simpson (2&1)	1
Sandy Lyle	0	Tom Kite (3&2)	1
Eamonn Darcy (1 hole)	1	Ben Crenshaw	0
Bernhard Langer (halved)	½	Larry Nelson (halved)	½
Severiano Ballesteros (2&1)	1	Curtis Strange	0
Ken Brown	0	Lanny Wadkins (3&2)	1
Gordon Brand Jr (halved)	½	Hal Sutton (halved)	½

22–24 September 1989, The Belfry, Sutton Coldfield, England

Captains: Tony Jacklin (Europe), Raymond Floyd (US)

EUROPE 14 – USA 14

Foursomes: Friday morning

N. Faldo & I. Woosnam (halved)	½	T. Kite & C. Strange (halved)	½
H. Clark & M. James	0	L. Wadkins & P. Stewart (1 hole)	1
S. Ballesteros & J. M. Olazábal (halved)	½	T. Watson & C. Beck (halved)	½
B. Langer & R. Rafferty	0	M. Calcavecchia & K. Green (2&1)	1

Fourballs: Friday afternoon

S. Torrance & G. Brand Jr (1 hole)	1	C. Strange & P. Azinger	0
H. Clark & M. James (3&2)	1	F. Couples & L. Wadkins	0
N. Faldo & I. Woosnam (2 holes)	1	M. Calcavecchia & M. McCumber	0
S. Ballesteros & J.M. Olazábal (6&5)	1	T. Watson & M. O'Meara	0

Foursomes: Saturday morning

I. Woosnam & N. Faldo (3&2)	1	L. Wadkins & P. Stewart	0
G. Brand Jr & S. Torrance	0	C. Beck & P. Azinger (4&3)	1
C. O'Connor Jr & R. Rafferty	0	M. Calcavecchia & K. Green (3&2)	1
S. Ballesteros & J.M. Olazábal (1 hole)	1	T. Kite & C. Strange	0

Fourballs: Saturday afternoon

N. Faldo & I. Woosnam	0	C. Beck & P. Azinger (2&1)	1
B. Langer & J.M. Cañizares	0	T. Kite & M. McCumber (2&1)	1
H. Clark & M. James (1 hole)	1	P. Stewart & C. Strange	0
S. Ballesteros & J.M. Olazábal (4&2)	1	M. Calcavecchia & K. Green	0

Singles: Sunday

Severiano Ballesteros	0	Paul Azinger (1 hole)	1
Bernhard Langer	0	Chip Beck (3&2)	1
José María Olazábal (1 hole)	1	Payne Stewart	0
Ronan Rafferty (1 hole)	1	Mark Calcavecchia	0
Howard Clark	0	Tom Kite (8&7)	1
Mark James (3&2)	1	Mark O'Meara	0
Christy O'Connor Jr (1 hole)	1	Fred Couples	0
José María Cañizares (1 hole)	1	Ken Green	0
Gordon Brand Jr	0	Mark McCumber (1 hole)	1
Sam Torrance	0	Tom Watson (3&1)	1
Nick Faldo	0	Lanny Wadkins (1 hole)	1
Ian Woosnam	0	Curtis Strange (2 holes)	1

27–29 September 1991, Ocean Course, Kiawah Island, South Carolina

Captains: Bernard Gallacher (Europe), Dave Stockton (US)

USA 14½ – EUROPE 13½

Fourballs: Friday morning

S. Ballesteros & J.M. Olazábal (2&1)	1	P. Azinger & C. Beck	0
B. Langer & M. James	0	R. Floyd & F. Couples (2&1)	1
D. Gilford & C. Montgomerie	0	L. Wadkins & H. Irwin (4&2)	1
N. Faldo & I. Woosnam	0	P. Stewart & M. Calcavecchia (1 hole)	1

Foursomes: Friday afternoon

S. Torrance & D. Feherty (halved)	½	L. Wadkins & M. O'Meara (halved)	½
S. Ballesteros & J.M. Olazábal (2&1)	1	P. Azinger & C. Beck	0
S. Richardson & M. James (5&4)	1	C. Pavin & M. Calcavecchia	0
N. Faldo & I. Woosnam	0	R. Floyd & F. Couples (5&3)	1

Foursomes: Saturday morning

D. Feherty & S. Torrance	0	H. Irwin & L. Wadkins (4&2)	1
M. James & S. Richardson	0	M. Calcavecchia & P. Stewart (1 hole)	1
N. Faldo & D. Gilford	0	P. Azinger & M. O'Meara (7&6)	1
S. Ballesteros & J.M. Olazábal (3&2)	1	F. Couples & R. Floyd	0

Fourballs: Saturday afternoon

I. Woosnam & P. Broadhurst (2&1)	1	P. Azinger & H. Irwin	0
B. Langer & C. Montgomerie (2&1)	1	C. Pavin & S. Pate	0
M. James & S. Richardson (3&1)	1	L. Wadkins & W. Levi	0
S. Ballesteros & J.M. Olazábal (halved)	½	P. Stewart & F. Couples (halved)	½

Singles: Sunday

Nick Faldo (2 holes)	1	Raymond Floyd	0
David Feherty (2&1)	1	Payne Stewart	0
Colin Montgomerie (halved)	½	Mark Calcavecchia (halved)	½
José María Olazábal	0	Paul Azinger (2 holes)	1
Steven Richardson	0	Corey Pavin (2&1)	1
Severiano Ballesteros (3&2)	1	Wayne Levi	0
Ian Woosnam	0	Chip Beck (3&1)	1
Paul Broadhurst (3&1)	1	Mark O'Meara	0

Sam Torrance	0	Fred Couples (3&2)	1
Mark James	0	Lanny Wadkins (3&2)	1
Bernhard Langer (halved)	½	Hale Irvin (halved)	½
David Gilford (halved	½	Steve Pate (halved)	½

24–26 September 1993, The Belfry, Sutton Coldfield, England
Captains: Bernard Gallacher (Europe), Tom Watson (US)
USA 15 – EUROPE 13

Fourballs: Friday morning

S. Torrance & M. James	0	L. Wadkins & C. Pavin (4&3)	1
I. Woosnam & B. Langer (7&5)	1	P. Azinger & P. Stewart	0
S. Ballesteros & J.M. Olazábal	0	T. Kite & D. Love III. (2&1)	1
N. Faldo & C. Montgomerie (4&3)	1	R. Floyd & F. Couples	0

Foursomes: Friday afternoon

I. Woosnam & P. Baker (1 hole)	1	J. Gallagher Jr & L. Janzen	0
B. Langer & B. Lane	0	L. Wadkins & C. Pavin (4&2)	1
N. Faldo & C. Montgomerie (halved)	½	P. Azinger & F. Couples (halved)	½
S. Ballesteros & J.M. Olazábal (4&3)	1	D. Love III. & T. Kite	0

Foursomes: Saturday morning

N. Faldo & C. Montgomerie (3&2)	1	L. Wadkins & C. Pavin	0
B. Langer & I. Woosnam (2&1)	1	F. Couples & P. Azinger	0
P. Baker & B. Lane	0	R. Floyd & P. Stewart (3&2)	1
S. Ballesteros & J.M. Olazábal (2&1)	1	D. Love III. & T. Kite	0

Fourballs: Saturday afternoon

N. Faldo & C. Montgomerie	0	J. Cook & C. Beck (1 hole)	1
M. James & C. Rocca	0	C. Pavin & J. Gallagher Jr (5&4)	1
I. Woosnam & P. Baker (6&5)	1	F. Couples & P. Azinger	0
J.M. Olazábal & J. Haeggman	0	R. Floyd & P. Stewart (2&1)	1

Singles: Sunday

Ian Woosnam (halved)	½	Fred Couples (halved)	½
Barry Lane	0	Chip Beck (1 hole)	1
Colin Montgomerie (1 hole)	1	Lee Janzen	0

Peter Baker (2 holes)	1	Corey Pavin	0
Joakim Haeggman (1 hole)	1	John Cook	0
Mark James	0	Payne Stewart (3&2)	1
Costantino Rocca	0	Davis Love III. (1 hole)	1
Severiano Ballesteros	0	Jim Gallagher Jr (3&2)	1
José María Olazábal	0	Raymond Floyd (2 holes)	1
Bernhard Langer	0	Tom Kite (5&3)	1
Nick Faldo (halved)	½	Paul Azinger (halved)	½
Sam Torrance*	½	Lanny Wadkins	½

*Torrance withdrawn at start of day

22–24 September 1995, Oak Hill Country Club, Rochester, New York
Captains: Bernard Gallacher (Europe), Lanny Wadkins (US)
EUROPE 14½ – USA 13½

Foursomes: Friday morning

N. Faldo & C. Montgomerie	0	C. Pavin & T. Lehman (1 hole)	1
S. Torrance & C. Rocca (3&2)	1	J. Haas & F. Couples	0
H. Clark & M. James	0	D. Love III. & J. Maggert (4&3)	1
B. Langer & P.-U. Johansson (1 hole)	1	B. Crenshaw & C. Strange	0

Fourballs: Friday afternoon

D. Gilford & S. Ballesteros (4&3)	1	B. Faxon & P. Jacobsen	0
S. Torrance & C. Rocca	0	J. Maggert & L. Roberts (6&5)	1
N. Faldo & C. Montgomerie	0	F. Couples & D. Love III. (3&2)	1
B. Langer & P.-U. Johansson	0	C. Pavin & P. Mickelson (6&4)	1

Foursomes: Saturday morning

N. Faldo & C. Montgomerie (4&2)	1	C. Strange & J. Haas	0
S. Torrance & C. Rocca (6&5)	1	D. Love III. & J. Maggert	0
I. Woosnam & P. Walton	0	L. Roberts & P. Jacobsen (1 hole)	1
B. Langer & D. Gilford (4&3)	1	C. Pavin & T. Lehman	0

Fourballs: Saturday afternoon

S. Torrance & C. Montgomerie	0	B. Faxon & F. Couples (4&2)	1
I. Woosnam & C. Rocca (3&2)	1	D. Love III. & B. Crenshaw	0
S. Ballesteros & D. Gilford	0	J. Haas & P. Mickelson (3&2)	1
N. Faldo & B. Langer	0	C. Pavin & L. Roberts (1 hole)	1

Singles: Sunday

Severiano Ballesteros	0	Tom Lehman (4&3)	1
Howard Clark (1 hole)	1	Peter Jacobsen	0
Mark James (4&3)	1	Jeff Maggert	0
Ian Woosnam (halved)	½	Fred Couples (halved)	½
Costantino Rocca	0	Davis Love III. (3&2)	1
David Gilford (1 hole)	1	Brad Faxon	0
Colin Montgomerie (3&1)	1	Ben Crenshaw	0
Nick Faldo (1 hole)	1	Curtis Strange	0
Sam Torrance (2&1)	1	Loren Roberts	0
Bernhard Langer	0	Corey Pavin (3&2)	1
Philip Walton (1 hole)	1	Jay Haas	0
Per-Ulrik Johansson	0	Phil Mickelson (2&1)	1

26–28 September 1997, Valderrama GC, Sotogrande, Spain

Captains: Severiano Ballesteros (Europe), Tom Kite (US)
EUROPE 14½ – USA 13½

Fourballs: Friday morning

J. M. Olazábal & C. Rocca (1 up)	1	D. Love III. & P. Mickelson	0
N. Faldo & L. Westwood	0	F. Couples & B. Faxon (1 up)	1
J. Parnevik & P.-U. Johansson (1 up)	1	T. Lehman & J. Furyk	0
C. Montgomerie & B. Langer	0	T. Woods & M. O'Meara (3&2)	1

Foursomes: Friday afternoon

C. Rocca & J. M. Olazábal	0	S. Hoch & L. Janzen (1 up)	1
B. Langer & C. Montgomerie (5&3)	1	M. O'Meara & T. Woods	0
N. Faldo & L. Westwood (3&2)	0	J. Leonard & J. Maggert	1
J. Parnevik & I. Garrido (halved)	½	T. Lehman & P. Mickelson (halved)	½

Foursomes: Saturday morning

C. Montgomerie & D. Clarke (1 up)	1	F. Couples & D. Love III	0
I. Woosnam & T. Bjørn (2&1)	1	J. Leonard & B. Faxon	0
N. Faldo & L. Westwood (2&1)	1	T. Woods & M. O'Meara	0
J.M. Olazábal & I. Garrido (halved)	½	P. Mickelson & T. Lehman (halved)	½

Fourballs: Saturday afternoon

C. Montgomerie & B. Langer (1 up)	1	L. Janzen & J. Furyk	0
N. Faldo & L. Westwood	0	S. Hoch & J. Maggert (2&1)	1
J. Parnevik & I. Garrido (halved)	½	J. Leonard & T. Woods (halved)	½
J.M. Olazábal & C. Rocca (5&4)	1	D. Love III. & F. Couples	0

Singles: Sunday

Ian Woosnam	0	Fred Couples (8&7)	1
Per-Ulrik Johansson (3&2)	1	Davis Love III	0
J. Parnevik	0	Mark O'Meara (5&4)	1
Darren Clarke	0	Phil Mickelson (2&1)	1
Costantino Rocca (4&2)	1	Tiger Woods	0
Thomas Bjørn (halved)	½	Justin Leonard (halved)	½
Ignacio Garrido	0	Tom Lehman (7&6)	1
Bernhard Langer (2&1)	1	Brad Faxon	0
Lee Westwood	0	Jeff Maggert (3&2)	1
José María Olazábal	0	Lee Janzen (1 up)	1
Nick Faldo	0	Jim Furyk (3&2)	1
Colin Montgomerie (halved)	½	Scott Hoch (halved)	½

24–26 September 1999, The Country Club, Brookline, Massachusetts

Captains: Mark James (Europe), Ben Crenshaw (US)
EUROPE 13½ – USA 14½

Foursomes: Friday morning

D. Duval & P. Mickelson	0	P. Lawrie & C. Montgomerie (3&2)	1
T. Lehman & T. Woods	0	S. García & J. Parnevik (2&1)	1
D. Love III. & P. Stewart (halved)	½	M. Á. Jiménez & P. Harrington (halved)	½
J. Maggert & H. Sutton (3&2)	1	D. Clarke & L. Westwood	0

Fourballs: Friday afternoon

J. Furyk & P. Mickelson	0	S. García & J. Parnevik (1 up)	1
J. Leonard & D. Love III. (halved)	½	P. Lawrie & C. Montgomerie (halved)	½
J. Maggert & H. Sutton	0	M. Á. Jiménez & J. M. Olazábal (2&1)	1
D. Duval & T. Woods	0	D. Clarke & L. Westwood	1

Foursomes: Saturday morning

J. Maggert & H. Sutton (1 up)	1	P. Lawrie & C. Montgomerie	0
J. Furyk & M. O'Meara	0	D. Clarke & L. Westwood (3&2)	1
S. Pate & T. Woods (1 up)	1	M. Á. Jiménez & P. Harrington	0
J. Leonard & P. Stewart	0	S. García & J. Parnevik (3&2)	1

Fourballs: Saturday afternoon

P. Mickelson & T. Lehman (2&1)	1	D. Clarke & L. Westwood	0
D. Love III. & D. Duval (halved)	½	S. García & J. Parnevik (halved)	½
J. Leonard & H. Sutton (halved)	½	M. Á. Jiménez & J. M. Olazábal (halved)	½
S. Pate & T. Woods	0	P. Lawrie & C. Montgomerie (2&1)	1

Singles: Sunday

Tom Lehman (3&2)	1	Lee Westwood	0
Davis Love III. (6&5)	1	Jean van de Velde	0
Phil Mickelson (4&3)	1	Jarmo Sandelin	0
Hal Sutton (4&2)	1	Darren Clarke	0
David Duval (5&4)	1	Jesper Parnevik	0
Tiger Woods (3&2)	1	Andrew Coltart	0
Steve Pate (2&1)	1	Miguel Ángel Jiménez	0
Mark O'Meara	0	Padraig Harrington (1 up)	1
J. Furyk (4&3)	1	Sergio García	0
Jeff Maggert	0	Paul Lawrie (4&3)	1
Justin Leonard (halved)	½	José María Olazábal (halved)	½
Payne Stewart	0	Colin Montgomerie (1 up)	1

27–29 September 2002, The Belfry, Sutton Coldfield, England
Captains: Sam Torrance (Europe), Curtis Strange (US)
EUROPE 15½ – USA 12½

Fourballs: Friday morning

T. Woods & P. Azinger	0	D. Clarke & T. Bjørn (1 up)	1
D. Duval & D. Love III	0	S. García & L. Westwood (4&3)	1
S. Hoch & J. Furyk	0	C. Montgomerie & B. Langer (4&3)	1
P. Mickelson & D. Toms (1 up)	1	P. Harrington & N. Fasth	0

Foursomes: Friday afternoon

H. Sutton & S. Verplank (2&1)	1	D. Clarke & T. Bjørn	0
T. Woods & M. Calcavecchia	0	S. García & L. Westwood (2&1)	1
P. Mickelson & D. Toms	½	C. Montgomerie & B. Langer	½
S. Cink & J. Furyk (3&2)	1	P. Harrington & P. McGinley	0

Foursomes: Saturday morning

P. Mickelson & D. Toms (2&1)	1	P. Fulke & P. Price	0
J. Furyk & S. Cink	0	L. Westwood & S. García (2&1)	1
S. Verplank & S. Hoch	0	C. Montgomerie & B. Langer (1 up)	1
T. Woods & D. Love III. (4&3)	1	D. Clarke & T. Bjørn	0

Fourballs: Saturday afternoon

M. Calcavecchia & D. Duval (1 up)	1	N. Fasth & J. Parnevik	0
P. Mickelson & D. Toms	0	C. Montgomerie & P. Harrington (2&1)	1
T. Woods & D. Love III. (1 up)	1	S. García & L. Westwood	0
S. Hoch & J. Furyk	½	D. Clarke & P. McGinley	½

Singles: Sunday

Scott Hoch	0	Colin Montgomerie (5&4)	1
David Toms (1 up)	1	Sergio García	0
David Duval	½	Darren Clarke	½
Hal Sutton	0	Bernhard Langer (4&3)	1
Mark Calcavecchia	0	Padraig Harrington (5&4)	1
Stewart Cink	0	Thomas Bjørn (2&1)	1
Scott Verplank (2&1)	1	Lee Westwood	0

Paul Azinger	½	Niclas Fasth	½
J. Furyk	½	Paul McGinley	½
Davis Love III	½	Pierre Fulke	½
Phil Mickelson	0	Phillip Price (3&2)	1
Tiger Woods	½	Jesper Parnevik	½

17–19 September 2004, Oakland Hills Country Club, Bloomfield Township, Michigan

Captains: Bernhard Langer (Europe), Hal Sutton (US)
EUROPE 18½ – USA 9½

Fourballs: Friday morning

P. Mickelson & T. Woods	0	C. Montgomerie & P. Harrington (2&1)	1
D. Love III. & C. Campbell	0	D. Clarke & M.Á. Jiménez (5&4)	1
C. Riley & S. Cink	½	P. McGinley & L. Donald	½
D. Toms & J. Furyk	0	S. García & L. Westwood (5&3)	1

Foursomes: Friday afternoon

J. Haas & C. DiMarco (3&2)	1	M.Á. Jiménez & T. Levet	0
D. Love III. & F. Funk	0	C. Montgomerie & P. Harrington	1
P. Mickelson & T. Woods	0	D. Clarke & L. Westwood	1
K. Perry & S. Cink	0	S. García & L. Donald (2&1)	1

Fourballs: Saturday morning

J. Haas & C. DiMarco	½	S. García & L. Westwood	½
T. Woods & C. Riley (4&3)	1	D. Clarke & I. Poulter	0
J. Furyk & C. Campbell	0	P. Casey & D. Howell	1
S. Cink & D. Love III. (3&2)	1	C. Montgomerie & P. Harrington	0

Foursomes: Saturday afternoon

J. Haas & C. DiMarco	0	D. Clarke & L. Westwood (5&4)	1
P. Mickelson & D. Toms	1	M.Á. Jiménez & T. Levet	0
J. Furyk & F. Funk	0	S. García & L. Donald (1 up)	1
D. Love III. & T. Woods	0	P. Harrington & P. McGinley	1

Singles: Sunday

Tiger Woods (3&2)	1	Paul Casey	0
Phil Mickelson	0	Sergio García	1
Davis Love III. (halved)	½	Darren Clarke (halved)	½
Jim Furyk (6&4)	1	David Howell	0
Kenny Perry	0	Lee Westwood (1 up)	1
David Toms	0	Colin Montgomerie (1 up)	1
Chad Campbell (5&3)	1	Luke Donald	0
Chris DiMarco (1 up)	1	Miguel Ángel Jiménez	0
Fred Funk	0	Thomas Levet (1 up)	1
Chris Riley	0	Ian Poulter (3&2)	1
Jay Haas	0	Padraig Harrington (1 up)	1
Stewart Cink	0	Paul McGinley (3&2)	1

24–26 September 2006, The K Club, Straffan, Co. Kildare, Ireland

Captains: Ian Woosnam (Europe), Tom Lehman (US)

EUROPE 18½ – USA 9½

Fourballs: Friday morning

P. Harrington & C. Montgomerie	1	T. Woods & J. Furyk (2&1)	0
P. Casey & R. Karlsson	½	S. Cink & J.J. Henry	½
S. García & J.M. Olazábal	1	D. Toms & B. Wetterich (3&2)	0
D. Clarke & L. Westwood	1	P. Mickelson & C. DiMarco (1 up)	0

Foursomes: Friday afternoon

P. Harrington & P. McGinley	½	C. Campbell & Z. Johnson	½
D. Howell & H. Stenson	½	S. Cink & D. Toms	½
L. Westwood & C. Montgomerie	½	P. Mickelson & C. DiMarco	½
L. Donald & S. García	1	T. Woods & J. Furyk (2 up)	0

Fourballs: Saturday morning

P. Casey & R. Karlsson	½	S. Cink & J.J. Henry	½
S. García & J.M. Olazábal	1	P. Mickelson & C. DiMarco (3&2)	0
L. Westwood & D. Clarke	1	T. Woods & J. Furyk (3&2)	0
H. Stenson & P. Harrington	0	S. Verplank & Z. Johnson (2&1)	1

Foursomes: Saturday afternoon

S. García & L. Donald	1	P. Mickelson & D. Toms (2&1)	0
C. Montgomerie & L. Westwood	½	C. Campbell & V. Taylor	½
P. Casey & D. Howell	1	S. Cink & Z. Johnson (5&4)	0
P. Harrington & P. McGinley	0	J. Furyk & T. Woods (3&2)	1

Singles: Sunday

Colin Montgomerie	1	David Toms (1 up)	0
Sergio García	0	Stewart Cink (4&3)	1
Paul Casey	1	J. Furyk (2&1)	0
Robert Karlsson	0	Tiger Woods (3&2)	1
Luke Donald	1	Chad Campbell (2&1)	0
Paul McGinley	½	J.J. Henry	½
Darren Clarke	1	Zach Johnson (3&2)	0
Henrik Stenson	1	Vaughn Taylor (4&3)	0
David Howell	1	Brett Wetterich (5&4)	0
José María Olazábal	1	Phil Mickelson (2&1)	0
Lee Westwood	1	Chris DiMarco (2 up)	0
Padraig Harrington	0	Scott Verplank (4&3)	1

19–21 September 2008, Valhalla GC, Louisville, Kentucky

Captains: Nick Faldo (Europe), Paul Azinger (US)

EUROPE 11½ – USA 16½

Foursomes: Friday morning

P. Mickelson & A. Kim	½	P. Harrington & R. Karlsson	½
J. Leonard & H. Mahan	1	H. Stenson & P. Casey (3&2)	0
S. Cink & C. Campbell	1	J. Rose & I. Poulter (1 up)	0
J. Furyk & K. Perry	½	L. Westwood & S. García	½

Fourballs: Friday afternoon

P. Mickelson & A. Kim	1	P. Harrington & G. McDowell (2 up)	0
S. Stricker & B. Curtis	0	I. Poulter & J. Rose (4&2)	1
J. Leonard & H. Mahan	1	S. García & M. Á. Jiménez (4&3)	0
J. B. Holmes & B. Weekley	½	L. Westwood & S. Hansen	½

Foursomes: Saturday morning

S. Cink & C. Campbell	0	I. Poulter & J. Rose (4&3)	1
J. Leonard & H. Mahan	½	M.Á. Jiménez & G. McDowell	½
P. Mickelson & A. Kim	0	H. Stenson & O. Wilson (2&1)	1
J. Furyk & K. Perry	1	P. Harrington & R. Karlsson (3&1)	0

Fourballs: Saturday afternoon

J.B. Holmes & B. Weekley	1	L. Westwood & S. Hansen (2&1)	0
B. Curtis & S. Stricker	½	S. García & P. Casey	½
J. Furyk & K. Perry	0	I. Poulter & G. McDowell (1 up)	1
P. Mickelson & H. Mahan	½	H. Stenson & R. Karlsson	½

Singles: Sunday

Anthony Kim	1	Sergio García (5&4)	0
Hunter Mahan	½	Paul Casey	½
Justin Leonard	0	Robert Karlsson (5&3)	1
Phil Mickelson	0	Justin Rose (3&2)	1
Kenny Perry	1	Henrik Stenson (3&2)	0
Boo Weekley	1	Oliver Wilson (4&2)	0
J. B. Holmes	1	Søren Hansen (2&1)	0
Jim Furyk	1	Miguel Ángel Jiménez (2&1)	0
Stewart Cink	0	Graeme McDowell (2&1)	1
Stever Stricker	0	Ian Poulter (3&2)	1
Ben Curtis	1	Lee Westwood (2&1)	0
Chad Campbell	1	Padraig Harrington (2&1)	0

1–4 October 2010, The Celtic Manor Resort, Newport, Wales

Captains: Colin Montgomerie (Europe), Corey Pavin (US)
EUROPE 14½ – USA 13½

Session 1 (Friday/Saturday): Fourballs

L. Westwood & M. Kaymer (3&2)	1	P. Mickelson & D. Johnson	0
R. McIlroy & G. McDowell (halved)	½	S. Cink & M. Kuchar (halved)	½
I. Poulter & R. Fisher	0	S. Stricker & T. Woods (2 up)	1
L. Donald & P. Harrington	0	B. Watson & J. Overton (3&2)	1

Session 2 (Saturday): Foursomes

M. Jimenez & P. Hanson	0	T. Woods & S. Stricker (4&3)	1
E. Molinari & F. Molinari	0	Z. Johnson & H. Mahan (2 up)	1
L. Westwood & M. Kaymer (halved)	½	J. Furyk & R. Fowler (halved)	½
P. Harrington & R. Fisher (3&2)	1	P. Mickelson & D. Johnson	0
I. Poulter & L. Donald (2&1)	1	B. Watson & J. Overton	0
G. McDowell & R. McIlroy	0	S. Cink & M. Kuchar (1 up)	1

Session 3 (Saturday and Sunday): Foursomes

L. Donald & L. Westwood (6&5)	1	S. Stricker & T. Woods	0
G. McDowell & R. McIlroy (3&1)	1	Z. Johnson & H. Mahan	0

Session 3 (Saturday and Sunday): Fourballs

P. Harrington & R. Fisher (2&1)	1	J. Furyk & D. Johnson	0
P. Hanson & M. Jimenez (2 Up)	1	B. Watson & J. Overton	0
E. Molinari & F. Molinari (halved)	½	S. Cink & M. Kuchar (halved)	½
I. Poulter & M. Kaymer (2&1)	1	P. Mickelson & R. Fowler	0

Session 4 (Monday): Singles

Lee Westwood	0	Steve Stricker (2&1)	1
Rory McIlroy (halved)	½	Stewart Cink (halved)	½
Luke Donald (1 up)	1	Jim Furyk	0
Martin Kaymer	0	Dustin Johnson (6&4)	1
Ian Poulter (5&4)	1	Matt Kuchar	0
Ross Fisher	0	Jeff Overton (3&2)	1
Miguel Ángel Jimenez (4&3)	1	Bubba Watson	0
Francesco Molinari	0	Tiger Woods (4&3)	1
Edoardo Molinari (halved)	½	Rickie Fowler (halved)	½
Peter Hanson	0	Phil Mickelson (4&2)	1
Padraig Harrington	0	Zach Johnson (3&2)	1
Graeme McDowell (3&2)	1	Hunter Mahan	0

Ryder Cup:
Summary of Results,
1927–1981

		US scores first
1927	Worcester CC, Worcester, Massachusetts	9½ – 2½
1929	Moortown GC, Leeds, England	5 – 7
1931	Scioto CC, Columbus, Ohio	9 – 3
1933	Southport & Ainsdale GC, England	5½ – 6½
1935	Ridgewood CC, Ridgewood, New Jersey	9 – 3
1937	Southport & Ainsdale GC, England	8 – 4
	No matches played because of World War II	
1947	Portland Golf Club, Portland, Oregon	11 – 1
1949	Ganton GC, Scarborough, England	7 – 5
1951	Pinehurst CC, Pinehurst, North Carolina	9½ – 2½
1953	Wentworth GC, Wentworth, England	6½ – 5½
1955	Thunderbird CC, Palm Springs, California	8 – 4
1957	Lindrick GC, Yorkshire, England	4½ – 7½
1959	Eldorado CC, Palm Desert, California	8½ – 3½
1961	Royal Lytham & St Annes, England	14½ – 9½
1963	East Lake CC, Atlanta, Georgia	23 – 9
1965	Royal Birkdale GC, Southport, England	19½ – 12½
1967	Champions GC, Houston, Texas	23½ – 8½
1969	Royal Birkdale GC, Southport, England	16 – 16
1971	Old Warson CC, St. Louis, Missouri	18½ – 13½
1973	Muirfield, Scotland	19 – 13
1975	Laurel Valley GC, Ligonier, Pennsylvania	21 – 11
1977	Royal Lytham & St Annes, England	12½ – 7½
1979	The Greenbrier, West Virginia	17 – 11
1981	Walton Health GC, Surrey, England	18½ – 9½

Acknowledgements

For whatever reason, Ken Brown said no. Don't ask me why – he just didn't want to talk about the Ryder Cup. Shame really, it would have been good to get the nitty gritty on The Greenbrier. Thankfully, Ken's reticence wasn't at all typical of the response I received from everybody else I approached for *Two Tribes*. Having just written a book about football, it never ceases to amaze me just how different and more open people are in the game of golf.

Golfers really are a different species to the rest of the planet. It always strikes me as remarkable how they have an inherent knack of being able to recall everything about any given round of golf, even if it was twenty or thirty years ago; the club they hit, the yardage, what the stimpmeter was reading – they have it all there in their heads, logged like some mini-golf computer. Now that, in itself, makes a writer's job a bit easier, but not as much the interviewees themselves. Throughout the course of this book, there have been scores of people who have given so freely of their time to talk about what the Ryder Cup has meant to them and I owe a huge debt of gratitude to the likes of Lanny Wadkins, Tom Watson, Ray Floyd, Peter Jacobsen, Hale Irwin, Tom Kite, Loren Roberts, Mark McCumber, Tom Lehman, Tony Jacklin, Bernard Gallacher, Mark James, Costantino Rocca, Howard Clark, Paul Way, Phil Price, Lee Westwood, Paul McGinley, Peter Baker, Gordon Brand Jr, Ian Poulter, Sam Torrance and Graeme McDowell.

Thanks also to all of the administrators, agents and golf clubs that helped out, including Gordon Simpson, Mitchell Platts and Frances

Jennings at the European Tour, Nat Sylvester, Maureen Roberts, David Wright and Sandy Jones at the PGA, Julius Mason and Una Jones at the PGA of America, Jim Awtrey, Sue Le Beau at South Staffordshire Golf Club, the wonderful Colin Snape and Ken Schofield, Kelly Fray, Rick Fehr, Julian Sheldon at Sky, Martin Hardy, Chubby Chandler and everyone at ISM, Guy Kinnings, Jane Brooks and Mark Booker at IMG. If I have forgotten anyone – and it's highly probable I have – then I apologise fully.

Thanks also to the people have helped out not just with this book but with previous efforts too, including Jonathan Taylor, Paul Hawksbee and Andy Jacobs, John Pawsey for all his help over the years and Richard Milbank, Toby Mundy, Sarah Norman, Sachna Hanspal and everyone at Atlantic. The ever-dependable Lizzie Stephenson also warrants a huge mention because without her this book would still be a series of taped conversations stuffed in a drawer.

On the family and friends front there is, as ever, a wealth of people who helped out in one way or another. So thank you to Sara Leatherland and John Davison at Kanoti, John Martin, Chris Payne and Michael Dennington at Identity, Iestyn George, Tim Southwell, Dan Davies, Mike Harris, Jock Howard, Graham Wray, Danny Crouch, Mark and Anne-Marie Leigh, Neil and Kellie Smith, Sally and J P Hamilton-Savory, Ruth and Chas Linn, and Mum and Dad for their continued enthusiasm despite not really being remotely interested in golf, ditto my brother Darren.

At home, as ever, there's some people I share my house with who make it all worthwhile. So to my children Betsy, Frank and Cissy, thanks for always messing my desk up before I start writing, stealing the stapler and using up all the paper in the printer to draw pictures of aliens in battle and horses frolicking. And to Ann, aka Mrs Gav, aka The Lovely Ann, thanks for putting up with me. Again. I love you honey.

Gavin Newsham
October 2010

Index